IMAGES
of America

PLUM BOROUGH

On the Cover: The Ladies Aid Society of Kerr Presbyterian Church gathers to have their photograph taken, sometime around 1948. Seen here are, from left to right, (seated) Grace Leonard (and her son), Clemma Ciceske, Loretta Green, Florence Richard, Stella Dible, Edna Wise, Janette Austin, Gayle Leroy, Annabelle Cook, Lizzie Bickerstaff, M. Kuhn, and Lyde Jeek; (standing) L. Foukes, Mabel Stephens, Margaret Mathius, Ida Cook, Lois Mullin, Jane Kuhn, A. Montgomery, Eleanor Skellive, Edna Mock, and Jane Kiser. (Courtesy of Allegheny Foothills Historical Society.)

IMAGES
of America

PLUM BOROUGH

Frank J. Kordalski Jr.

ARCADIA
PUBLISHING

ISBN 978-0-7385-7433-2

Published by Arcadia Publishing
Charleston, South Carolina

Printed in the United States of America

Library of Congress Control Number: 2010935102

For all general information, please contact Arcadia Publishing:
Telephone 843-853-2070
Fax 843-853-0044
E-mail sales@arcadiapublishing.com
For customer service and orders:
Toll-Free 1-888-313-2665

Visit us on the Internet at www.arcadiapublishing.com

This book is dedicated to the good people of Plum, both past and present. They have led the transition of the town from one of mining and agriculture to a bustling suburban oasis. Additionally, since Plum has such a rich agricultural heritage, this book is also dedicated to my "Pop-pop," Rudy. He taught me all I know about gardening and life on the farm.

Contents

Acknowledgments

There is a plethora of people to whom I must offer my most sincere thanks for aiding me in the publication of this book. First, I must thank the members of the Allegheny Foothills Historical Society. Without their blessing, it would have been quite difficult to complete this book. Second, many thanks go to the excellent staff at Arcadia—especially my editor, Erin Vosgien—whose help has been a tremendous blessing. Finally, to my family and friends—thank you for your support, for without it, I may have never embarked on this endeavor.

All images, unless otherwise noted, are courtesy of the archives of the Allegheny Foothills Historical Society.

INTRODUCTION

Although much has changed since World War II, Plum Borough still retains some of its original agricultural aura. Not as many farms exist, but when one travels on some of the roads through Plum, it is still possible at times to have the feeling that one is in the country.

On September 24, 1788, western Pennsylvania's Allegheny County was formed. What would later become known as the steel-producing capital of the country, Allegheny County was originally made up of seven townships, one of which was Plum. Originally extending as far south as Versailles (modern-day North Versailles Township), east to the county line, west to Pitt Township, and north to the Allegheny River, Plum Township was founded on December 18, 1788. Plum has shrunk slightly over the years, but still retains its status as one of the largest municipalities within Allegheny County and the Commonwealth of Pennsylvania.

Western Pennsylvania, not widely settled until the early 19th century, was riddled with Native American trails. These trails, cut by members of the Shawnee, Seneca, and Algonquian tribes (among others), served as Pennsylvania's original "superhighways" and would later be utilized by European colonists.

One of the earliest settlers of Plum was William McJunkin. The McJunkin family arrived from Ireland in 1788 and settled on a farm (which McJunkin named Greenfield) along present-day New Texas Road. Many Irish and Scotch-Irish immigrants followed suit. Later, English and German immigrants settled in the region. All of these groups helped Plum to become a successful farming community by 1900. Other early settlers included the Carpenter, Davidson, Kerr, McCracken, and Sharp families.

From the town's inception through the 1950s, agriculture played a vital role in Plum's economic life. Mining was another major industry, although it did not establish itself in the area until the late 19th century. Andrew Carnegie, along with several partners, purchased large tracts of coal-rich land in Plum; upon consolidating their interests, they formed the New York and Cleveland Gas Coal Company. Other mining operations came and went, including the mines of Barking, Logans Ferry, Plum Creek, Renton, and Unity. In conjunction with coal mining, drilling for gas and oil, which began in the 1890s, played a large role in the development of industry in Plum.

Industry in general would not have been able to flourish had it not been for the advent of the railroad. The Allegheny Valley Railroad, founded in 1852, was eventually absorbed by the Pennsylvania Railroad in 1910. The North Bessemer Rail Yard in neighboring Penn Hills Township was another major player on the region's industrial scene, employing over 200 men from Plum alone. This railroad system played a vital role in the shipment of coal and the development of the coal industry in the area. Other industries in the Allegheny River and Turtle Creek Valley soon followed suit.

Plum is a diverse community that has seen an explosion of growth in recent years. According to census records, between 1960 and 1970 Plum doubled in size, going from 10,241 to 21,955 residents. In 1980, the population rose to 25,392. It was during this period that a renewed interest in the community's history arose. The founding of the Allegheny Foothills Historical Society was spearheaded by a descendant of one of Plum's oldest families, Eleanor Carpenter Broome. The historical society was established on October 11, 1979, and Broome went on to serve as president of the organization for several years.

It was a dream of many to rebuild the old Carpenter-family log house, especially since the borough's bicentennial celebration was rapidly approaching. The Carpenters' log house was dismantled in 1958, and parts of it were used to build a log cabin in Pittsburgh's Point State Park. After much fundraising by volunteers, a ground breaking ceremony took place on September 27, 1981. The reconstructed homestead was dedicated by the council of Plum Borough as a heritage museum on May 30, 1988. The reconstruction campaign had the support of local government officials and also the support of over 100 active historical-society members. The reconstructed log house is meant to be "a memorial to the past and a museum for the future." Although the historical society accepts donated objects from all eras of Plum's history, the log house is meant to be a representation of life in early- and mid-19th-century Plum.

Much has happened since Plum's bicentennial celebration. Plum has continued to grow, and its citizens have become more interested in its history. The first weekend of October 2008, the Allegheny Foothills Historical Society hosted the 250th anniversary of Washington's encampment. This event—the largest to be put on by the historical society to date—garnered much community support. Several thousand people converged on Boyce Park for the two-day event.

It is from this increased interest in local history that this book emerges. It is not meant to be a comprehensive history of Plum; rather, it is meant to be a history told in broad strokes. If a place or topic of interest was omitted, it certainly was not intentional. Plum has too rich a history to be told through a few pages and pictures. Hopefully, this book will inspire the reader to go out and further explore Plum Borough's rich heritage.

One

Early History

Prior to the arrival of Europeans, southwestern Pennsylvania was home to several different Native American tribes. From approximately the 10th through the 17th century, the region was home to several villages belonging to the Monongahela tribe. A village from the Monongahela tribe was unearthed in 1909 near the home of William McJunkin by an archaeological team from the Carnegie Institute of Technology. The Monongahela tribe left the area around the 16th century, possibly forced farther west by other tribes such as the Shawnee and Algonquian. Another native village was excavated in 1966 by local resident Kirke Wilson; further excavations of Wilson's site were conducted under the supervision of the University of Pittsburgh's Department of Anthropology in 1976.

It was not until after General Forbes's successful 1758 campaign against Fort Duquesne that settlers began to immigrate to the area. In late 1758, a treaty that allowed colonial settlers to establish homes west of the Alleghenies was signed with the Iroquois at Fort Stanwix.

In his book *Indian Paths of Pennsylvania*, Paul A. Wallace identified and mapped out over 170 Native American trails in Pennsylvania. Many historians agree that General Forbes followed the Raystown Path, which ran from Paxtang (Harrisburg) to Fort Duquesne, on his march to capture the fort from the French. On July 10, 1758, Forbes wrote in a letter to William Pitt, "we are indebted to the Indians who have footpaths through these desearts [*sic*], by help of which we make our roads." It is believed that Forbes's original path went near Old Frankstown and Pierson Run Roads, through what is now Boyce Park. It was in Boyce Park that Plum Borough celebrated the 250th anniversary of Forbes's 1758 campaign,

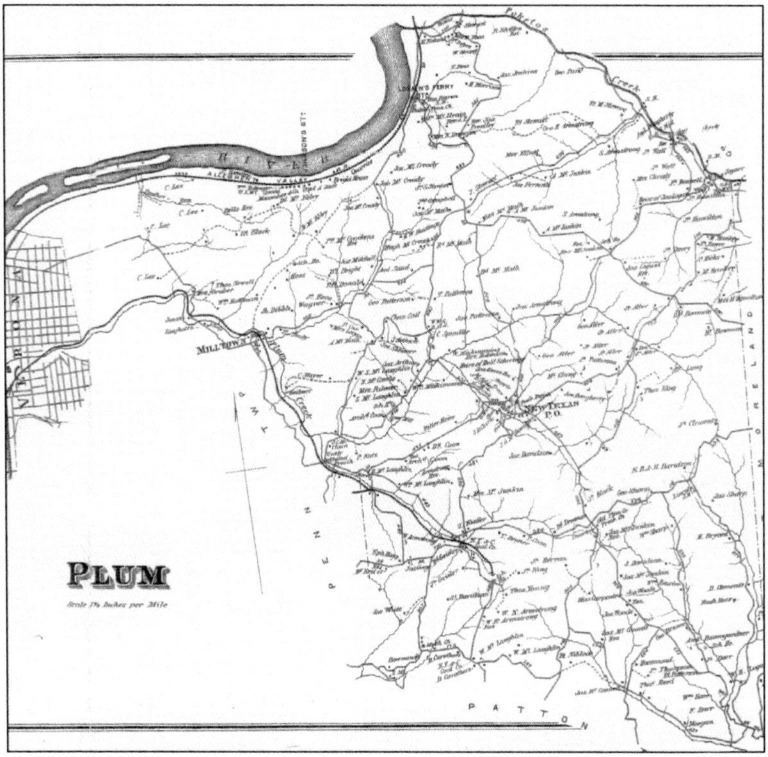

This early-20th-century map of Plum shows several communities, including New Texas, Logan's Ferry, and Milltown. Also shown are the names of many of the area's landowners at the time of the map's publication. Landowning members of the Carpenter, Davidson, McJunkin, and McLaughlin families are but a few of the names listed.

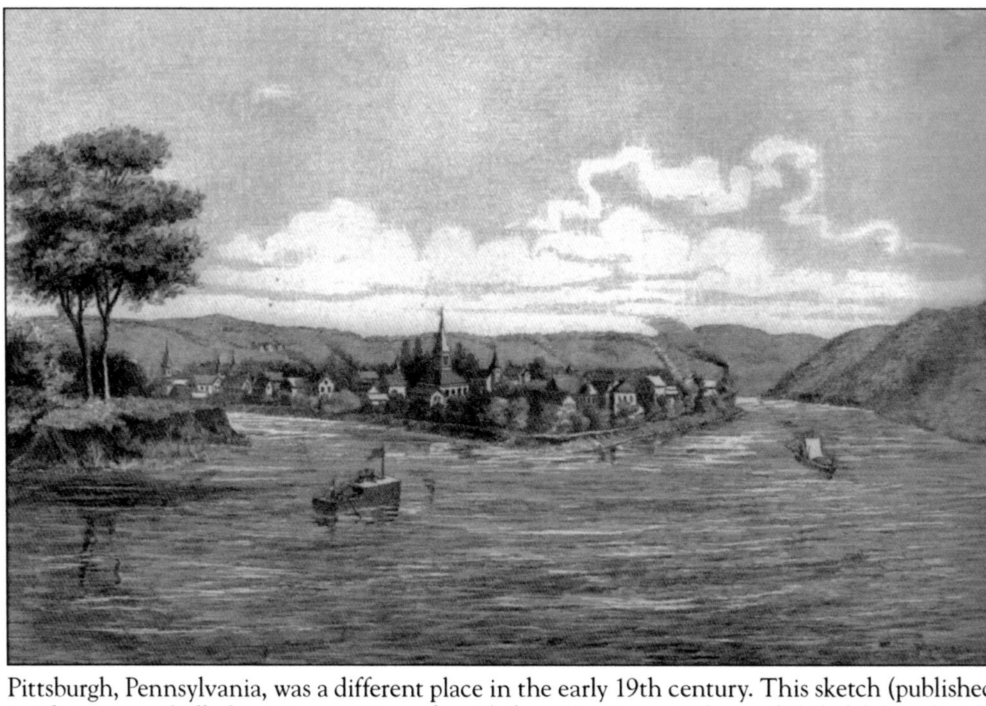

Pittsburgh, Pennsylvania, was a different place in the early 19th century. This sketch (published in *The History of Allegheny County, Pennsylvania*), from Mrs. James Gibson of Philadelphia, depicts Pittsburgh as it appeared around 1817. The book describes the growth of the country west of the Appalachians as being "something phenomenal."

Jeremiah Murry was the founder of neighboring Murrysville. However, like many of the other older families of the area (e.g., the McJunkins, Carpenters, Beattys, and Ramaleys), they were not confined to one community. When Jeremiah's daughter Jane married John Carpenter, Jeremiah presented the new husband and wife with a tract of land between present-day Pierson Run Road and New Texas Road in Plum.

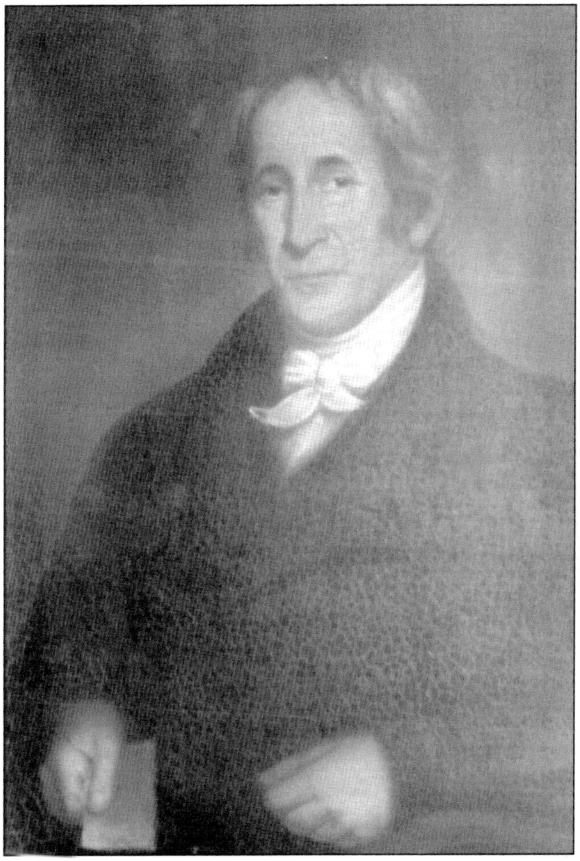

In 1755, Maj. Gen. Edward Braddock was tasked with driving the French from Fort Duquesne. This attack was to be part of a larger campaign against the French in America. On July 8, 1755, near Lincoln Way in present-day White Oak, Braddock's army made their last camp (recognized by this marker near White Oak community swimming pool) before crossing the Monongahela River. Braddock's campaign ended in failure. The wounded Braddock died on July 13, 1755.

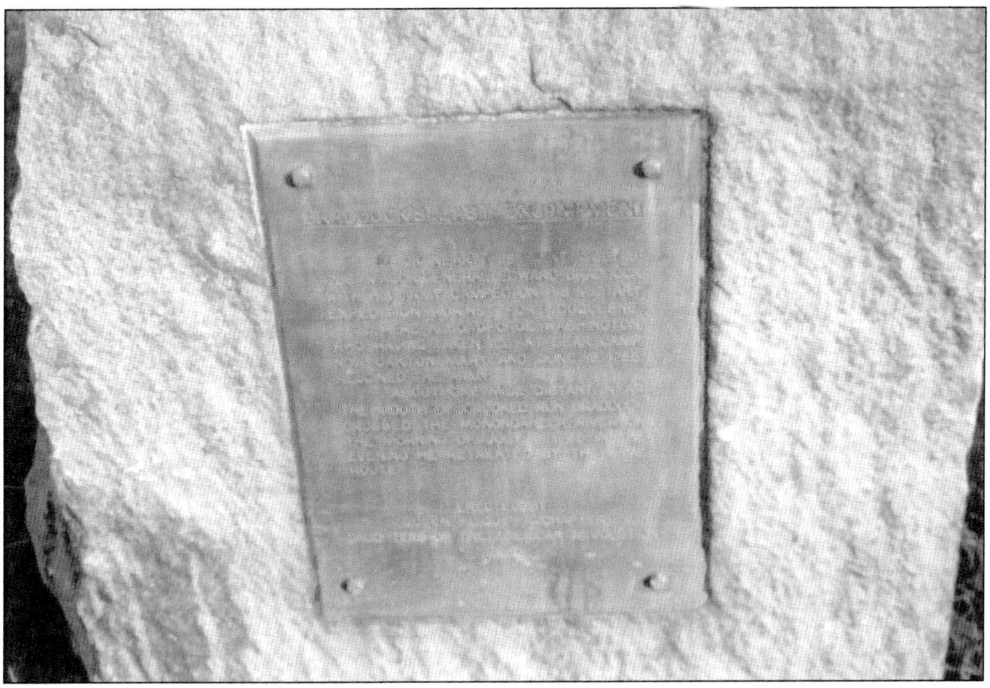

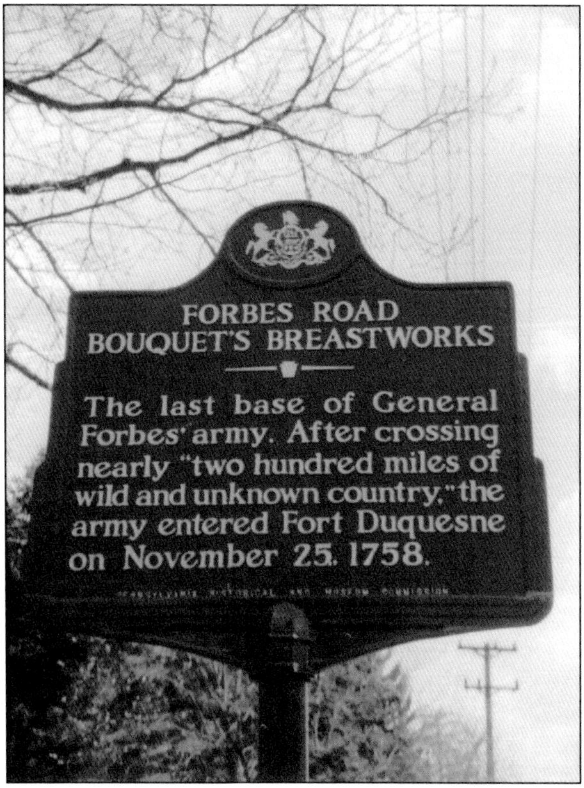

In 1758, Gen. John Forbes was given the responsibility of taking Fort Duquesne. Forbes decided to travel the Pennsylvanian route (which would come to bear his name) as opposed to the route that Braddock had taken (known as Braddock Road), which began in western Maryland. This decision led to political infighting between Pennsylvanians and Virginians, both of whom claimed the Ohio country for their own colonies. Forbes calmed the political storm by agreeing to improve Braddock's Road. In late November 1758, Forbes's army made its last base near Old Frankstown Road in present-day Plum (left). In early October 2008, the sign below was erected along one of the trails through Boyce Park. The sign went up immediately prior to the Allegheny Foothills Historical Society's celebration of the 250th anniversary of Washington's encampment in the area.

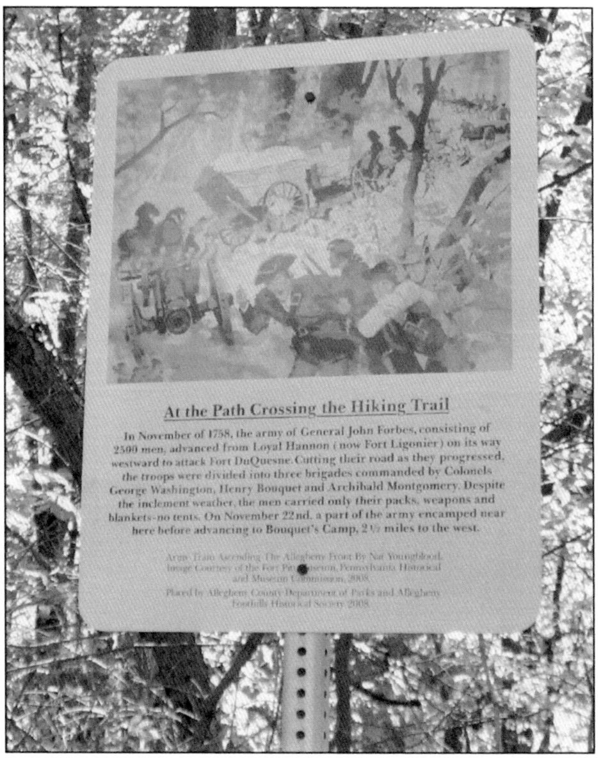

William McJunkin was one of the first permanent settlers in Plum Township. His naturalization papers (right) show that he was a native of Ireland and that he appeared before a circuit court in Pittsburgh on October 10, 1808, in order to be admitted as a citizen of the United States. A legal paper (below) dated April 28, 1824, bears the names of William McJunkin and various members of his family. The farm on which he settled is named Greenfield on the land-patent map of 1790. In his will, McJunkin left his land to his wife, Susannah, and son William and divided his remaining estate amongst his five daughters and three sons.

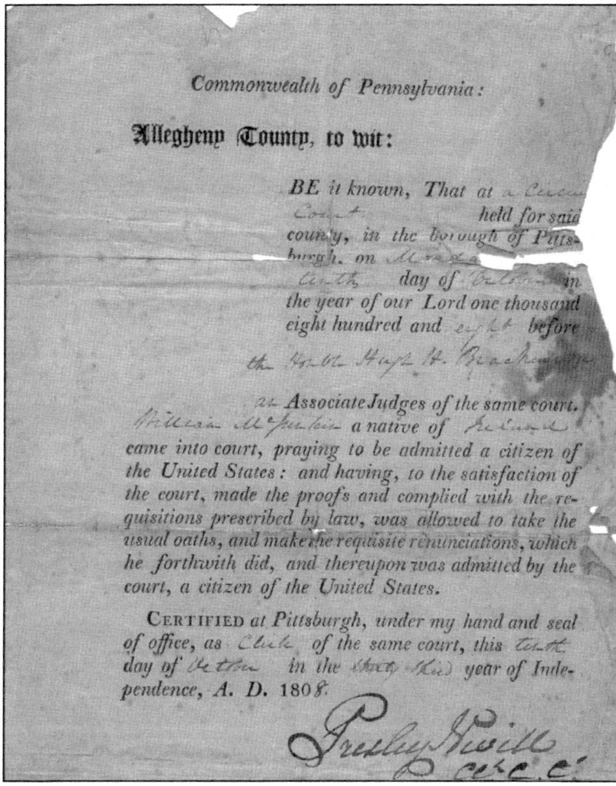

Commonwealth of Pennsylvania:

Allegheny County, to wit:

BE it known, That at a Circuit Court *held for said county, in the borough of Pittsburgh, on* Monday *tenth day of* October *in the year of our Lord one thousand eight hundred and* eight *before* the Honble Hugh H. Brackenridge *as Associate Judges of the same court,* William McJunkin *a native of* Ireland *came into court, praying to be admitted a citizen of the United States: and having, to the satisfaction of the court, made the proofs and complied with the requisitions prescribed by law, was allowed to take the usual oaths, and make the requisite renunciations, which he forthwith did, and thereupon was admitted by the court, a citizen of the United States.*

CERTIFIED *at Pittsburgh, under my hand and seal of office, as* Clerk *of the same court, this* tenth *day of* October *in the* thirty third *year of Independence, A. D. 180*8.

Presley Nevill

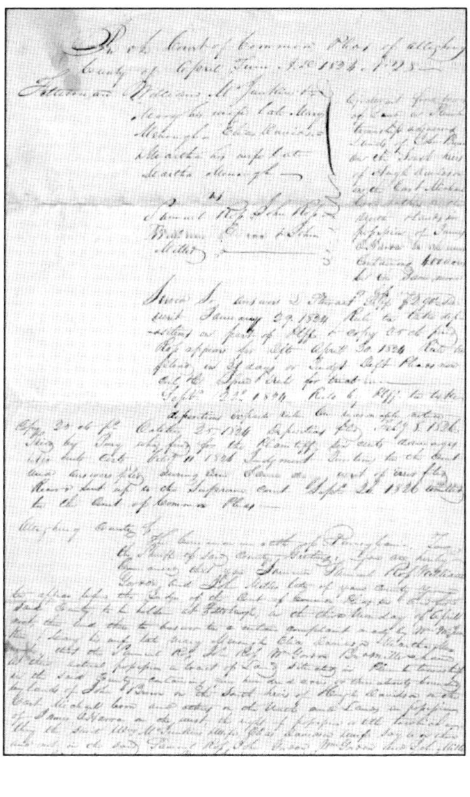

an Allowance proportiond to
two miles North from Forbes
of Turtle Creek, Including an
the Fort. now Westmoreland
1773 —
unto the

Not long after the founding of the United States, land patents were being granted for parcels west of the Allegheny Mountains. Had it not been for the success of the British Empire and its colonies in the Seven Years' War (the French and Indian War) from 1754 to 1763, such expansion may not have been possible. Immigration to the lands west of the Alleghenies was generally low prior to the beginning of the 19th century. However, there were still brave souls willing to face the challenges of the frontier. This image of a remnant of an original deed from the late 18th century reads as follows: "An allowance proportioned to six [percent] . . . two miles North from Forbes's old ro[ad] . . . of Turtle Creek, including an im . . . old Fort, now Westmoreland County . . . 1773 . . . Signed . . . nto the Secretary's office the 7th June 1790 . . . for Daniel Broadhead, Esq . . . Edw'd Lynch."

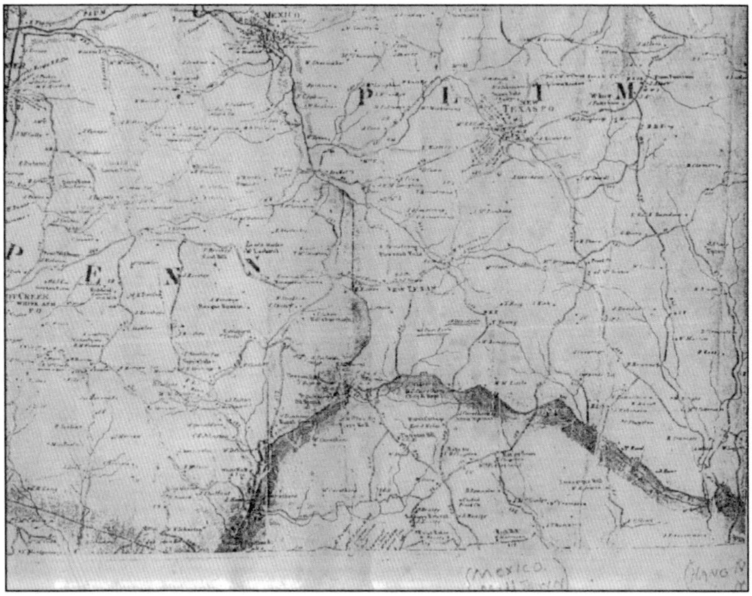

This map of Plum Township appeared in the 1876 *Atlas of the County of Allegheny, Pennsylvania*. When Allegheny County was first formed, Plum was one its original townships. While all of the original townships have shrunk in size (as has Plum), Plum Borough has remained the largest borough in the county and one of the largest boroughs in the state.

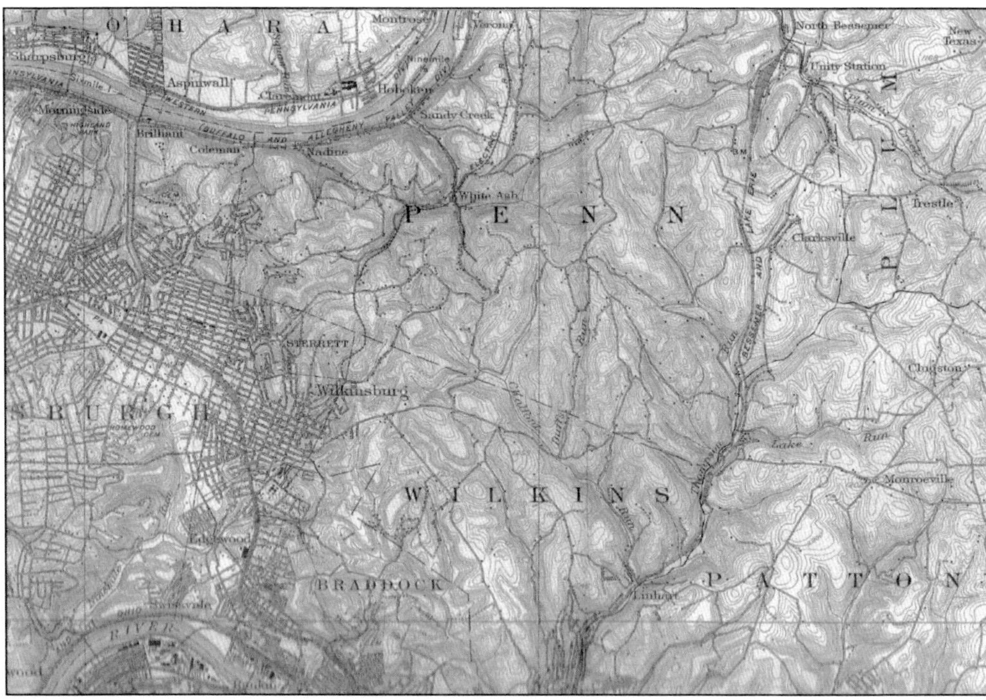

Southern Plum can be seen on this 1949 printing of a 1907 topographical survey of the area. The survey shows that modern-day Monroeville was still known by its former name of Patton and that modern-day Penn Hills was still known as Penn. This map was printed seven years before Plum changed its status from a township to a borough.

National and state maps usually only have major cities and larger towns labeled on them. Because Plum was still largely rural at the time, it is not surprising that it was not yet "on the map" in this example from 1912. One can see the importance of train transportation, however, as several rail lines are shown.

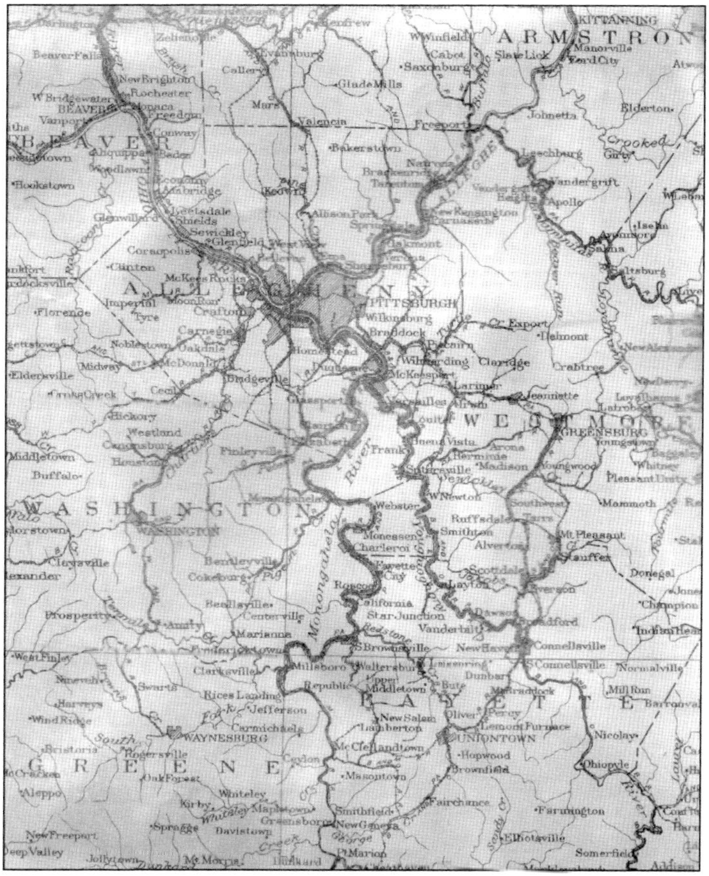

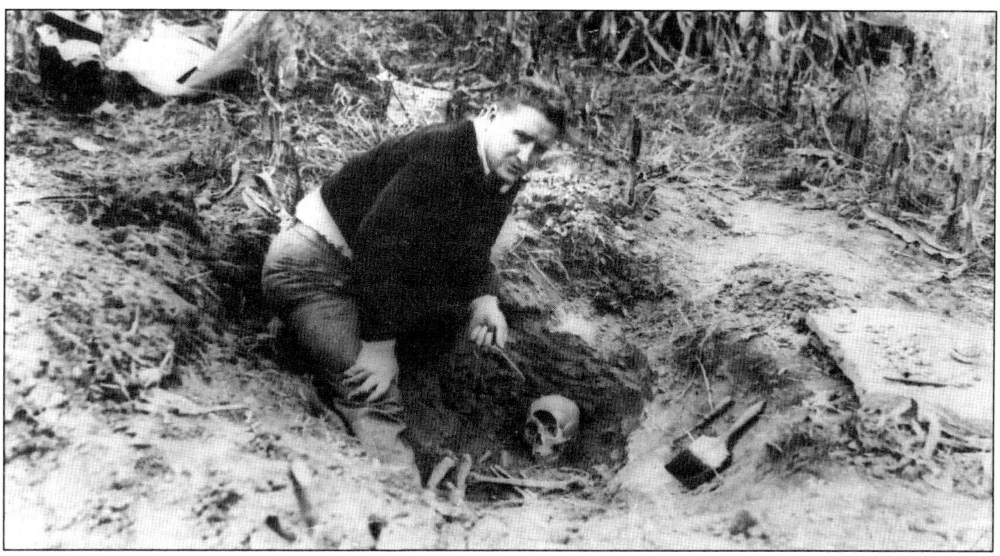

On October 8, 1909, Glenn Hoskin discovered a Native American's remains on the McJunkin family farm. The corpse's feet and hands were missing, and the body was buried with a stone pipe, a pendant with two inlaid stones, and a 16-inch-long spear. Eart Raum and Mr. Mascara were also present at the excavation.

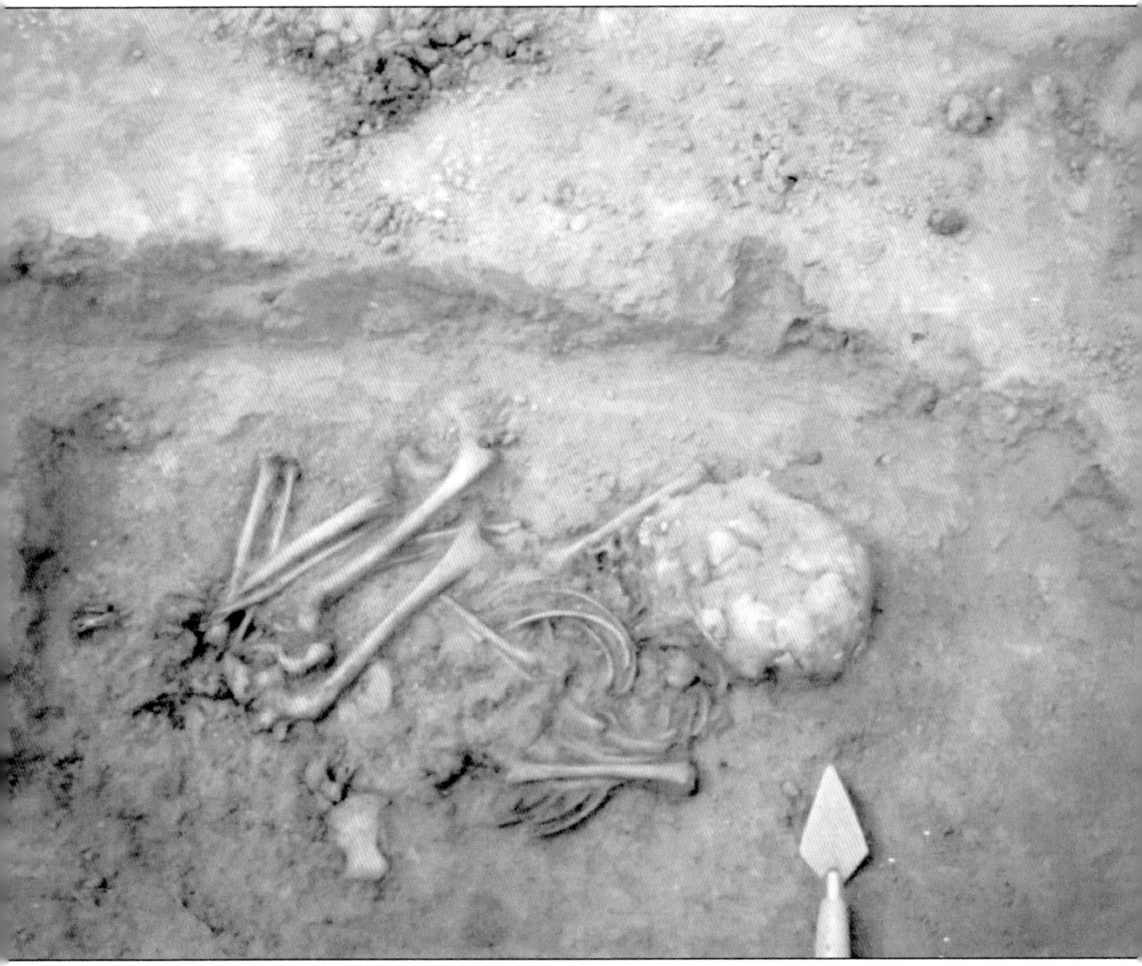

Additional archaeological digs were conducted in Plum in 1966 and 1976. Both occurred in Boyce Park, where another Native American burial site and village had been discovered. The 1966 dig was conducted by Plum resident Kirke Wilson, while the 1976 dig was overseen by University of Pittsburgh anthropologist Richard George. The village seems to have been a short-lived settlement due to the relatively small number of artifacts found. However, a large number of arrowheads, burial mounds, and a stockade were also found, suggesting a battle may have occurred here. A number of Native American paths crisscrossed the area. These paths included the Raystown Path, the Byerly Path, and the Frankstown Path. The Byerly Path was a north-south route while both the Raystown and Frankstown Paths were east-west routes. This picture shows one of the Boyce Park excavations.

Two

AGRICULTURE

From the town's founding until well into the 20th century, agriculture had been the primary business of Plum residents. In fact, in the early 19th century, Allegheny County boasted some 4,881 farms. In the early days, corn, oats, beef, poultry, and hay were all staples of local farms. The typical farm in those days averaged 50 to 100 acres. Dairy cattle and horses were a necessity.

By the 1940s, Plum hosted a farm show. The Plum Township Farm Show began in 1941. For two days in the fall, Plum Township High School opened its doors so the local residents could showcase the fruits of their labors. The farm show was a popular venue throughout the 1940s.

Throughout this first half of the 20th century, one could visit Plum—only 15 miles from downtown Pittsburgh—and feel as though they were traveling through the rural countryside miles and miles from anywhere. However, the agricultural aura of the town was about to change. The housing boom that was initiated by the returning World War II veterans caught up to Plum in the 1950s. Regency Park, Frankstown Acres, Holiday Park, and other housing developments have their roots in this housing boom.

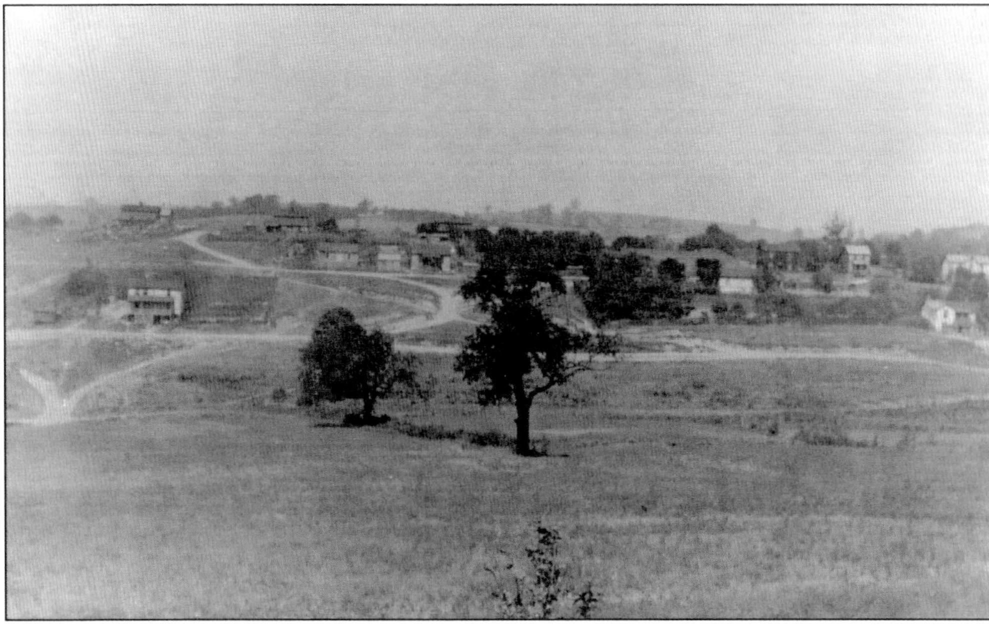

These photographs of Center were taken from the Pierson Run Road area. Center was originally known as Trestle and was home to Plum's first coal mine. By the 1890s, there was a stable constructed to house the mules that were used to haul the coal cars in the nearby mine. During the great migration of the late 19th and early 20th centuries, many immigrants from east-central Europe were attracted to Center because of the employment opportunities in the nearby mines. Fishing in Plum Creek was a popular form of entertainment in the early days of the community. Center was also home to a swimming pool, aptly named Center Beach.

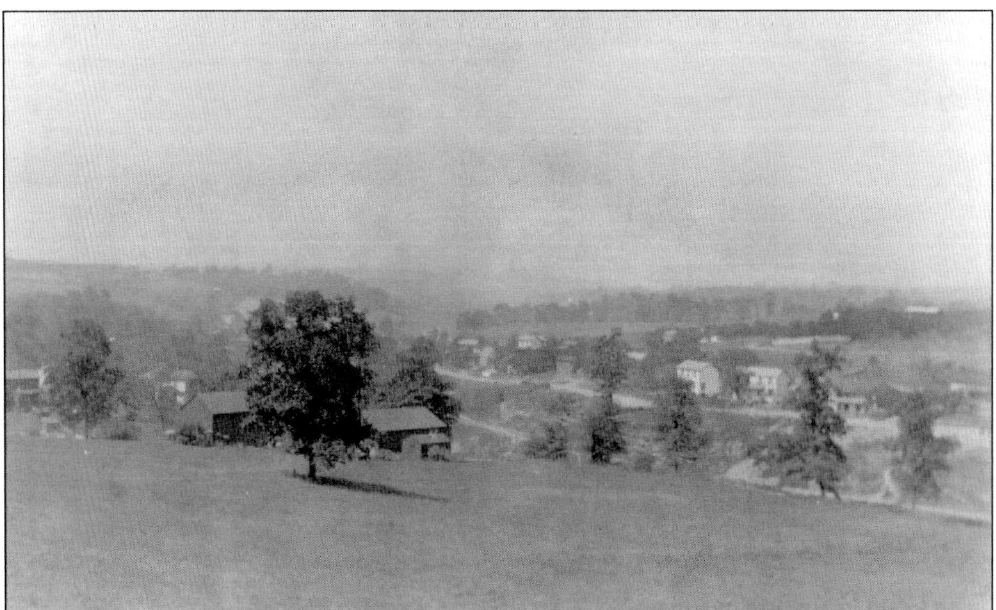

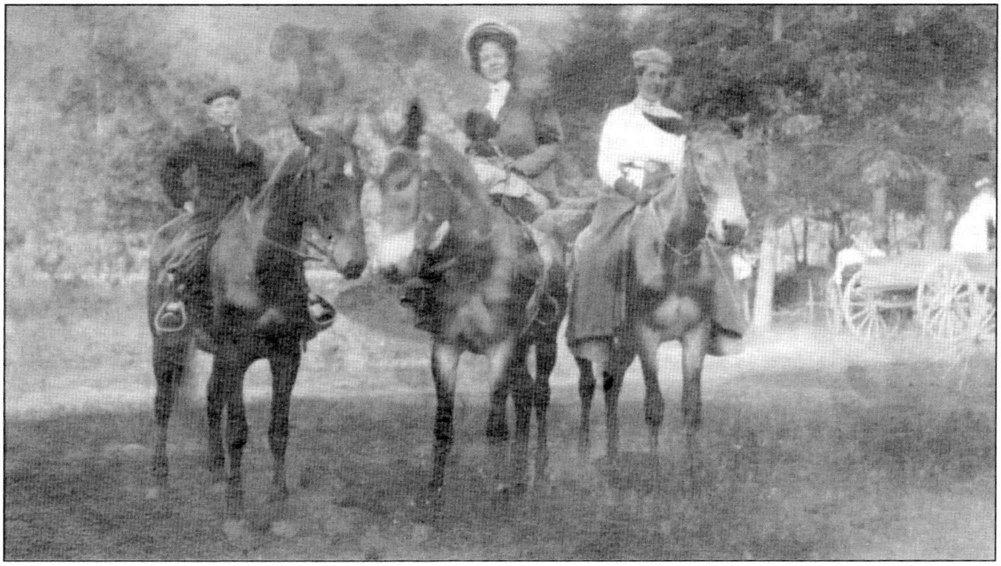

Pictured are three local residents posing for a picture while on horseback. Prior to the advent of the automobile, horses, wagons, and buggies were the primary modes of transportation. Farmers utilized horses on their farms, both for farm work and for transporting their goods to market. During the winter, it was also common for one of the farmers to hitch up the sleigh and transport the local children to school during particularly bad weather.

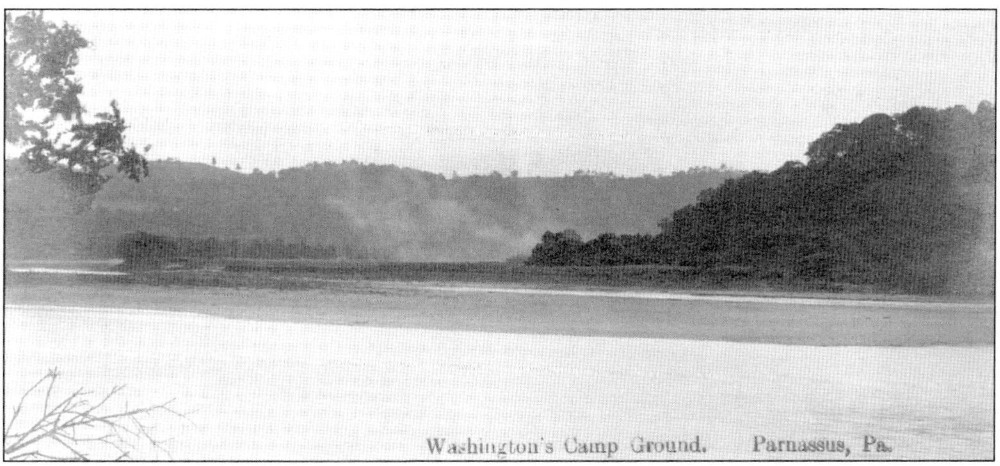

This picture reminds one of what the country looked like in the 19th century. This postcard photograph was taken along the Allegheny River near the Parnassus area (Parnassus being the neighborhood that stretches from the base of the Logans Ferry area through to southern New Kensington). This postcard labels the image as "Washington's Camp Ground," which perhaps is in reference to George Washington traveling on the Allegheny on his way to Fort Le Boeuf, near Erie. (Courtesy of Gary Rogers.)

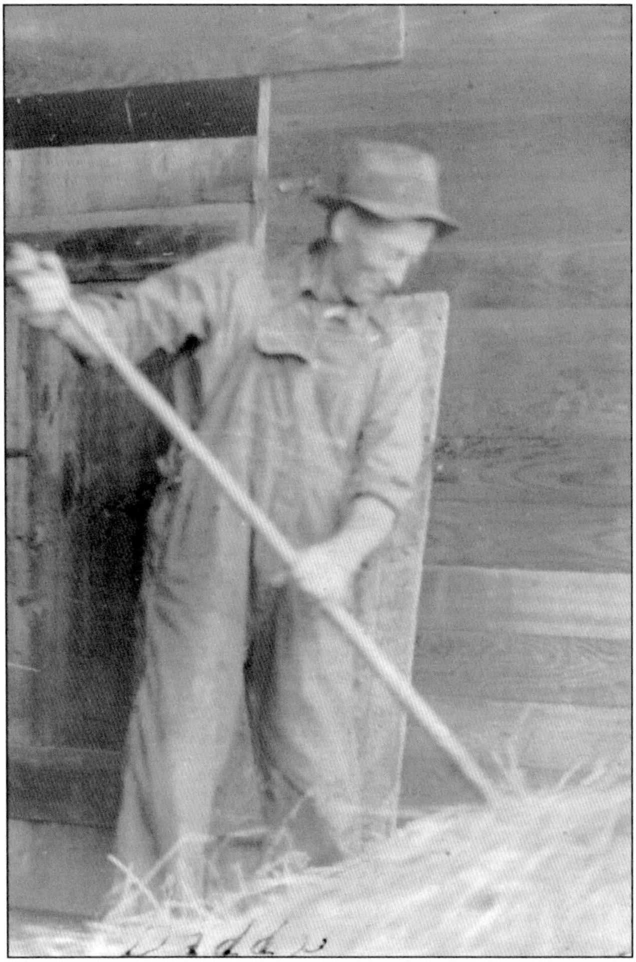

Hay, there! William Carpenter is seen moving the hay in his barn. Hay was a necessity for the feeding of livestock. The Carpenter farm focused more on dairy farming by the early 1900s. In addition to hay, dairy, beef, poultry, oats, and corn were other popular yields from Plum's farms.

During the summer of 1938, William Carpenter is shown relaxing on the lawn in front of his homestead. There was probably not much time for such repose, however. By early autumn, farmers (and farmers' wives, of course) began canning food. Jam was a popular byproduct of fresh fruit. Smoking meat was also a popular way of preserving food.

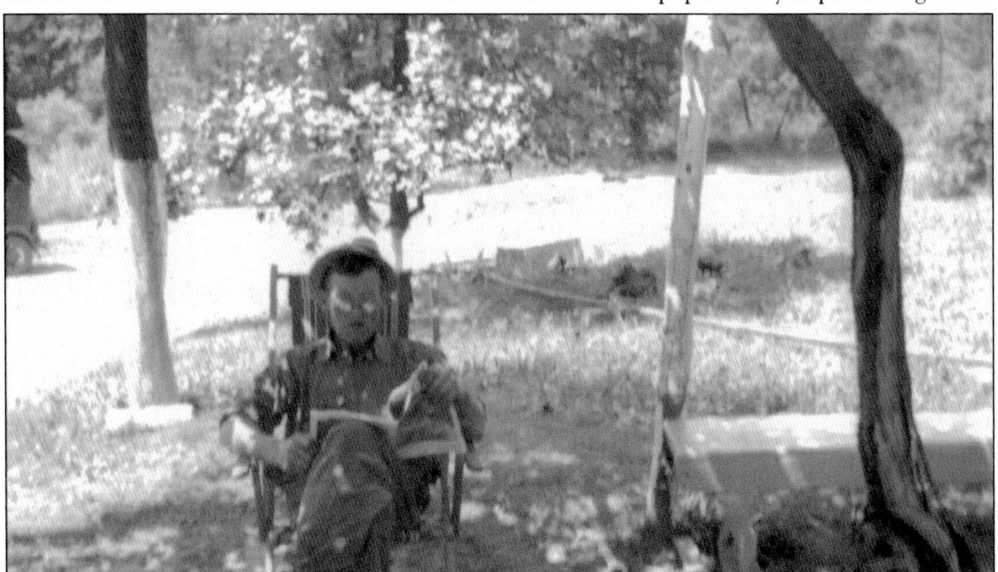

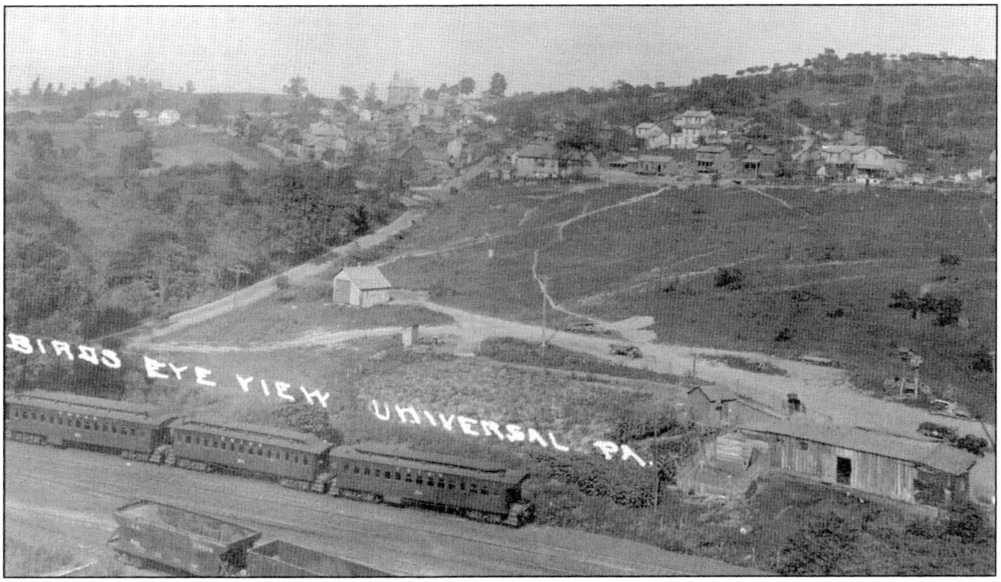

This picture of the community of Universal provides a view of the industrial, agricultural, commercial, and residential all in one photograph. Universal lies within the boundaries of the neighboring township of Penn Hills. At the founding of Allegheny County, the majority of the land now comprising Penn Hills was split between Plum Township and Pitt Township. On January 16, 1850, Penn Hills (then called Adams) was formed. (Courtesy of Gary Rogers.)

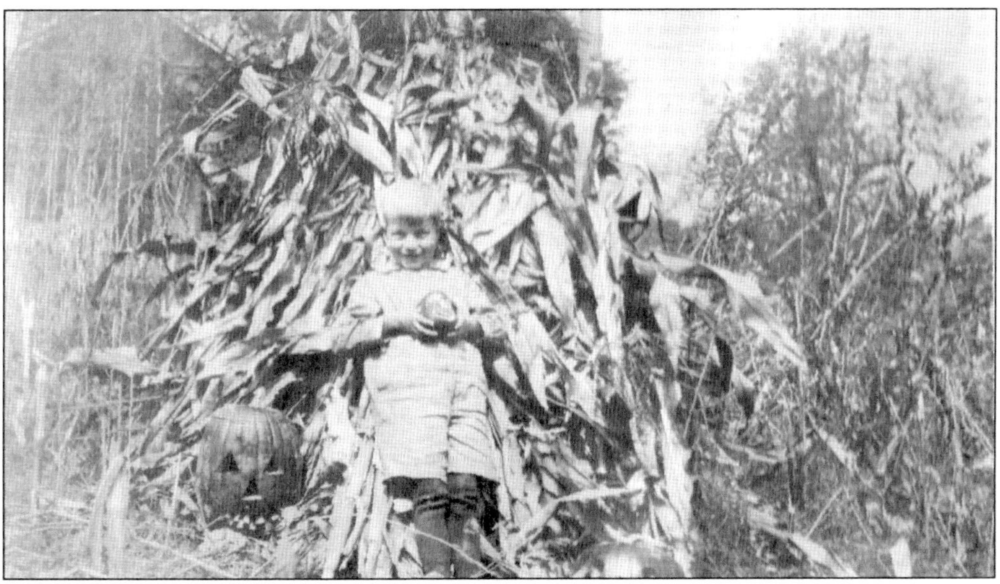

Even in the early part of the 20th century, carving pumpkins and using cornstalks as decorations for Halloween were popular activities during the month of October. This tradition may have been brought to Plum by the community's rich Irish and British heritage. Throughout the British Isles, there has been a long tradition of carving lanterns from vegetables. However, the carved vegetable lantern does not become associated specifically with Halloween until 1866.

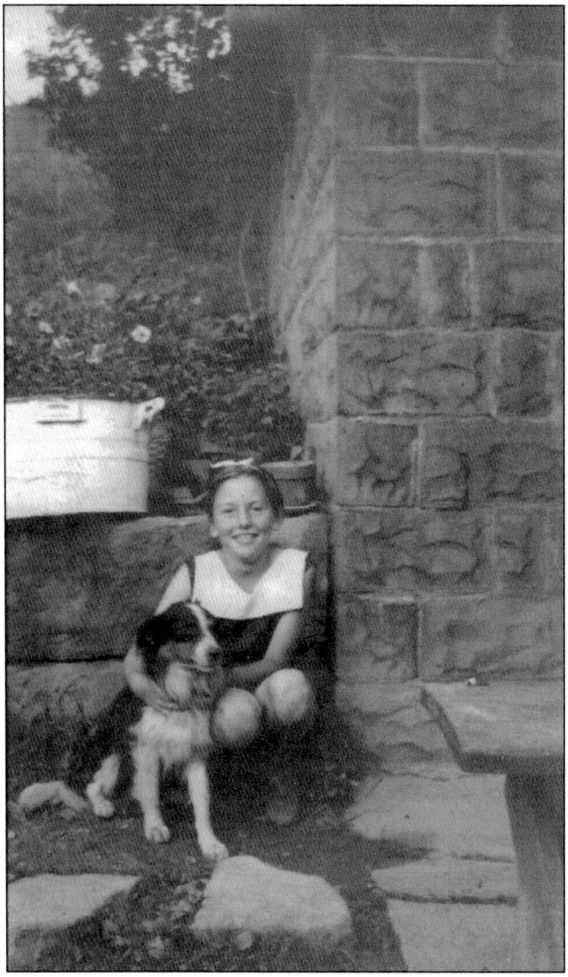

In the late 1930s, Eleanor Carpenter Broome and Barney (left) pose in front of the springhouse next to the Carpenter-family homestead. Around this time, this was a dairy farm. Government regulations of the era mandated updates to the storage of dairy products, and the cement walls of the springhouse were added (the water running below the springhouse served as Mother Nature's natural refrigeration). Below, pictured munching on grapes are, from left to right, Grace Klingensmith, Eleanor Carpenter, and Martha Brodmerkel. The Carpenter barn can be seen in the background. This barn served as a year-round storage center. Hay and straw were stored in the loft while farming equipment was stored in the main part of the barn. The barn still stands today and serves as both a storage place for the Allegheny Foothills Historical Society and Allegheny County and also as a lecture hall for special historical-society events.

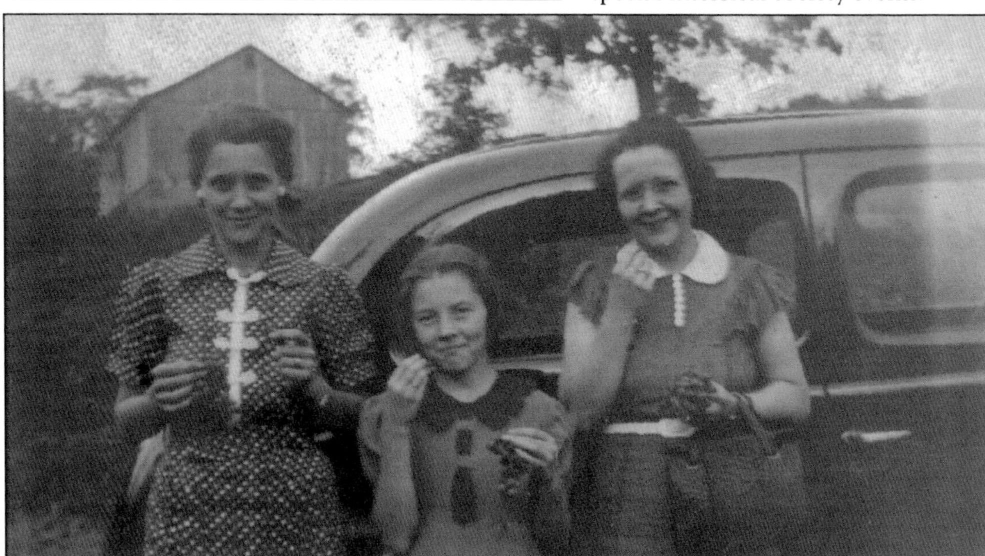

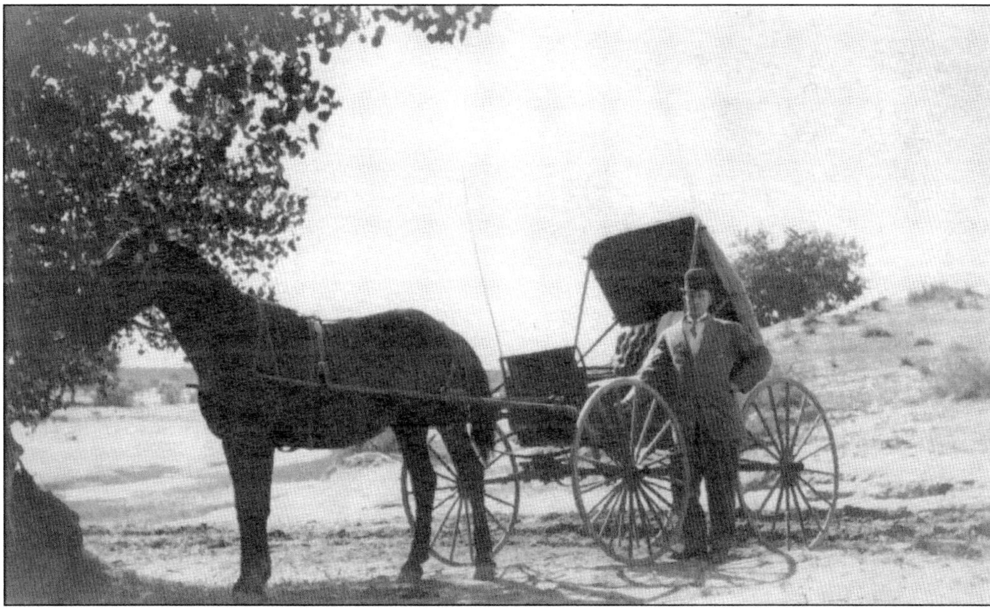

Members of the Ciceske family of Plum are seen here in two alternate modes of transportation. At the start of the 20th century, many roads were still unimproved; this was especially true in a rural community like Plum. It was in one of these early-model cars (below) that Guy R. Smith, first supervising principal of Plum Township Schools, drove around Plum to visit the various schools of the district. In fact, it was not until the 1920s that the Lincoln Highway— the nation's first series of roads designated as a highway—was formed. By then, while horses and buggies may still have been utilized (for necessity or for nostalgic reasons), motorized vehicles ruled the transportation industry.

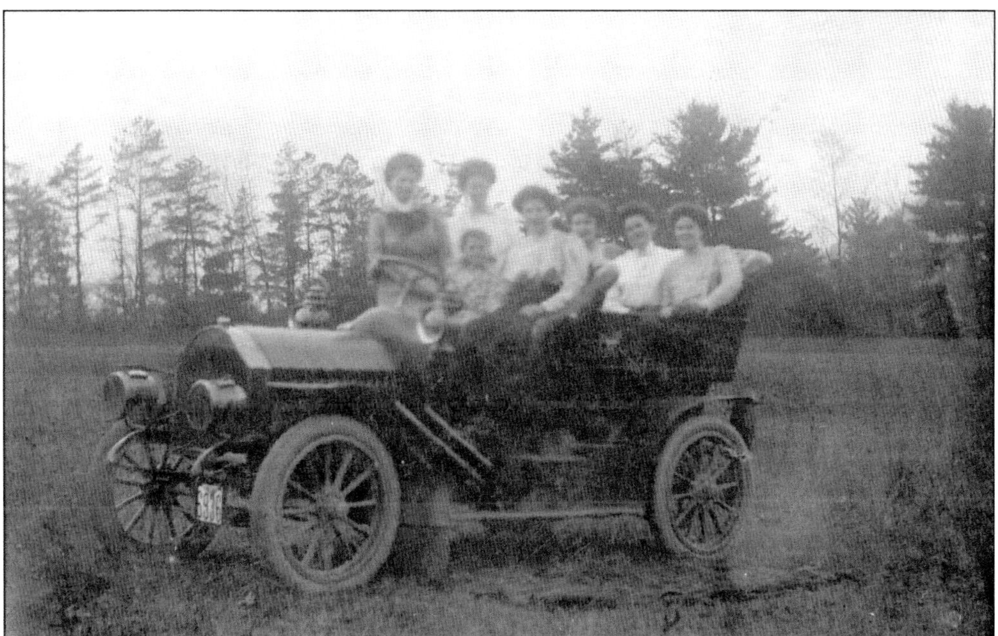

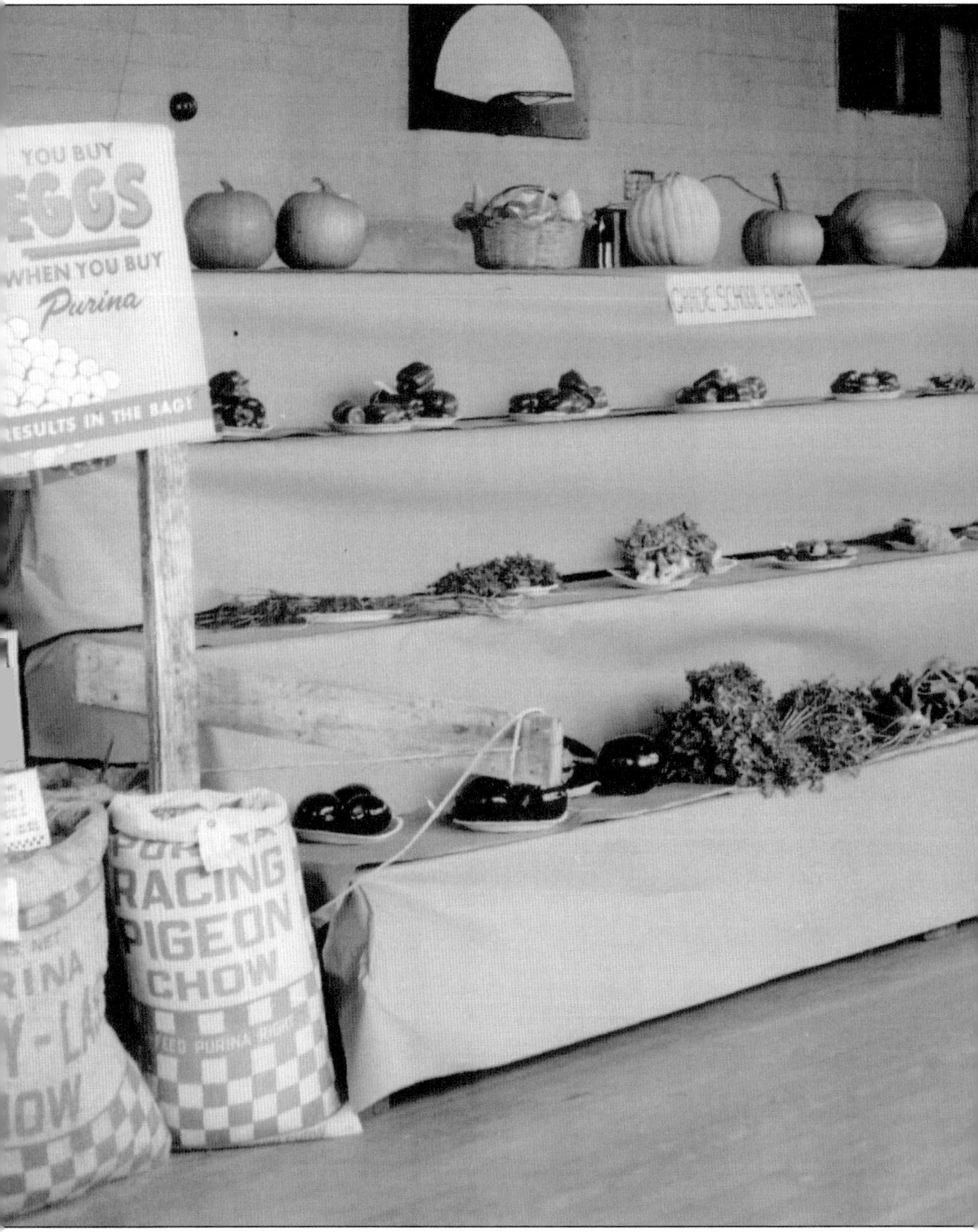

This picture, taken around 1945 or 1946, depicts the Plum Township Farm Show, which was popular during much of the 1940s. Beginning in the fall of 1941, Plum High School hosted the annual show. Residents could enter their prize livestock, crops, baked goods, and other fruits of their labors to be exhibited beside those of their neighbors. Prizes and ribbons were awarded to

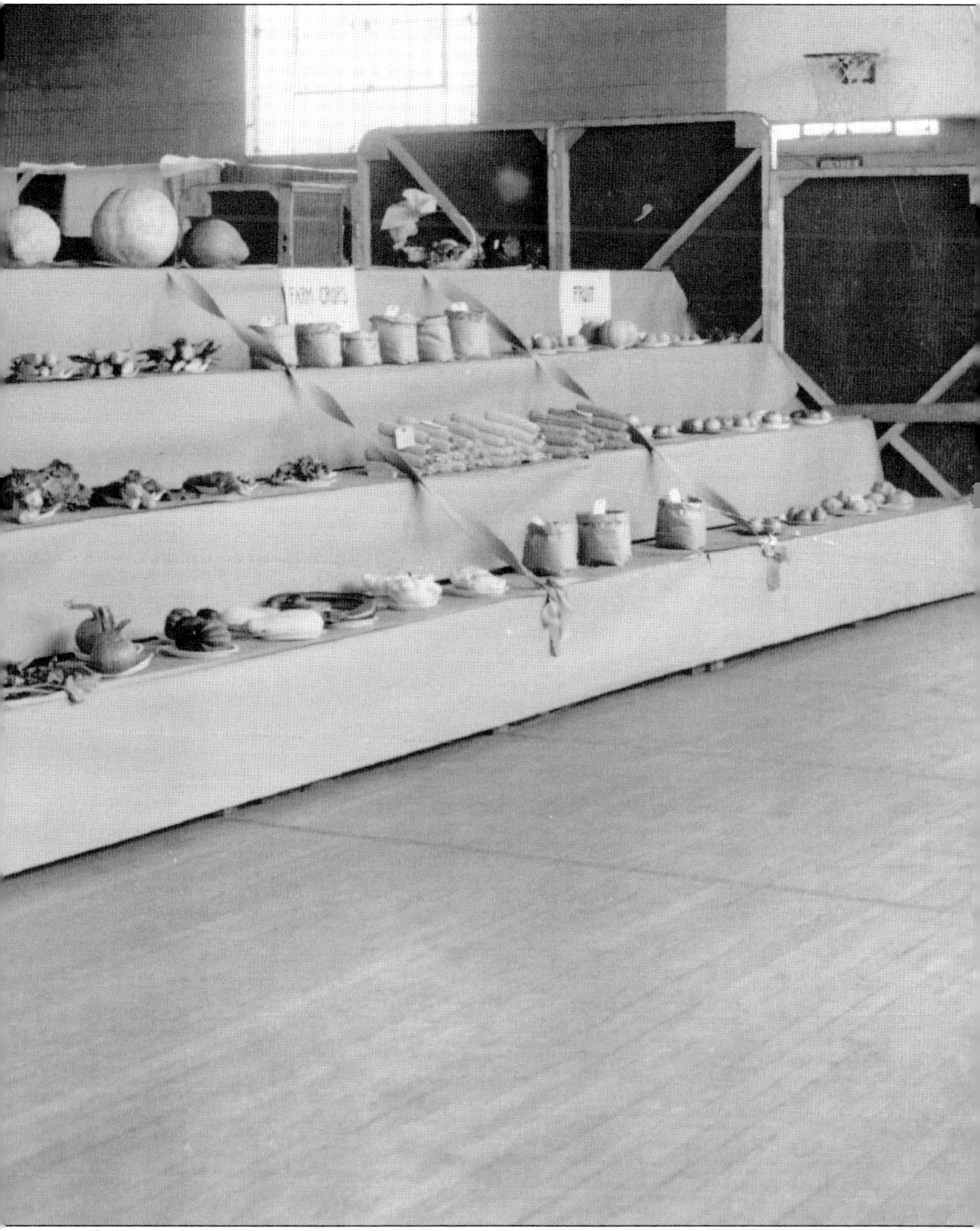

winning exhibitors. Unfortunately, this wonderful community event did not last very long. The farm show was discontinued in the late 1940s, but it had been a welcome and needed escape for a war-weary public.

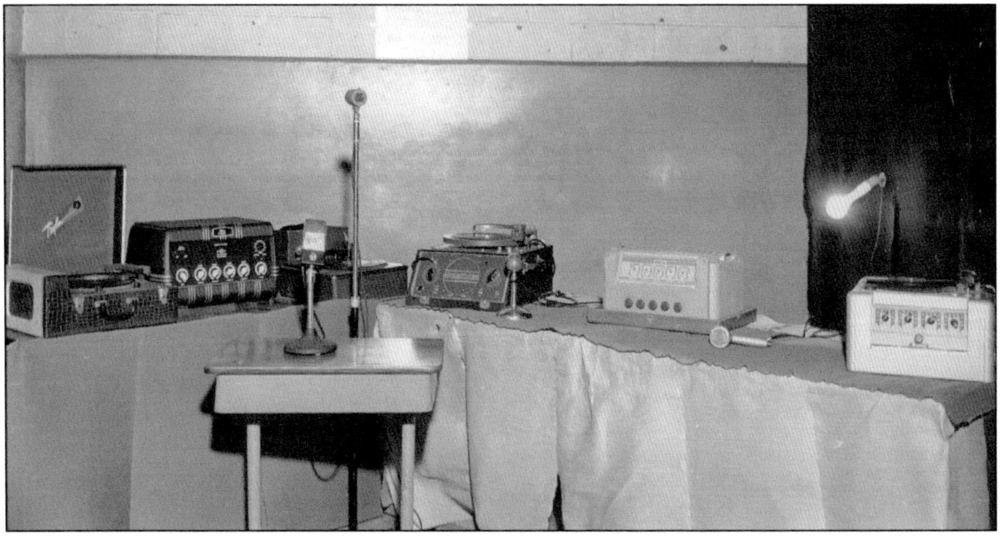

Pictured here is some of the new technology displayed at the 1945–1946 Plum Township Farm Show. The farm show was a popular venue for local residents to come together and learn about new technologies as well as to swap tried-and-true farming techniques. Of course, the farm show was a useful advertising tool for local businesses, which might have been able to provide some much needed services, such as banks offering loans, or mechanics offering farm equipment repair.

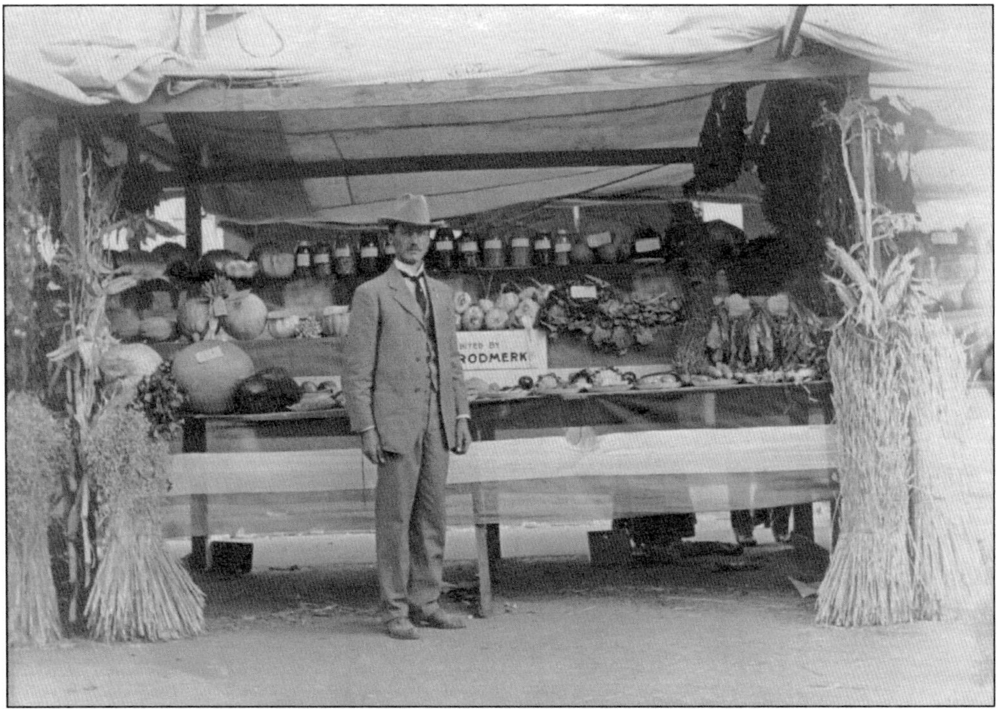

This gentleman displays some of his crops and other such wares. As the introduction to the 1946 farm show program states, the "farm show was inspired by desire on the part of many in our community to gather together at the end of a season of plenty to lay before our friends and neighbors the finest fruits of our labors and by doing so inspire others and encourage ourselves to even finer things."

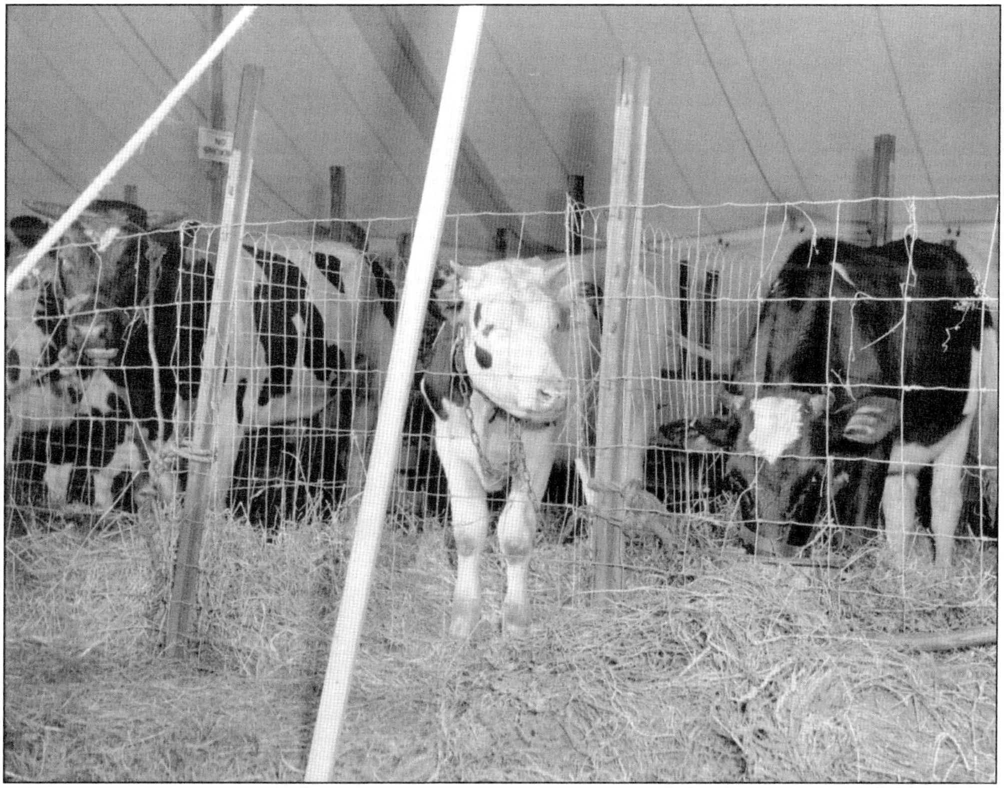

Pictured are cattle and various poultry on display, brought to the show by farmers vying for a famous blue ribbon. According to the rules and regulations of the farm show, "ribbons shall be awarded on all 1st, 2nd, and 3rd placings as called for in the premium list, provided the exhibit merits a placing." Commercial exhibits had their own set of rules. They had to be educational in nature, there could be no misrepresentation of products, and they had to remain set up for the duration of the show. The festivities were spread out over a three-day period.

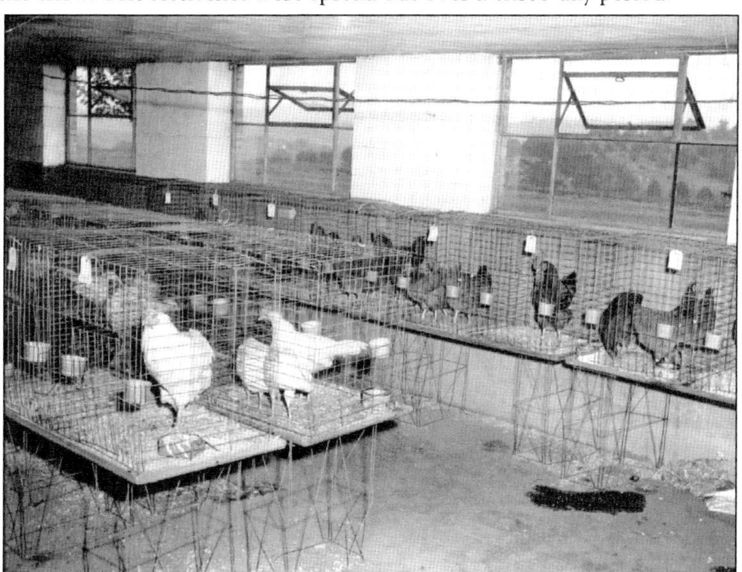

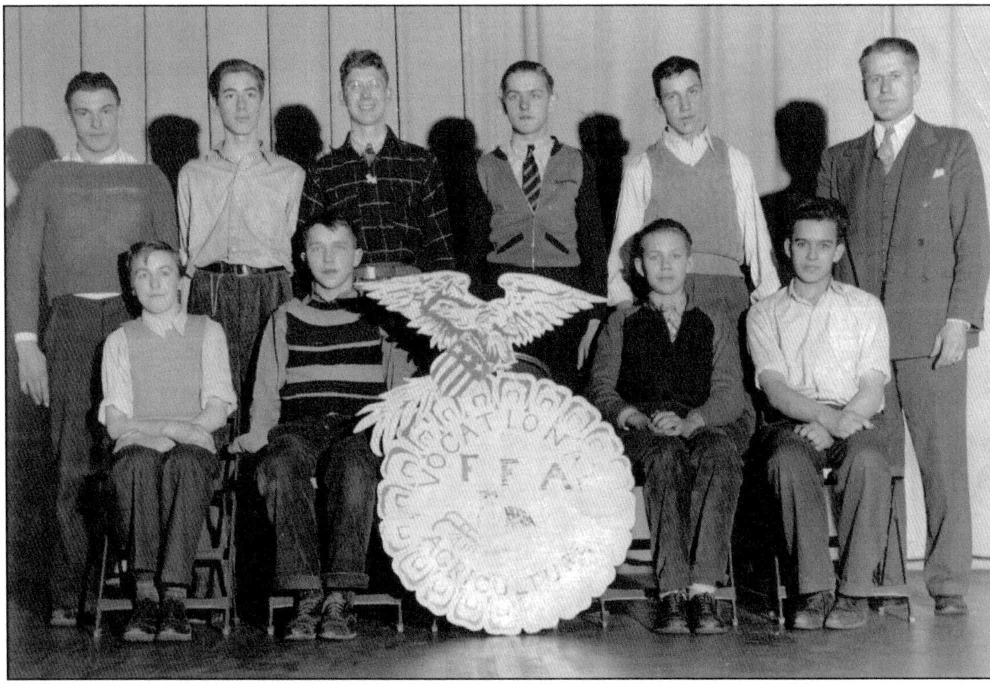

Around 1941, the first agriculture teacher poses for a photograph with his Plum Township High School students. The agriculture club was one of the many clubs students had to choose from when they attended the newly formed school. In 1941, the students could participate in the chorus, the news club, the library club, the sports club, and more.

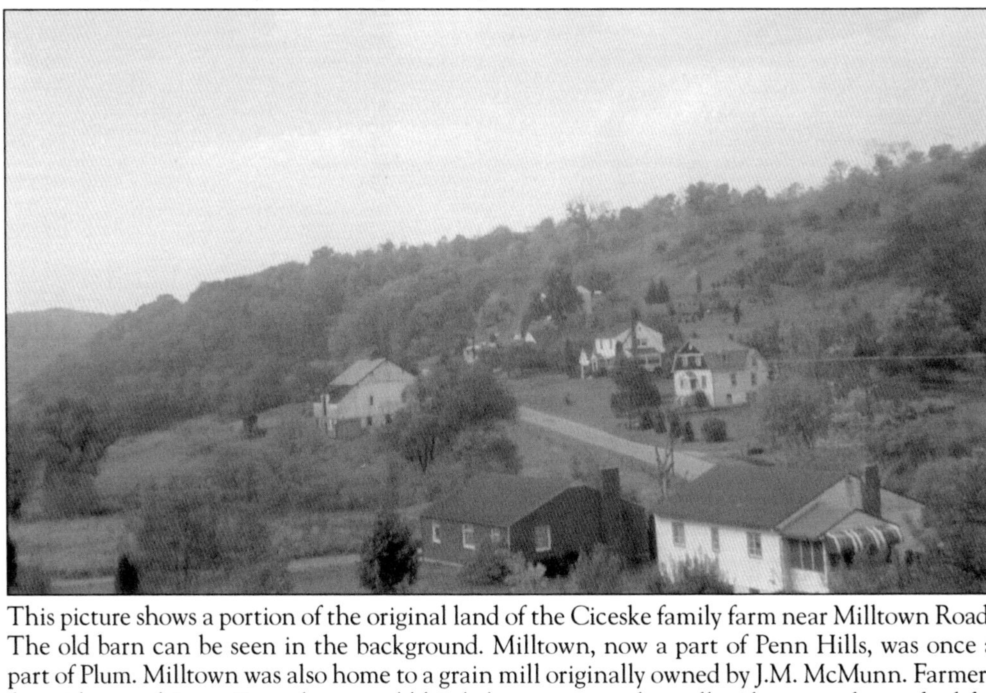

This picture shows a portion of the original land of the Ciceske family farm near Milltown Road. The old barn can be seen in the background. Milltown, now a part of Penn Hills, was once a part of Plum. Milltown was also home to a grain mill originally owned by J.M. McMunn. Farmers from Plum and Penn Townships would haul their grain to the mill to be ground into feed for their livestock.

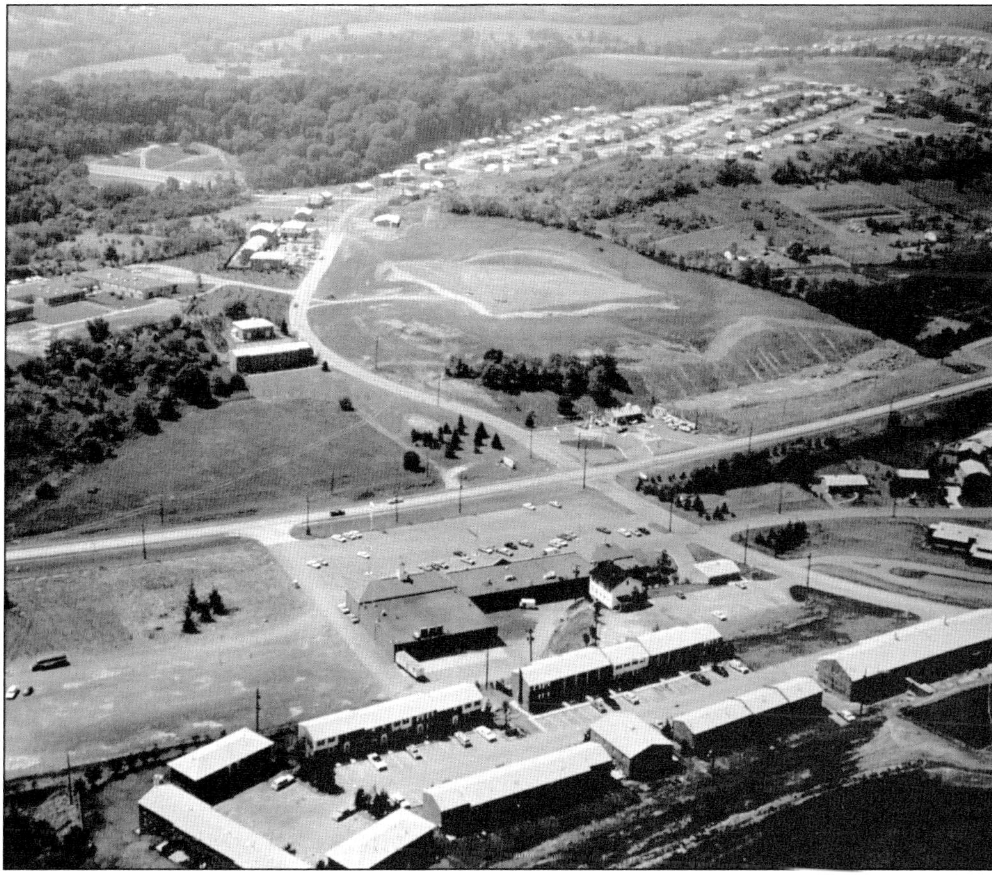

Holiday Park is the area of Plum that has seen the most rapid development recently. Around 1990, the development had a population of around 12,000. The total area of Holiday Park is 2,044 acres. Several reputable contractors were used in the development of the community. The name of the development was found by pouring over the real-estate sections of the nation's larger newspapers. A Los Angeles newspaper noted all of the special attractions and amenities of a housing development named Holiday Park, and this is how Plum's Holiday Park got its name. In the aerial view above, Holiday Park can be seen in the background. Below, a sign announces the availability of homes for sale there.

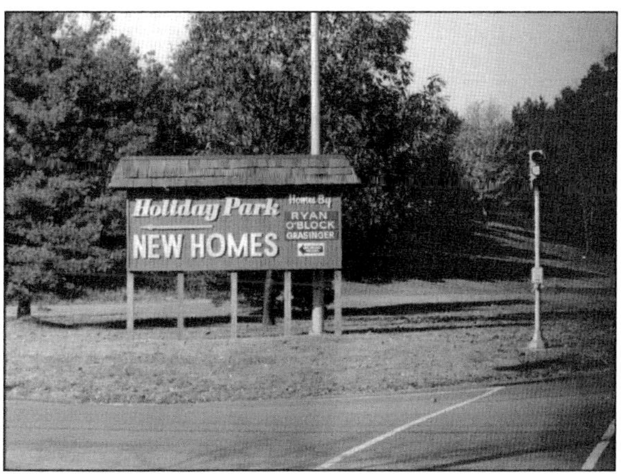

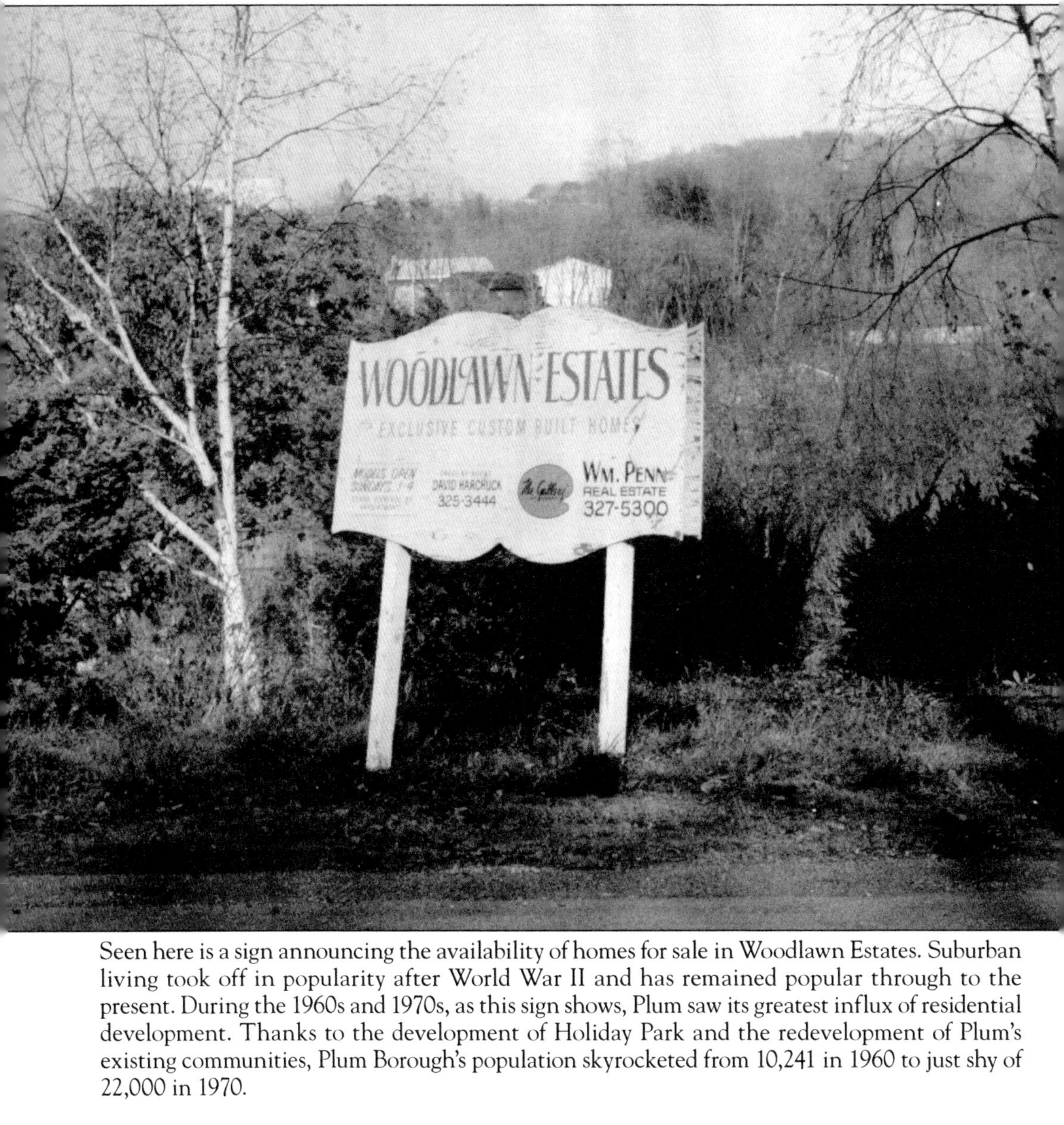

Seen here is a sign announcing the availability of homes for sale in Woodlawn Estates. Suburban living took off in popularity after World War II and has remained popular through to the present. During the 1960s and 1970s, as this sign shows, Plum saw its greatest influx of residential development. Thanks to the development of Holiday Park and the redevelopment of Plum's existing communities, Plum Borough's population skyrocketed from 10,241 in 1960 to just shy of 22,000 in 1970.

Three

Industry and Commerce

While not known as an industrial hub like many surrounding communities, Plum did have an active industrial base within its boundaries. Several of Plum's communities formed around coal mines. Railroads were the superhighways of the 19th century and flourished in conjunction with the mining industries. In Plum, other industries did not come about until after World War II. These included the oil and gas, manufacturing, and aluminum industries.

Family businesses played a major part in the commercial life of Plum. McLaughlin's Store in Unity, Jackson's Hardware of Center, Nesbit's Garage of New Texas, and Funfar's Garage of Center are all businesses dating from the early 20th century and before. Funfar's was in operation since 1924 and was the first service station in Plum. Jackson's Hardware dated from 1870.

As the town's population increased and the per capita income followed suit, the number of retail businesses also increased. Almost every community within Plum, dating back to the 19th century, had its own group of entrepreneurs. After the 1950s and the shift of large numbers of people from the cities to the suburbs, Plum saw an increase in retail centers, particularly along the Route 286 corridor.

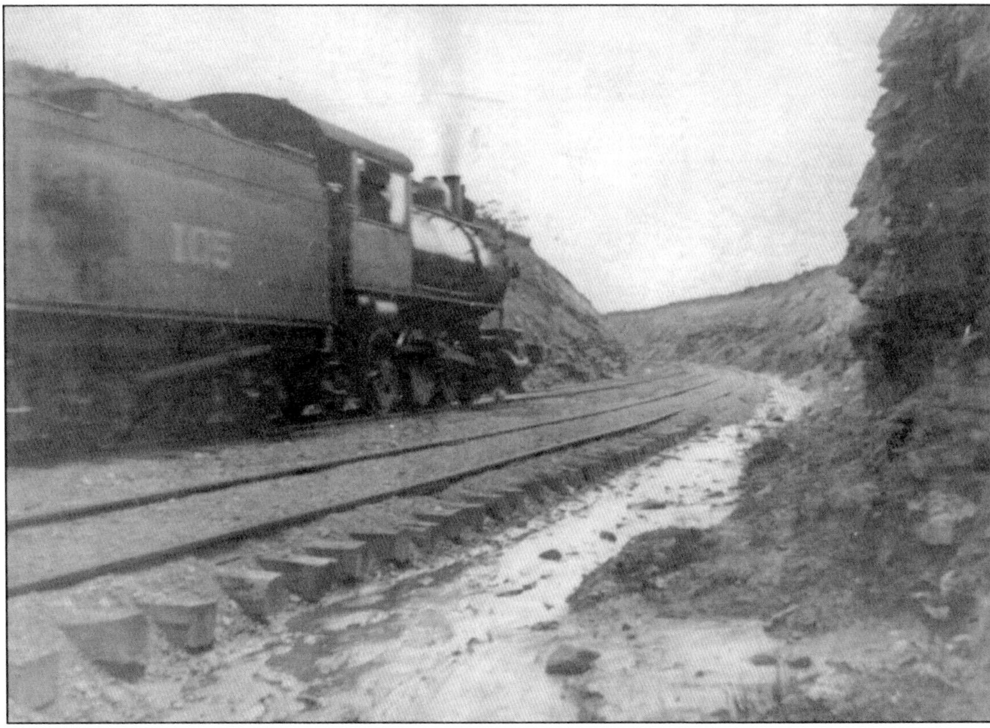

This undated photograph shows a locomotive traveling around the Bessemer Bend near East Oakmont. The railroad played a major part in the history of human civilization. It was the first high-speed mode of transportation ever used. Many rail yards and transportation hubs were in Plum's vicinity, including North Bessemer, Pitcairn, the Turtle Creek valley, and the tracks running along the Allegheny River valley.

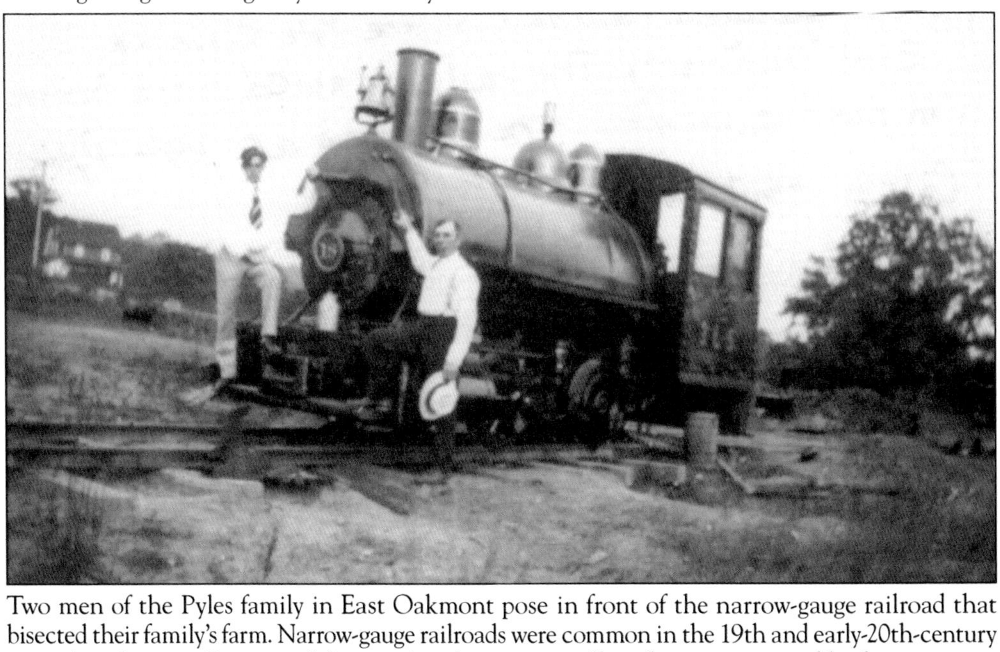

Two men of the Pyles family in East Oakmont pose in front of the narrow-gauge railroad that bisected their family's farm. Narrow-gauge railroads were common in the 19th and early-20th-century agricultural scene. One use of these railroads was in small coal mines operated by farm owners.

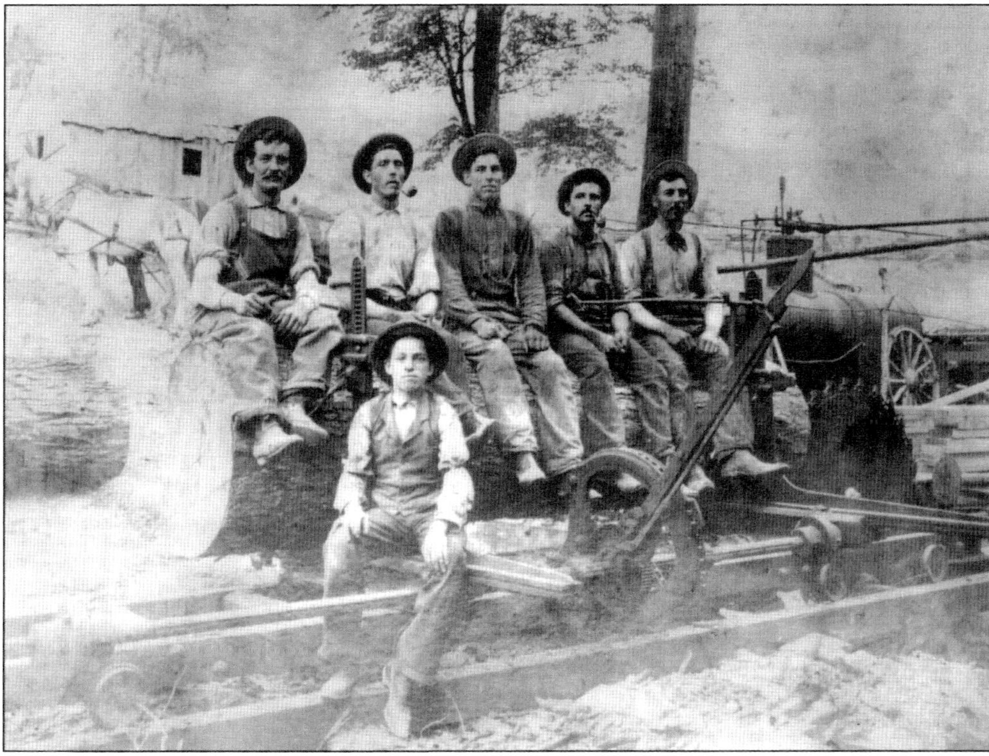

Pictured are railroad workers building the Bessemer tracks through East Oakmont. The North Bessemer Rail Yard near the Penn Hills–Plum border was the southern terminus of the Bessemer and Lake Erie Railroad Company's line (which originated from Conneaut, Ohio). From North Bessemer, Union Railroad serviced the blast furnaces of the Monongahela Valley.

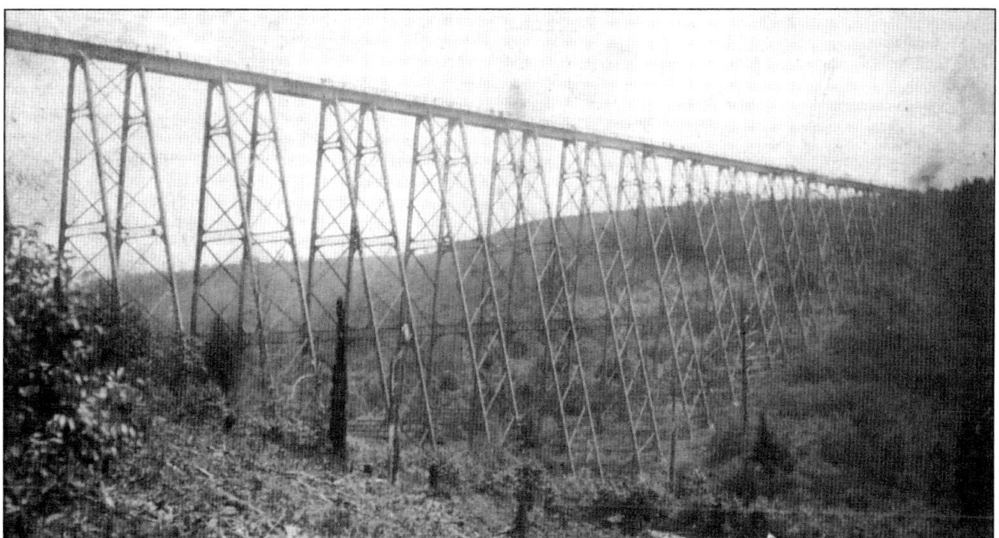

This coal trestle bridge stretched from Unity Station to Trestle (now known as the community of Center). As with many of the communities of Plum, the mining industry and the railroad played a major role in the growth of Unity. In 1902, there were only 13 homes in Unity, and the only telephone in the entire neighborhood was located in McLaughlin's Store.

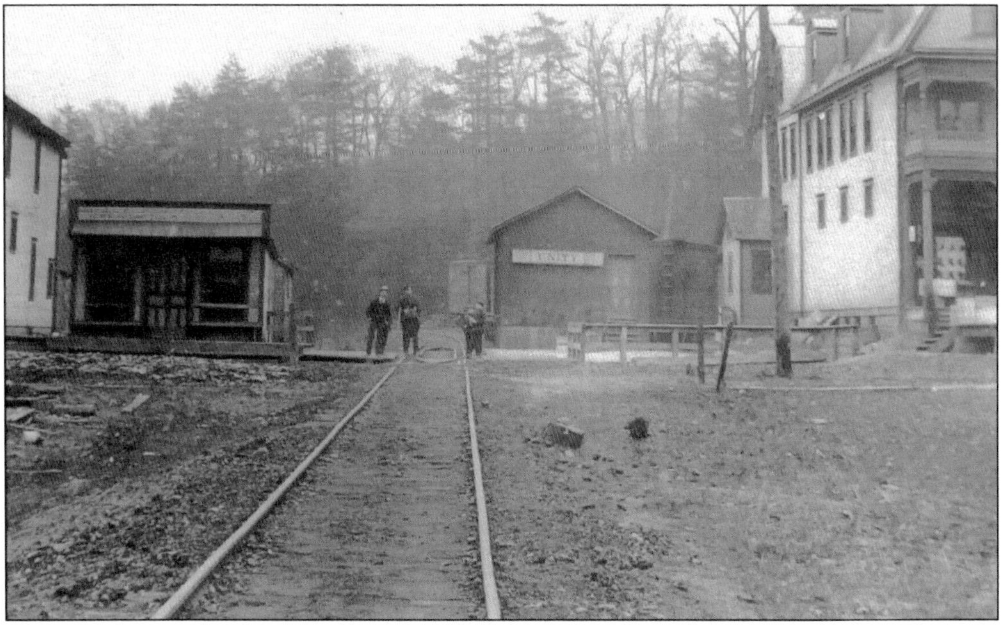

Several men stand near the tracks of what was known as Unity Station. Unity—on the western border of Plum near Penn Hills—was centered around the train station and the coal mine. McLaughlin's Store was the community general store. The Unity Volunteer Fire Department was created after a major fire destroyed several businesses. (Courtesy of Gary Rogers.)

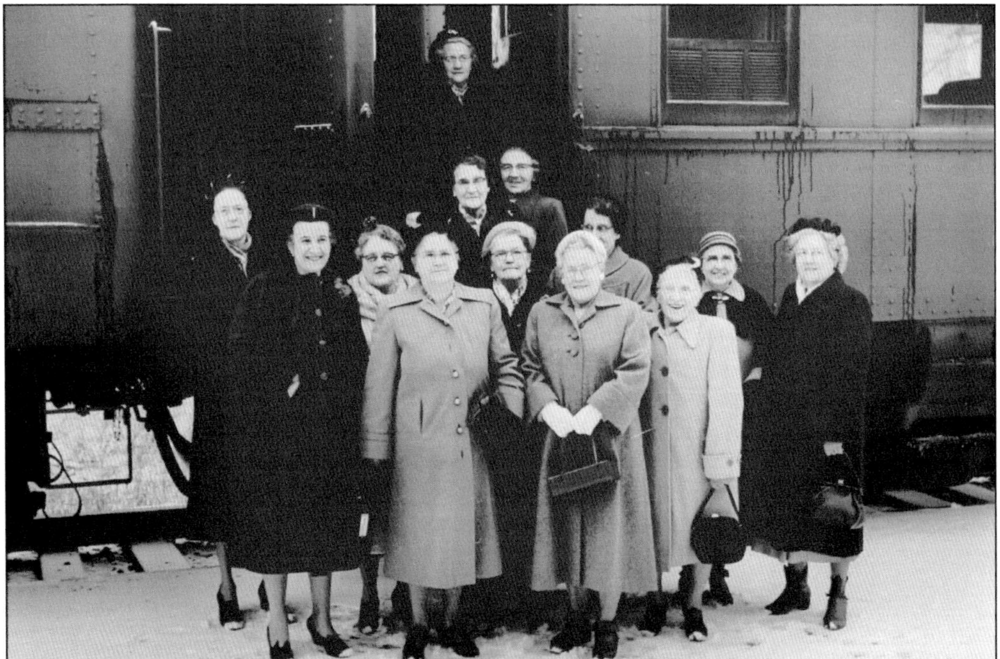

Pictured are members of the Ladies Society of the Brotherhood of Locomotive Firemen and Enginemen boarding Number 12 at Greenville, Pennsylvania. The society was founded on December 1, 1873, and initially offered insurance benefits to its members. In 1969, the union merged with three other unions in order to form the United Transportation Union.

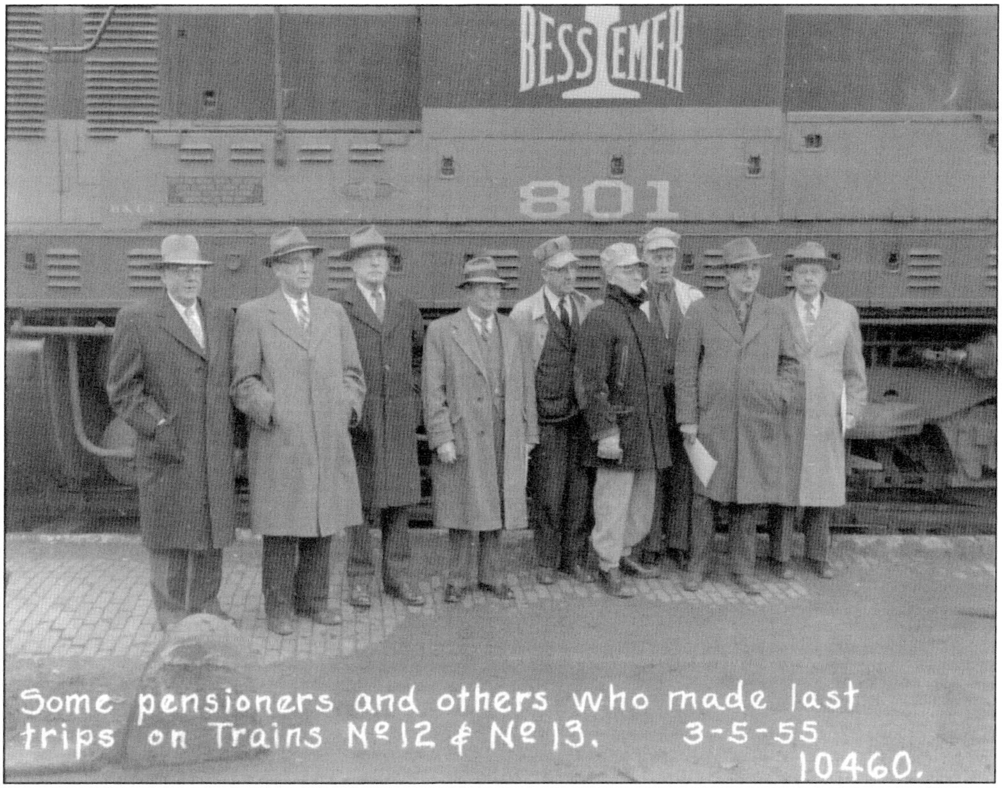

Shown are some pensioners, accompanied by other passengers, who made the last trips on trains No. 12 and No. 13 on March 5, 1955. Those shown in this picture are, from left to right, Mr. Wiesen, Mr. Buchanan, Mr. Gunther, Mr. Adams, Mr. Burns, Mr. Reitz, Mr. Dinehart, Mr. Reed, and Mr. Smith.

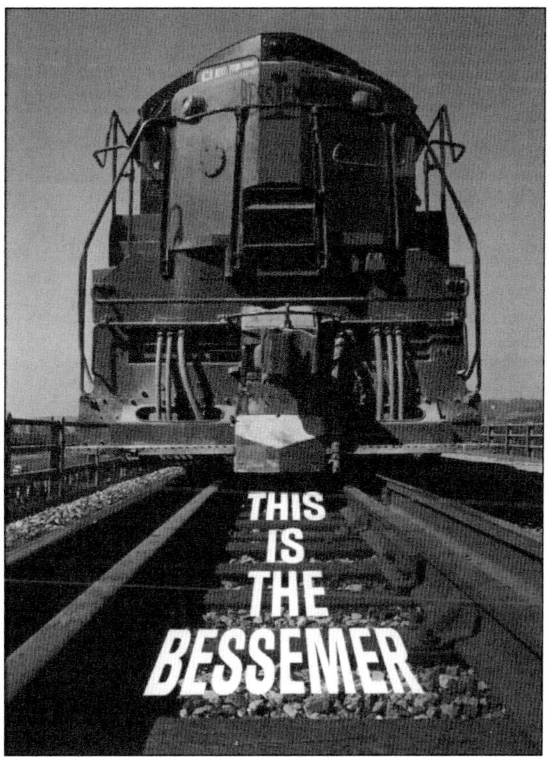

The title sheet of this magazine featuring the North Bessemer Rail Yard (located in Penn Hills, near the western border of Plum) prominently displays one of the engines that dominated the landscape of the area for many decades. The Bessemer Rail Yard was part of the Bessemer and Lake Erie Railroad Company, which extended from Conneaut, Ohio, and the steel mills of the upper Monongahela Valley such as the Clairton Works, Irvin Works, and Duquesne Works, among others.

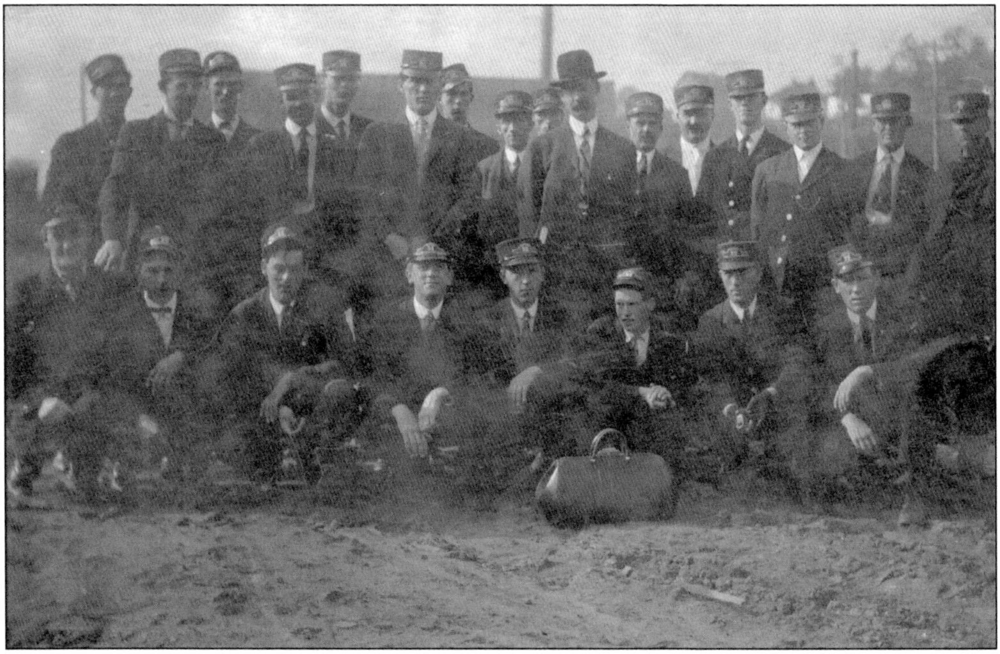

Above, Bessemer railroad workers pose in the rail yard. Below, workers pose on one of the Bessemer steam engines. The Bessemer and Lake Erie Railroad was established in 1900, a successor of the Bear Creek Railroad (founded in 1865). The Bessemer provided a vital link between the iron ore–receiving ports of Conneaut, Ohio and Erie, Pennsylvania and the steel capital of the world—the Pittsburgh metropolitan area. In addition to iron ore for steel-mill consumption, coal was a major freight for the railroad. In fact, on average, about 50 percent of the total tonnage handled by the railroad in the mid-20th century was coal. (Both courtesy of Gary Rogers.)

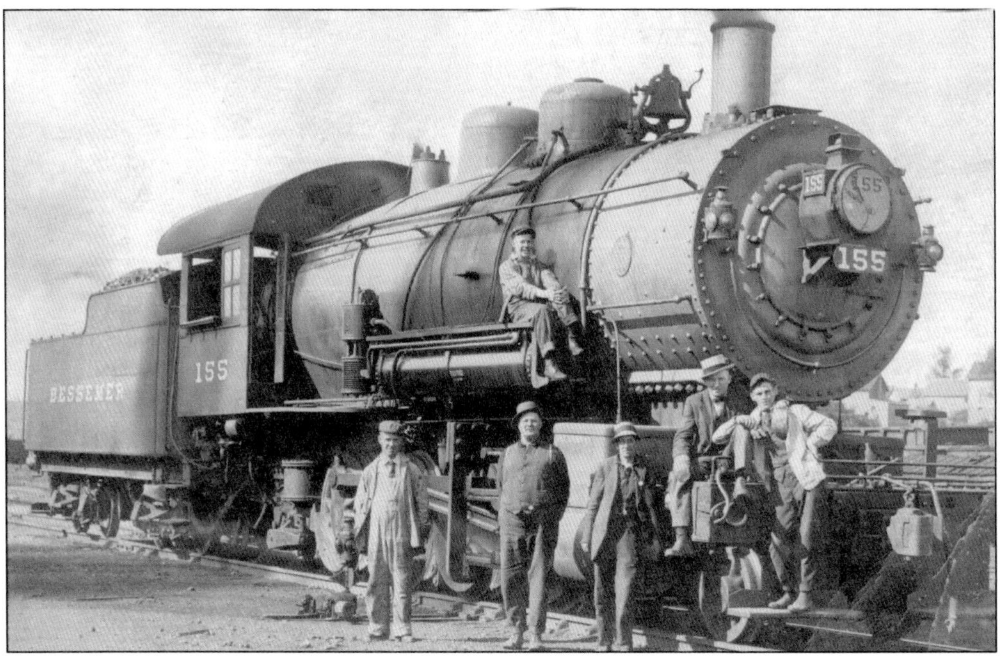

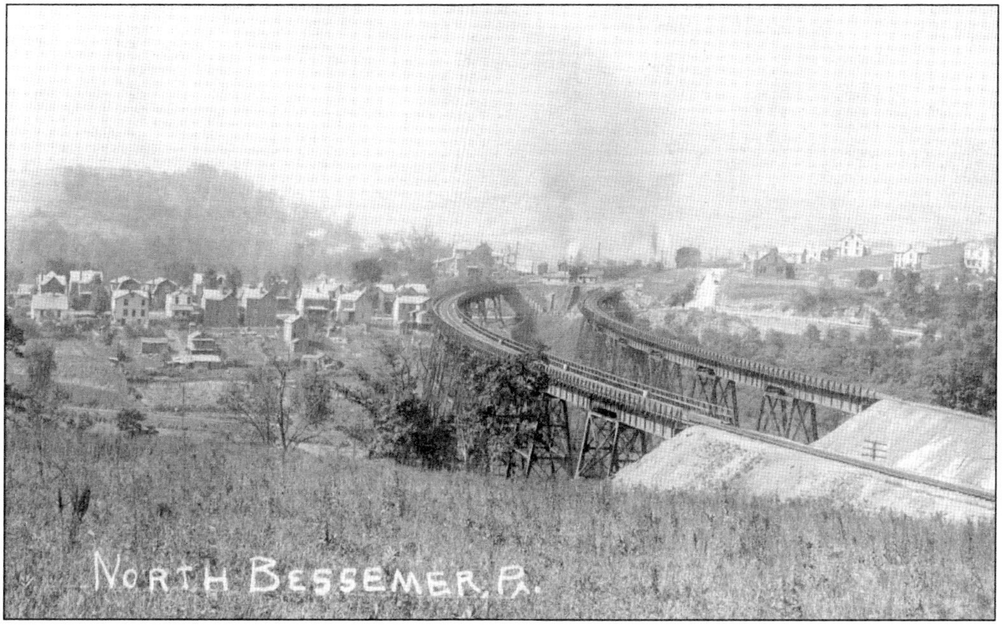

This undated photograph shows the North Bessemer rail bridge, a vital link for trains going to and from the North Bessemer Rail Yard. Much like the Horseshoe Curve outside of Altoona, the North Bessemer Bridge was considered to be a target for Axis espionage during World War II. To reduce the likelihood of it being attacked, the area around the bridge was backfilled; thus, the bridge was "buried." (Courtesy of Gary Rogers.)

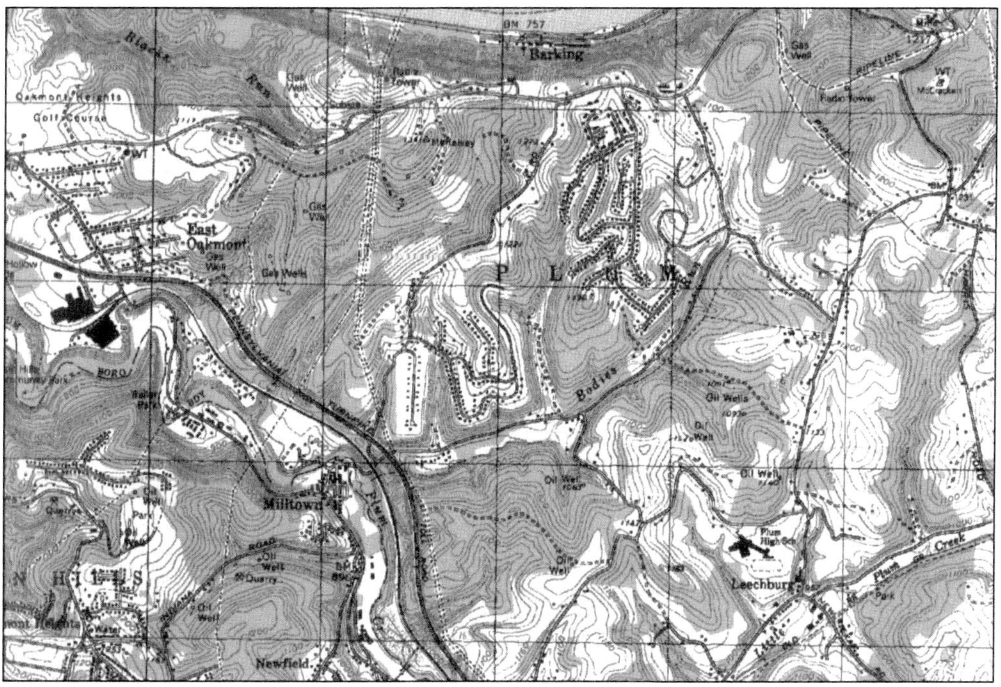

This topographical map of Plum was created by the US Geological Service in 1993. Shown in this portion of the map is the northern half of Plum Borough and the northern portion of neighboring Penn Hills Township. The Pennsylvania Turnpike (Interstate 76) can be seen on the left.

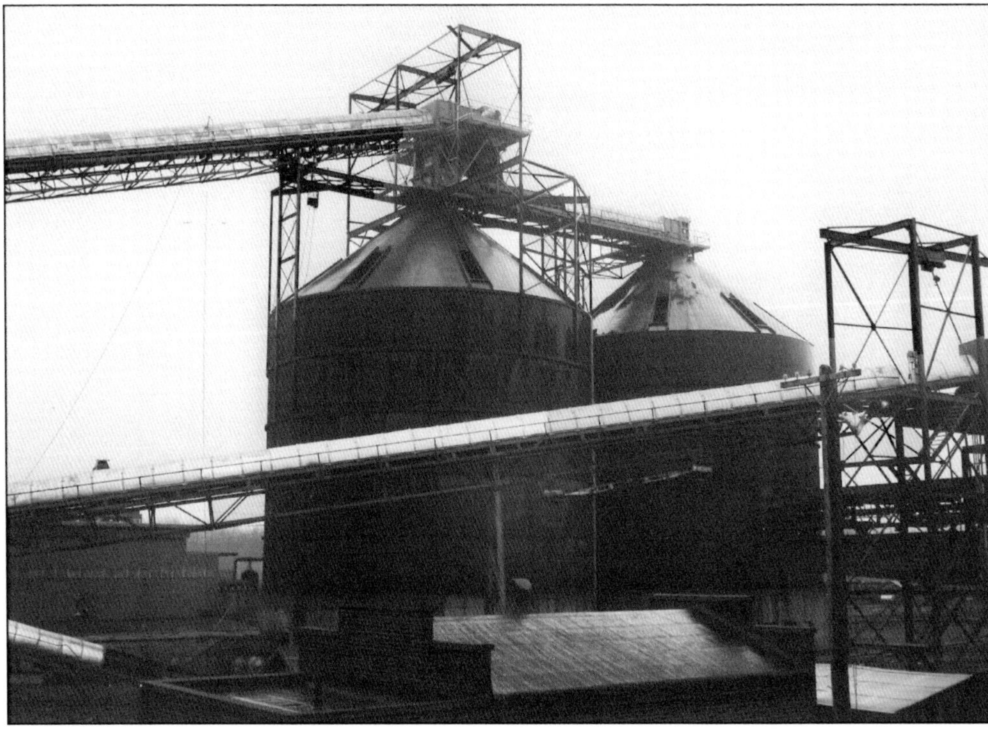

From its beginnings with William Coleman and Andrew Carnegie's initial venture in 1870, coal mining in Plum came a long way. This photograph depicts the large structures that eventually replaced the earlier, more primitive structures within the mining industry in Plum and around the country. Plum had three communities grow up around its coal mines—Barking, Logans Ferry, and Renton. In 1919, Allegheny-Pittsburgh Coal Company opened the mine in Logans Ferry, which operated until 1968. The Oakmont Mine was opened in 1917 by Hillman Coal and Coke Company. After a series of sales and mergers and the decline of the coal-using industries, the mine, then owned by the Wheeling Pittsburgh Steel Company, closed in 1979.

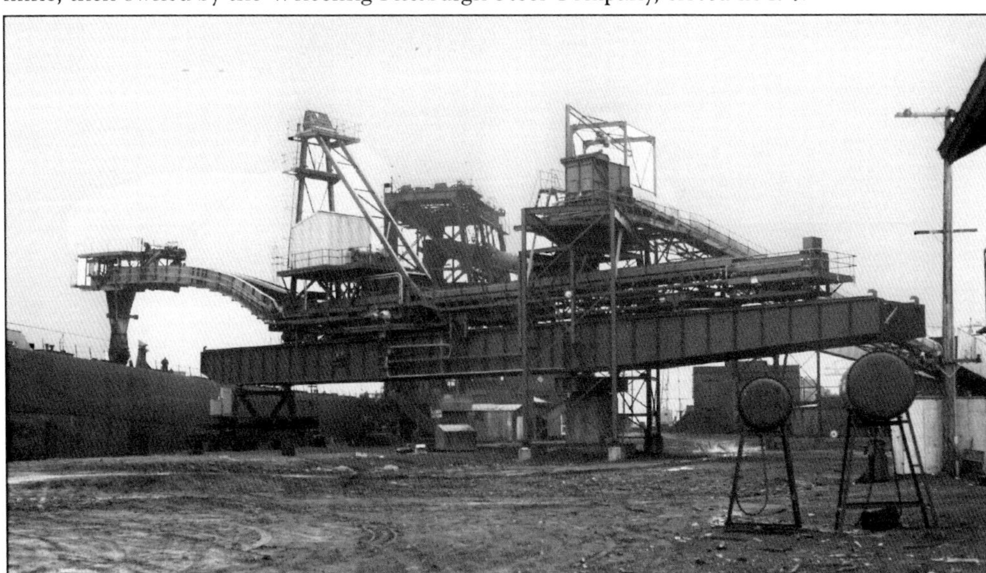

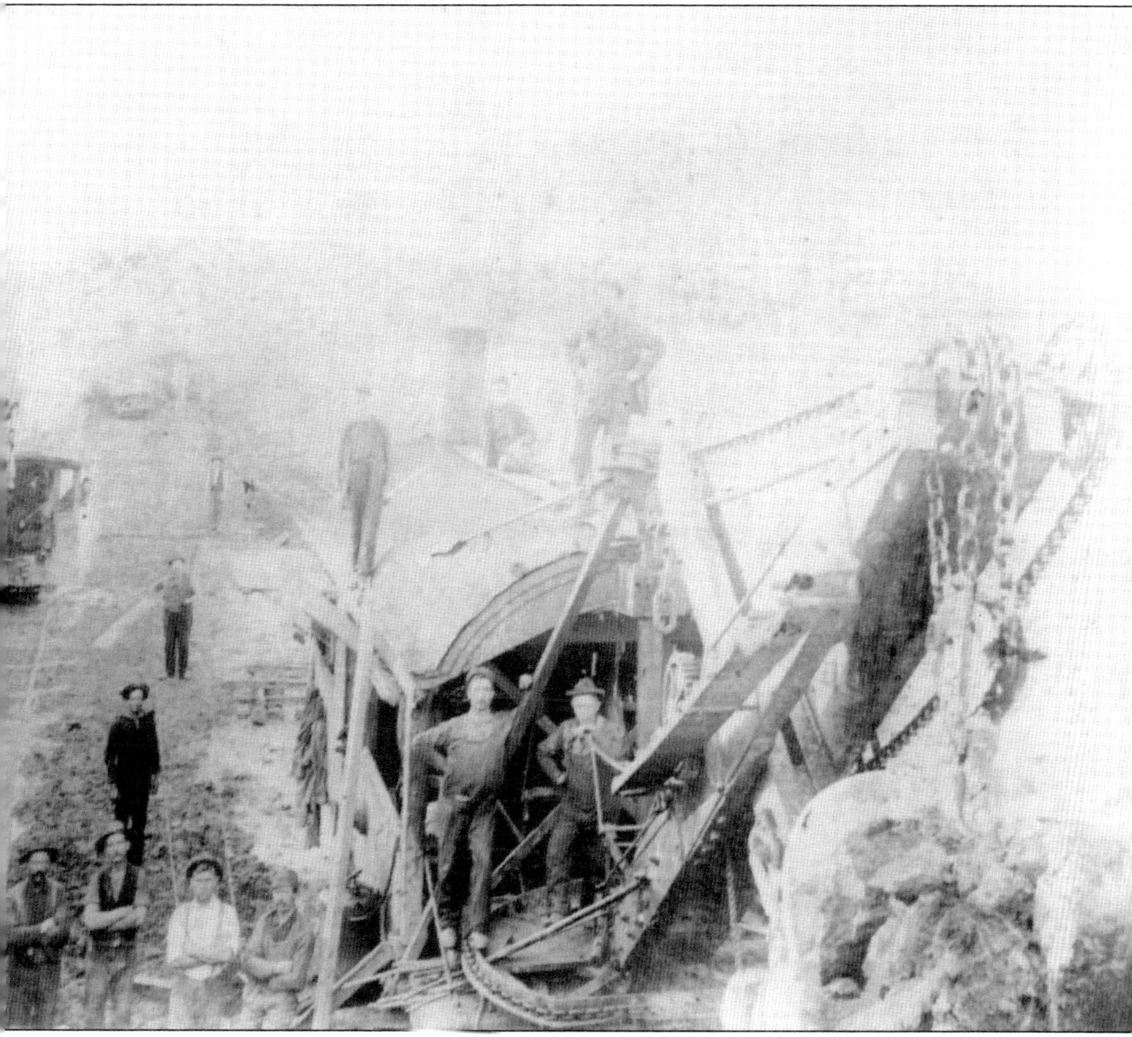

Workers pause to have their photograph taken. Such a sight was common in Plum during the late 19th and early 20th centuries. Around 1870, industrial leaders such as William Coleman and Andrew Carnegie bought large tracts of coal-rich property. They went on to consolidate their holdings to form the New York and Cleveland Gas Coal Company, one of the largest mining corporations in Western Pennsylvania. New York and Cleveland Company's holdings included several thousand acres that extended from the lines of the Pennsylvania Railroad to the lines of the Allegheny Valley Railroad. The coal extracted from Plum's mines was shipped as far away as Canada. Plum Creek Mine opened in 1872, and was located along Universal Road in the community of Unity. Originally under the ownership of Doak & Kier Company, it was later sold around 1901 to the Pittsburgh Coal Company.

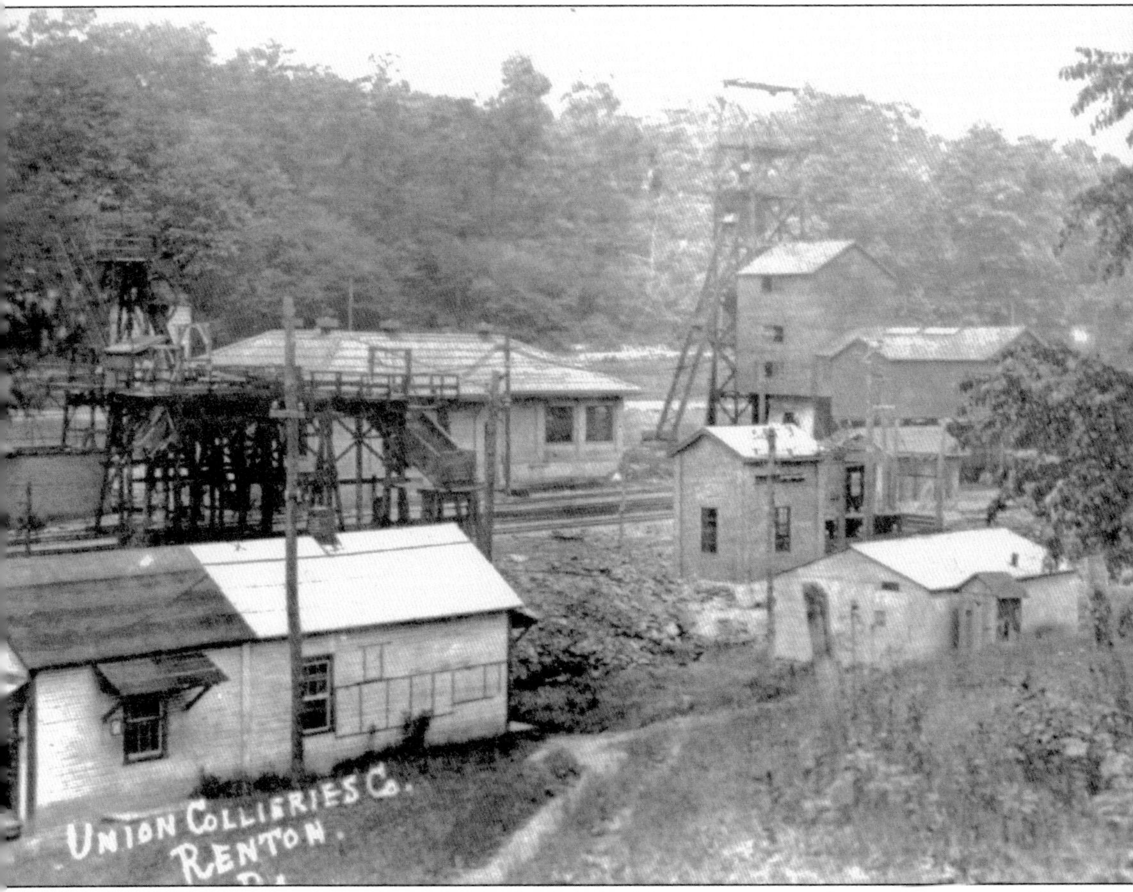

When the mine in Renton was opened, two possible names were submitted: Renton Calverly Company and Union Collieries Company. The former of the two won, with the name of the community being Renton. The community's namesake, Walter Renton Calverly, officially emigrated from Leeds, England, in 1917. Originally, two shafts were dug at Renton. The shafts ran to a depth of 512 feet, and an entrance could be found at the base of Hankey's Hill (which is one of the higher points in Allegheny County). Renton Mine, as held by Union Collieries Company, had several miles of railroad track within, and the extent of its operations ran from Renton to Unity. The mine ran along Saltsburg Road to Camp Joann, along Vandergrift Road, and under parts of the community of New Texas.

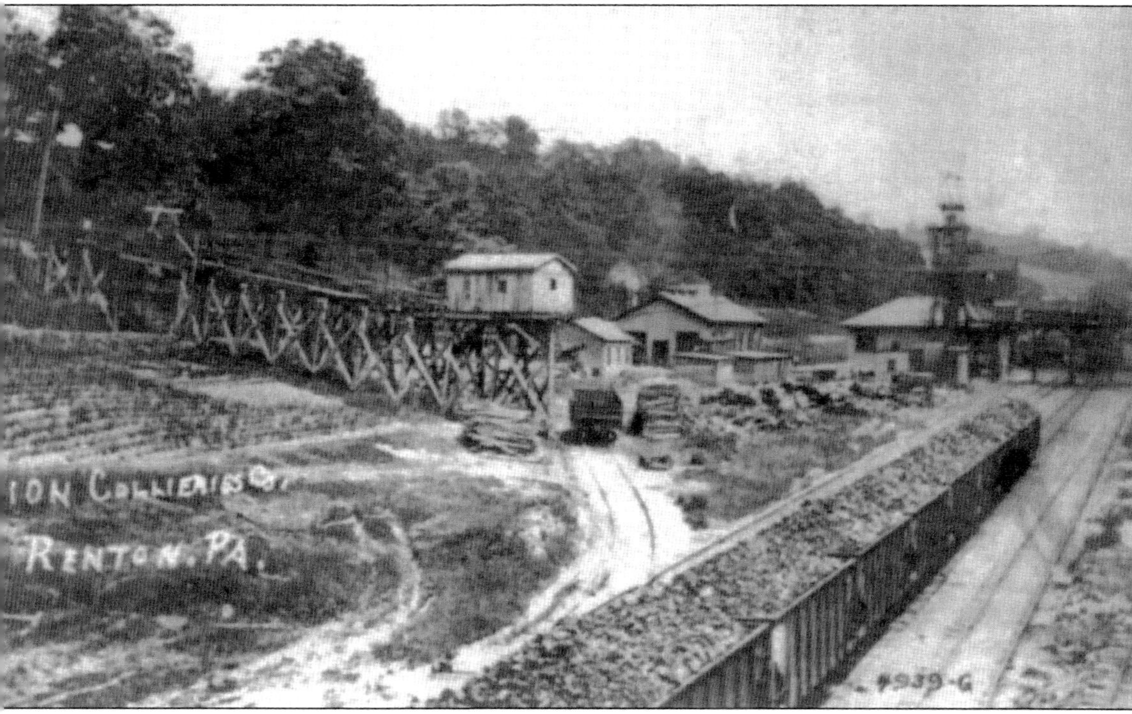

In this early-20th-century photograph, one can see the train tracks leading to and from Renton Mine. In 1916, Union Colliers Company purchased approximately 500 acres from the Zimmerman, Alter, and Clements families. Four drift mines were opened, and this was the beginning of Renton Mine and the surrounding community of Renton. However, a nearby mine caused the greater Plum community to be thrust into the national limelight. In 1897, United Mine Workers of America called a strike against the bituminous coal companies in several Northeast and Midwest states. Workers at the Plum Creek Mine in Unity were still on the job a week after the strike began. This thrust Plum and Plum Creek Mine into the national limelight as protestors and striking mineworkers camped out in Plum in order to try to persuade the miners to join the strike. The Plum workers (whether on their own or because of corporate influence, the author is unsure) never did join the national strike. (Courtesy of Gary Rogers.)

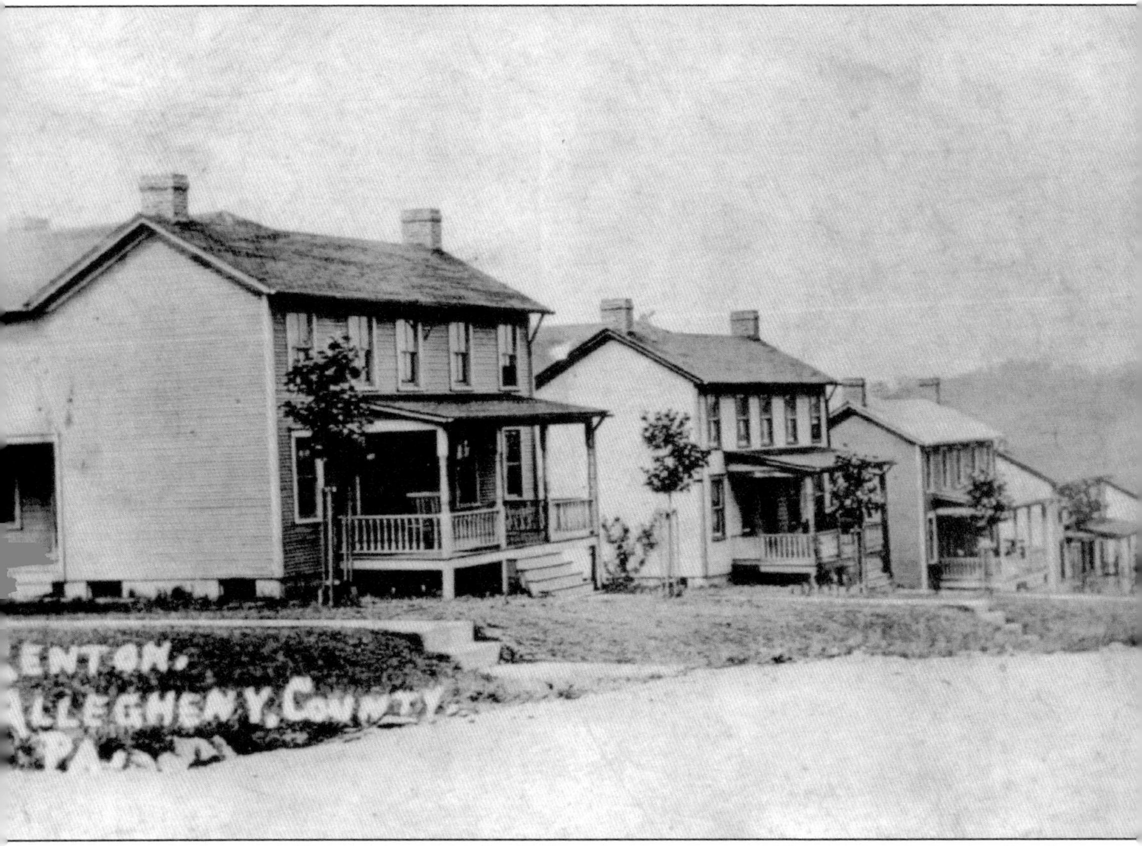

The community of Renton came with all the amenities one would expect to find in a close-knit village—churches, a school, and a store. The company store of Renton was owned by Renton Mine and managed by G.W. Matthews. The company store also housed a pool hall and a barber shop. The Renton Theatre—operated by Elizabeth Beckwith—also housed a dance hall on its upper level and was home to many parties and dances over the years. In addition to the company store, the mine also had company doctors. Dr. Hawes, Dr. Hobaugh, and Dr. K.V. Waite began serving the community in 1940. During the 1927 miners' strike at Renton Mine, the people of Renton "relocated" briefly. The coal mine forced the miners and their families out of the company-owned houses. During the strike, the mining families lived at what came to be known as "The Barracks" on the Miller Family farm.

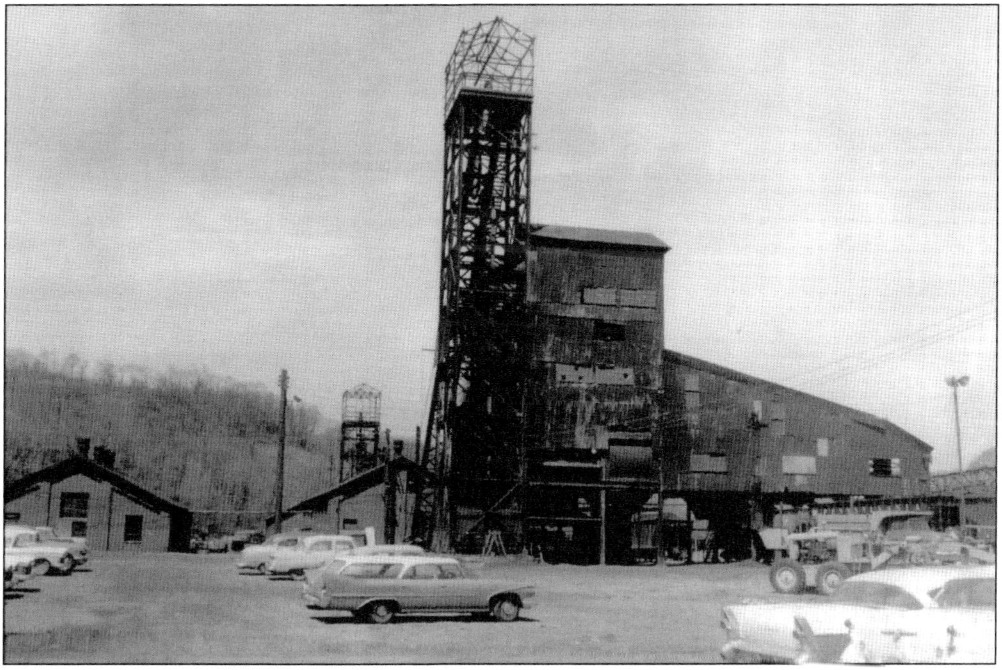

During its heyday, one would often find an advertisement for the Renton Mine in a local newspaper. It would read, "at our Renton Mine, you may obtain coal from 7:00 a.m. to 10:00 p.m. 1500 tons available of lump and egg per day. Quickest Loading—properly cleaned." During the days of coal furnaces, it was not uncommon for people with pickup trucks to make some extra money by hauling coal for residential customers.

Pictured is Renton Mine in its later years. As with many industries in the greater-Pittsburgh region, the 1970s and 1980s proved to be a dire time. Many of the clients of Plum's mines closed, and the mines soon followed. Renton Mine endured two decades of sporadic activity before closing in March 1987.

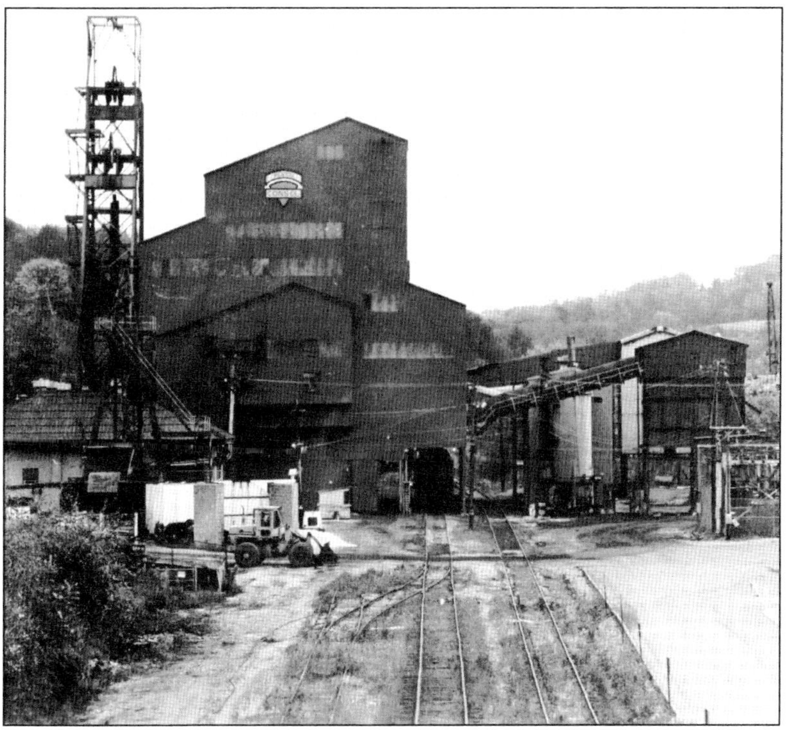

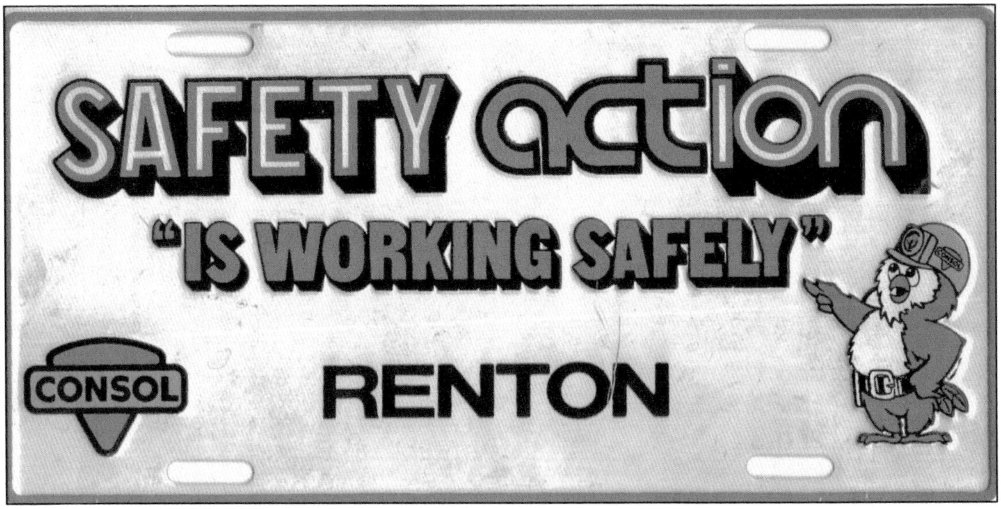

This souvenir license plate is from Renton Mine. In 1890, a miner at Plum Creek Mine could expect to get paid $1.35 for one 10-hour workday. In 1876, a team of eight horses pulled a three-ton lump of coal out of Plum Creek Mine. The lump was displayed in Pittsburgh during the Pittsburgh Exposition and later in Philadelphia.

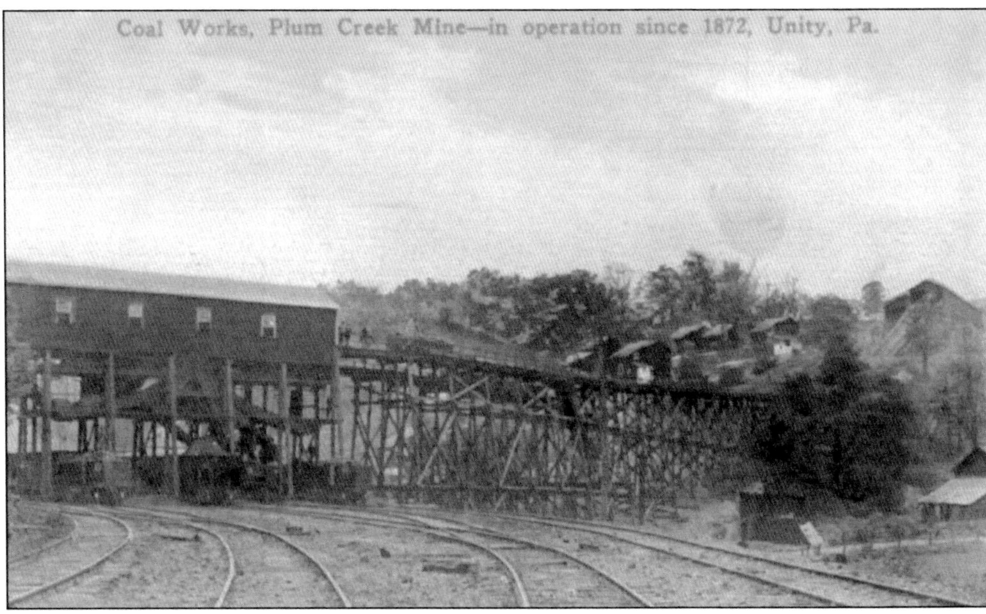

This postcard depicts Unity's Plum Creek Mine, which opened in 1872. Plum Creek was serviced by Allegheny Valley Railroad's Plum Creek line, affectionately known as "Old Plummy." The Allegheny Valley Railroad was founded in 1852; the Plum Creek line was established in 1872 and ran for 7.53 miles, from Verona to Unity. (Courtesy of Gary Rogers.)

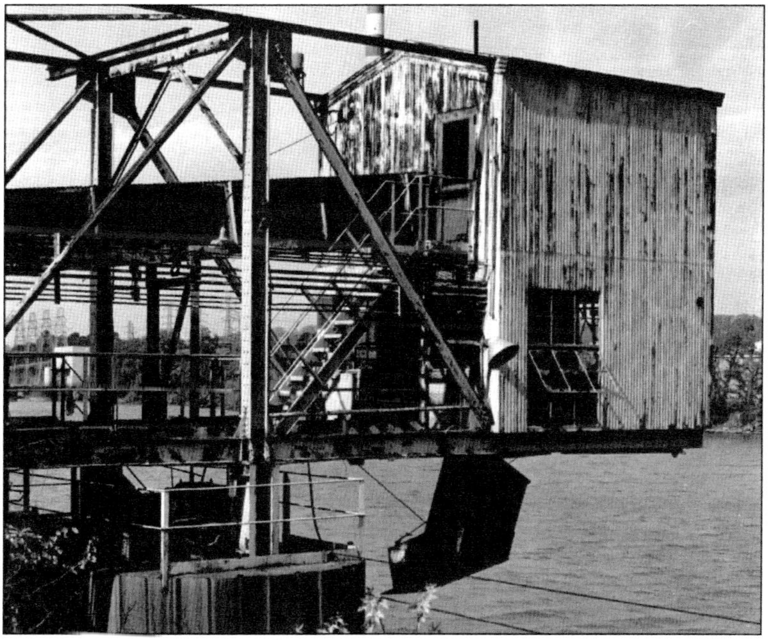

Situated along the Allegheny River, the community of Barking was a prime location for a mine. Additionally, it is only about 1.75 miles from the New Kensington border, an industrial hub in the Allegheny Valley. Barking's Oakmont Mine began operation in 1917 and was originally owned by Hillman Coal and Coke Company. Through a series of sales and consolidations, the Oakmont Mine came to be owned by the Harmar Coal Company, and the mine was operated in conjunction with the Harmar Mine in Harmarville. Prior to the opening of the Harmar Mine in 1948, coal from Oakmont Mine was loaded onto railcars and delivered to local businesses. After 1948, Oakmont Mine's coal was shipped downriver via barge, cleaned at a cleaning plant at Harmarville, reloaded onto barges, and shipped to mills belonging to Wheeling-Pittsburgh Steel.

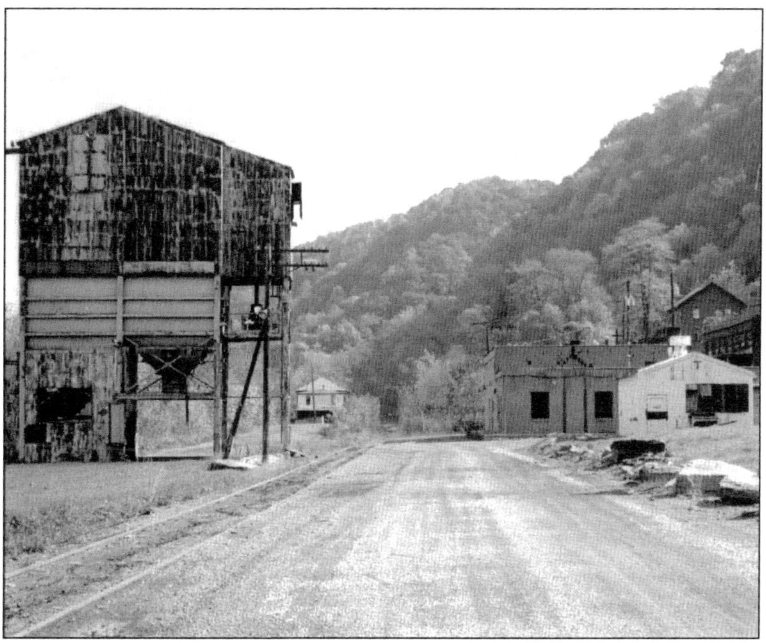

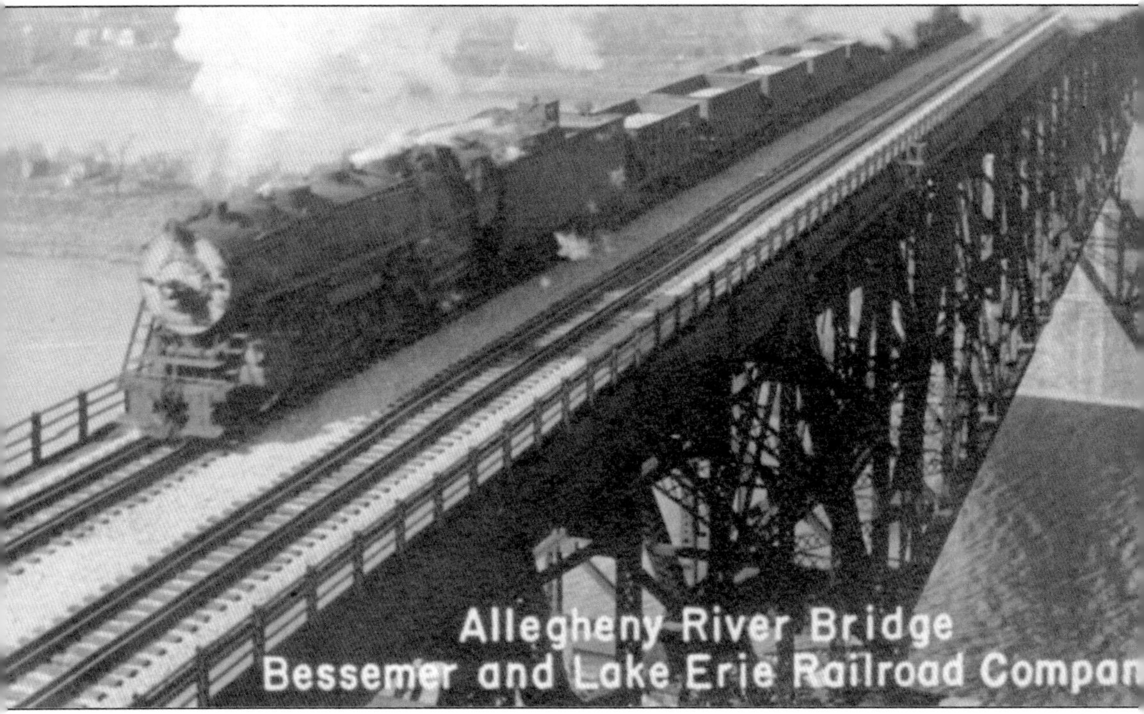

This bridge over the Allegheny River provided a link for the Bessemer and Lake Erie Railroad's lines on either side of the river. In addition to bridges, there was a tunnel going under the Allegheny. In 1919, West Penn Power Company began building a power plant in Springdale. This plant required 80,000 pounds of coal per hour. The supply of coal was easily acquired from the mine in Logans Ferry. The only issue was the transportation of the coal from one side of the river to the other. The power company decided to build a tunnel from the mine directly to the power plant. The tunnel, which really consisted of two parallel tunnels, was completed on April 20, 1921. The coal was pulled through the tunnel by an electric locomotive, dumped into a holding area on the Springdale side of the river, and then carried to the surface via a conveyor belt. (Courtesy of Gary Rogers.)

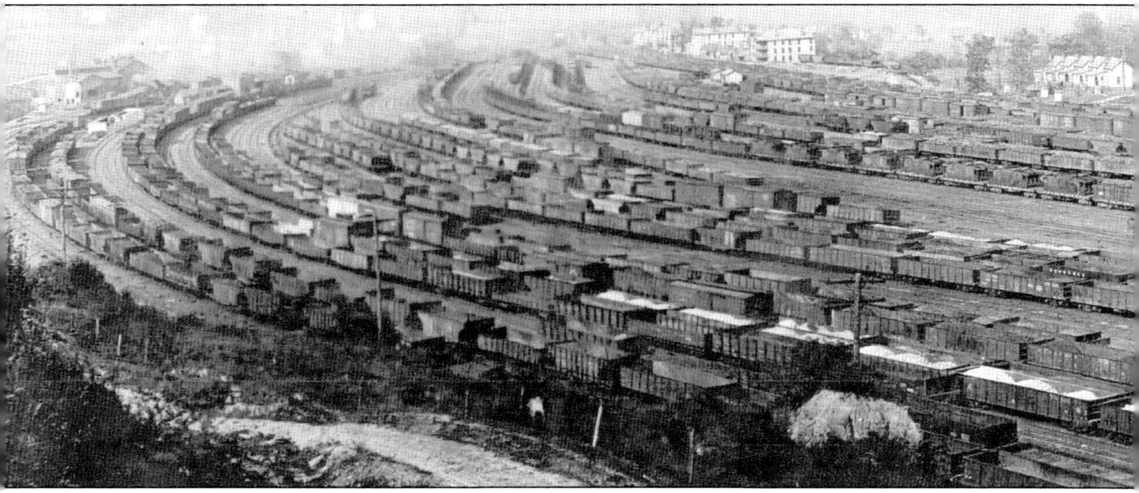

This aerial view depicts the Bessemer Rail Yard in all its industrial glory. Smaller rail lines connected to the Bessemer line all along its 200-plus-mile length. The land north of the Bessemer viaduct was owned by Henry Garlow and was largely agricultural. The Bessemer rail yard changed this rural community into a busy railroad terminal. The shops at the rail yard employed over 200 men from Plum. Greater Pittsburgh was not unfamiliar to the railroad scene. In addition to the Bessemer Rail Yard, other large local rail yards included Pitcairn in the Turtle Creek valley and Conway along the Ohio River near Beaver. Both Pitcairn and Conway went on to claim the title of "the largest"—Pitcairn being the largest terminal in the area at the turn of the century and Conway being the largest automated terminal by mid-century. (Courtesy of Gary Rogers.)

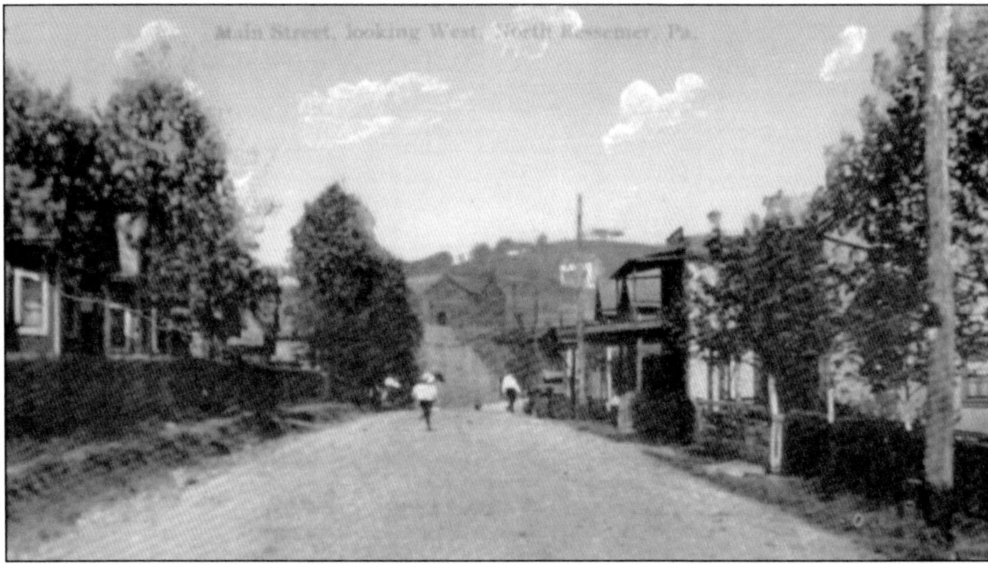

As with all of the industrial hubs in the area, North Bessemer had its own little community spring up around its industry. This westward-oriented, c. 1913 picture shows a snapshot of Main Street in North Bessemer. The Carnegie Library can be seen in the distance. (Courtesy of Gary Rogers.)

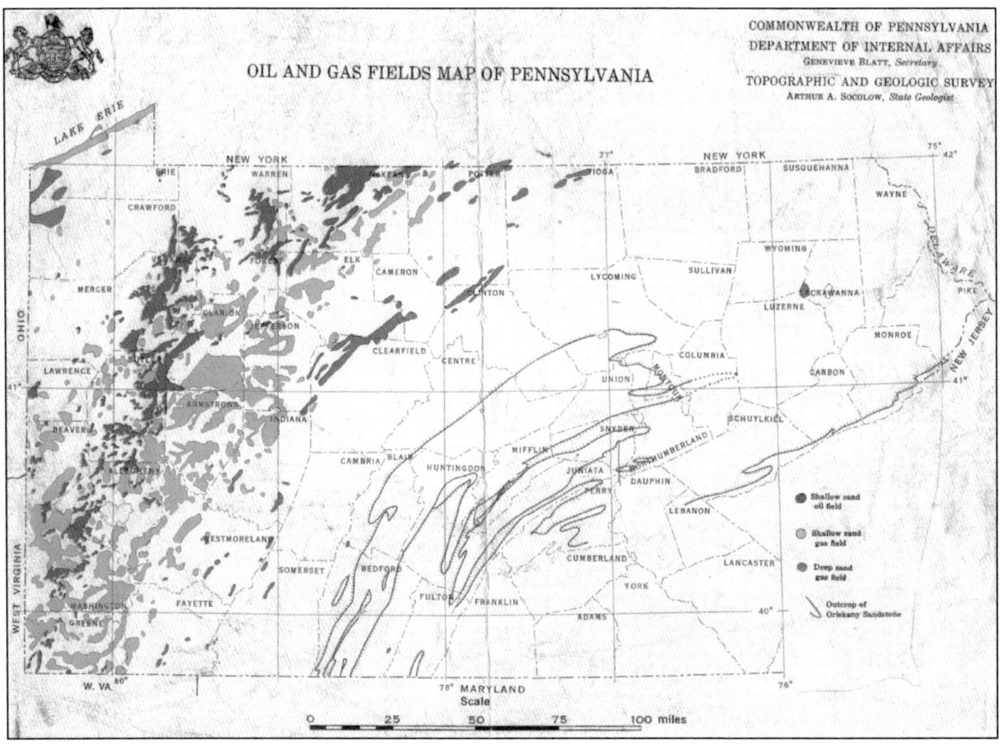

This map, created by the Pennsylvania Department of Internal Affairs and Topographic and Geologic Survey, shows oil and gas deposits throughout Pennsylvania. It shows that eastern Allegheny County and western Westmoreland County are home to both shallow sand oil fields and deep sand gas fields. Present-day Versailles Township—about 15 miles to the south of Plum—was another area that saw many gas wells erected.

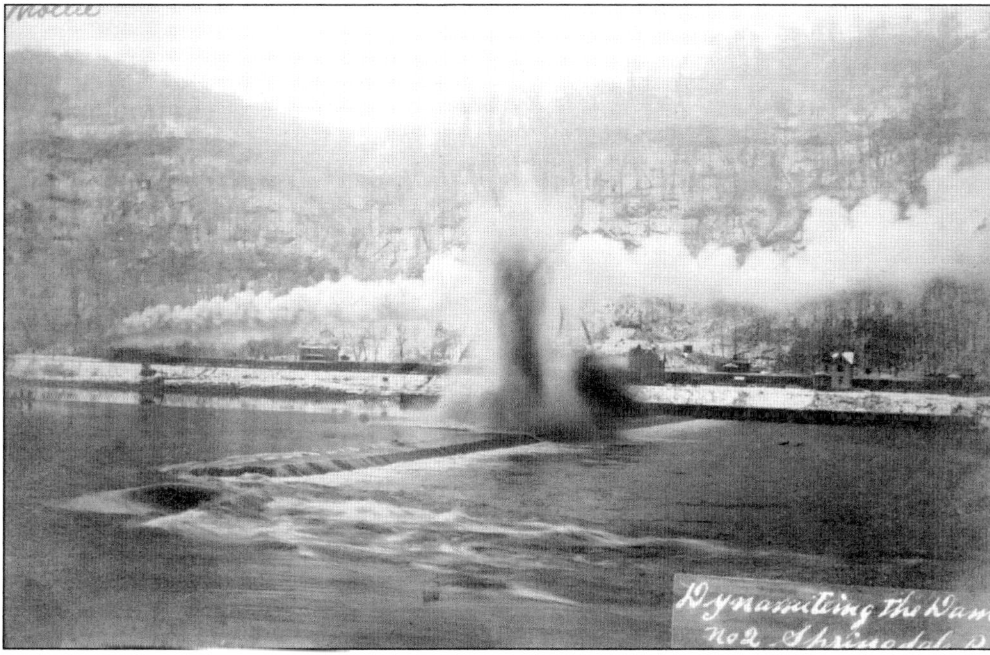

These photographs, taken from the Springdale shore of the Allegheny River, show the old dam being blown up by dynamite. Built between 1897 and 1904, this dam was replaced by the C.W. Bill Young Lock and Dam, which was built between 1932 and 1935 slightly downstream at the town of Cheswick. Within the Pittsburgh District of the Army Corps of Engineers—which encompasses an area between Pittsburgh and Templeton, Armstrong County—there is a series of eight locks and dams on the Allegheny River. The train in the background is traveling along the tracks that cut through the community of Barking. (Both courtesy of Gary Rogers.)

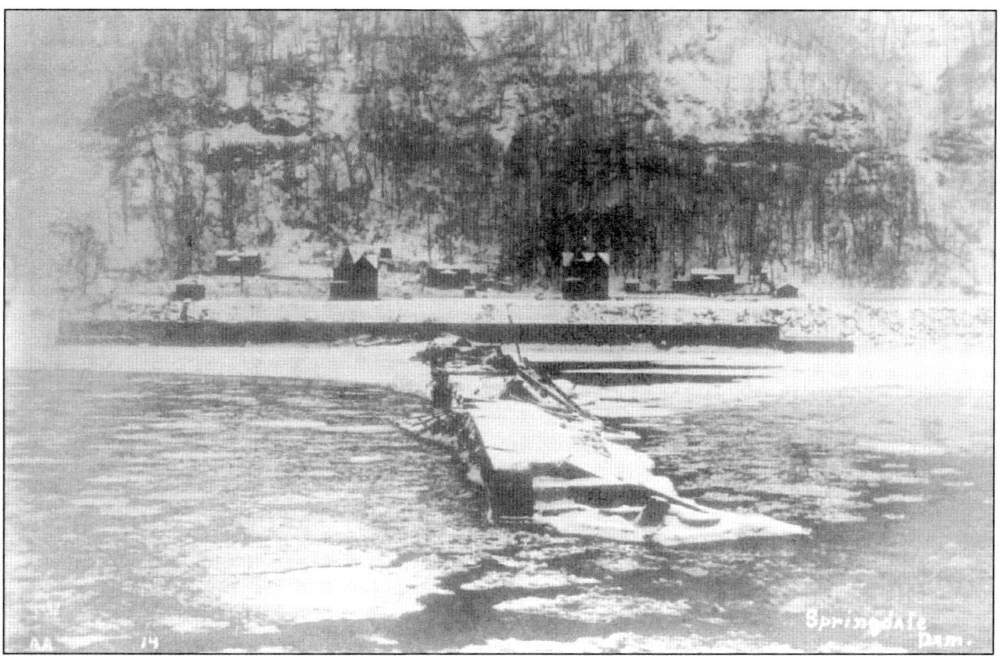

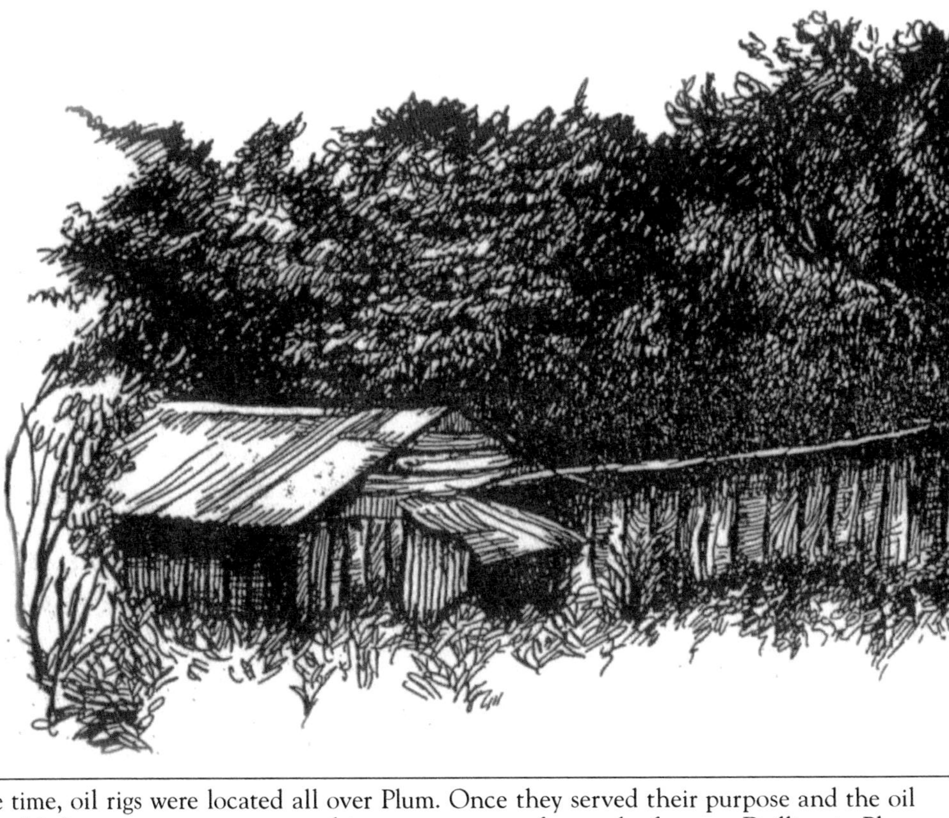

At one time, oil rigs were located all over Plum. Once they served their purpose and the oil reserves dried up, many were converted into water pumps for nearby farmers. Drilling in Plum began in the 1890s, and the first derricks were generally built of wood. After iron piping was introduced, derricks rose to heights of 60 to 90 feet. The families who owned the land where the

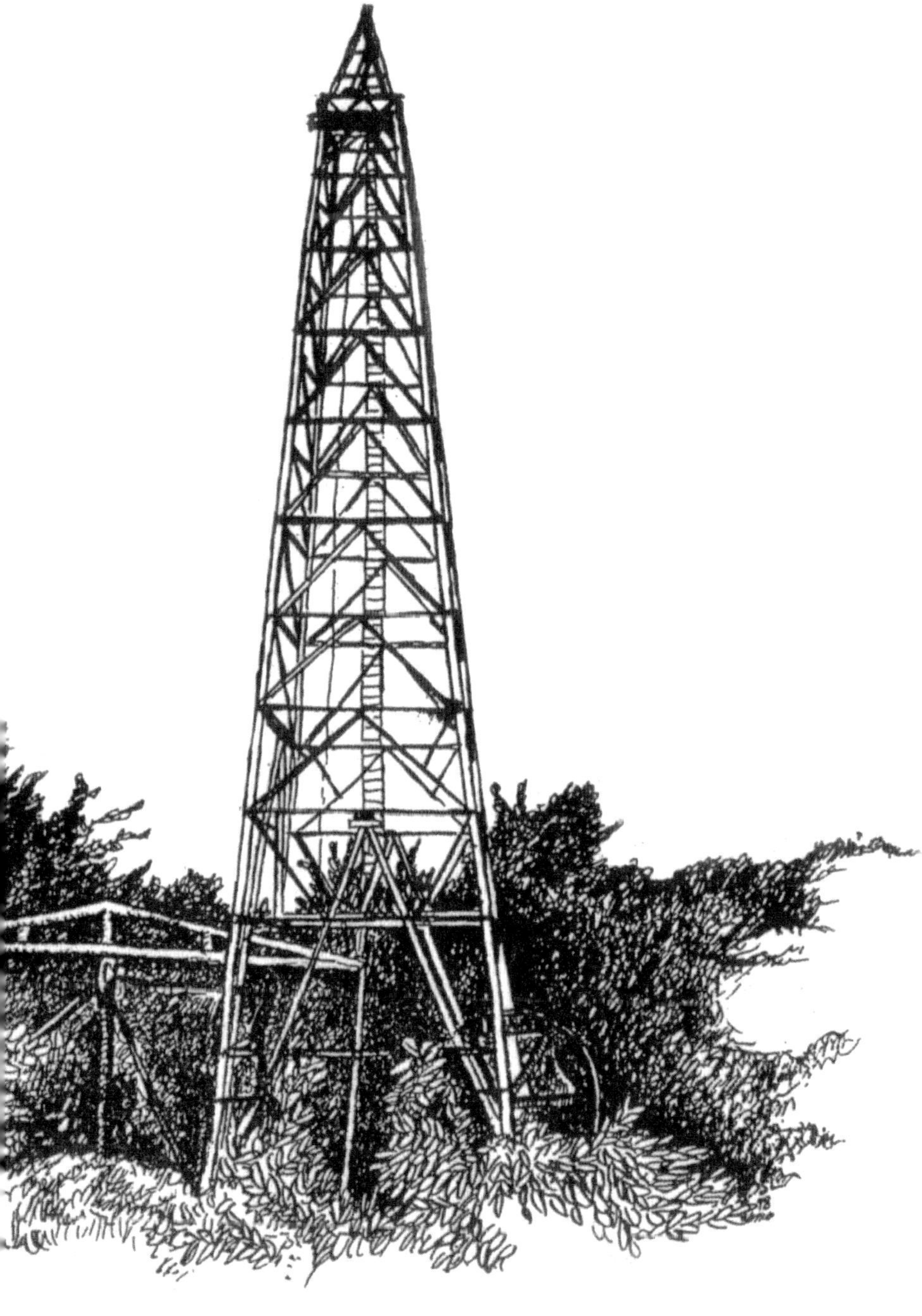

derricks were built usually utilized the commodities the derricks produced, and they also made a bit of money off them directly. The drilling industries waned in the mid-20th century, although a few small oil rigs can still be seen around Plum Borough today.

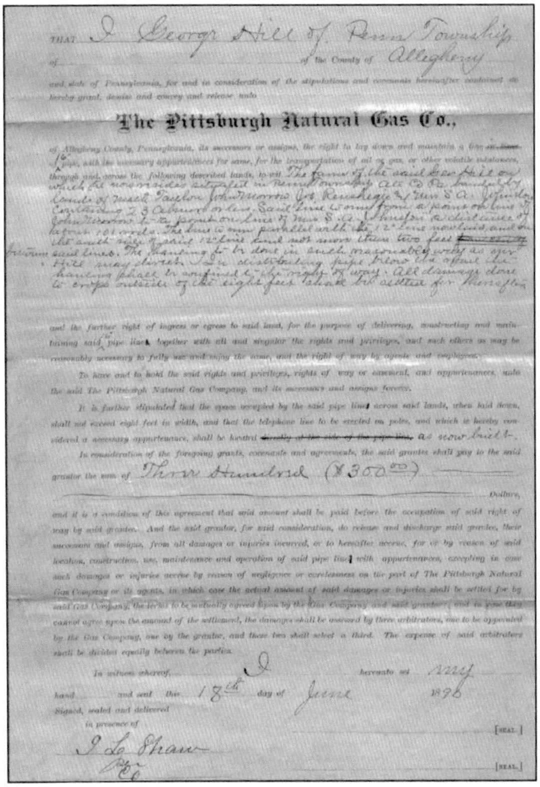

THAT I George Hill of Penn Township of the County of Allegheny and state of Pennsylvania, for and in consideration of the stipulations and covenants hereinafter contained do hereby grant, demise and convey and release unto

The Pittsburgh Natural Gas Co.,

of Allegheny County, Pennsylvania, its successors or assigns, the right to lay down and maintain a line ~~of lines~~ of 16" pipe, with the necessary appurtenances for same, for the transportation of oil or gas, or other volatile substances, through and across the following described lands, to wit: The farm of the said Geo Hill on which he now resides situated in Penn Township All Co Pa [illegible] [illegible] Containing [illegible] Acres more or less. Said line to run from a point on line of John Morrow to a point on line of Mrs S. A. Johnston a distance of about 101 rods. The line to run parallel with the 12" line now laid, and on the south side of said 12" line and not more than two feet ~~[illegible]~~ between said lines. The hauling to be done in such reasonable way as Geo Hill may direct. In distributing pipe along the [illegible] the hauling shall be confined to the right of way. All damage done to crops outside of the eight feet shall be settled for [illegible]

and the further right of ingress or egress to said land, for the purpose of delivering, constructing and maintaining said 16" pipe line, together with all and singular the rights and privileges, and such others as may be reasonably necessary to fully use and enjoy the same, and the right of way by agents and employees.

To have and to hold the said rights and privileges, rights of way or easement, and appurtenances, unto the said The Pittsburgh Natural Gas Company, and its successors and assigns forever.

It is further stipulated that the space occupied by the said pipe line across said lands, when laid down, shall not exceed eight feet in width, and that the telephone line to be erected on poles, and which is hereby considered a necessary appurtenance, shall be located ~~directly at the side of the pipe line~~ as now built.

In consideration of the foregoing grants, covenants and agreements, the said grantee shall pay to the said grantor the sum of Three Hundred ($300.00) Dollars,

and it is a condition of this agreement that said amount shall be paid before the occupation of said right of way by said grantee. And the said grantor, for said consideration, do release and discharge said grantee, their successors and assigns, from all damages or injuries incurred, or to hereafter accrue, for or by reason of said location, construction, use, maintenance and operation of said pipe line with appurtenances, excepting in case such damages or injuries accrue by reason of negligence or carelessness on the part of The Pittsburgh Natural Gas Company or its agents, in which case the actual amount of said damages or injuries shall be settled for by said Gas Company, the terms to be mutually agreed upon by the Gas Company and said grantor; and in case they cannot agree upon the amount of the settlement, the damages shall be assessed by three arbitrators, one to be appointed by the Gas Company, one by the grantor, and these two shall select a third. The expense of said arbitrators shall be divided equally between the parties.

In witness whereof, I hereunto set my hand and seal this 18th day of June 1890

Signed, sealed and delivered in presence of

I. L. Shaw

[SEAL.]

[SEAL.]

On June 18, 1890, a land grant was given to the Pittsburgh Natural Gas Company for a right of way to build a pipeline. It was during this time—the late 19th century—that drilling for oil and gas became popular in the region. Having an oil rig or gas pump on one's farm meant a steady source of additional income for the farmer.

With the rise in the population of residential development Holiday Park, commercial centers were soon to follow. Holiday Park Shopping Center, located on Route 286, is still in operation today and has a mix of retail stores, various service providers, and restaurants. Pennsylvania Route 286 takes on many different names during its 67-mile trek northeast past Indiana, PA. The portion in Plum is called Golden Mile Highway.

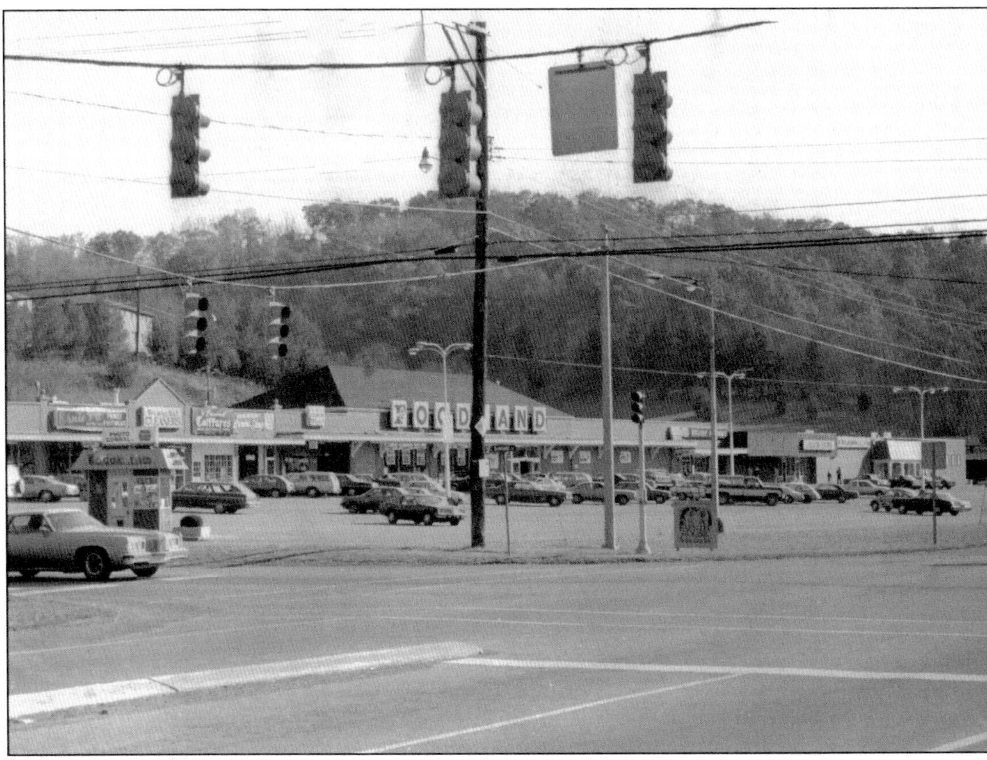

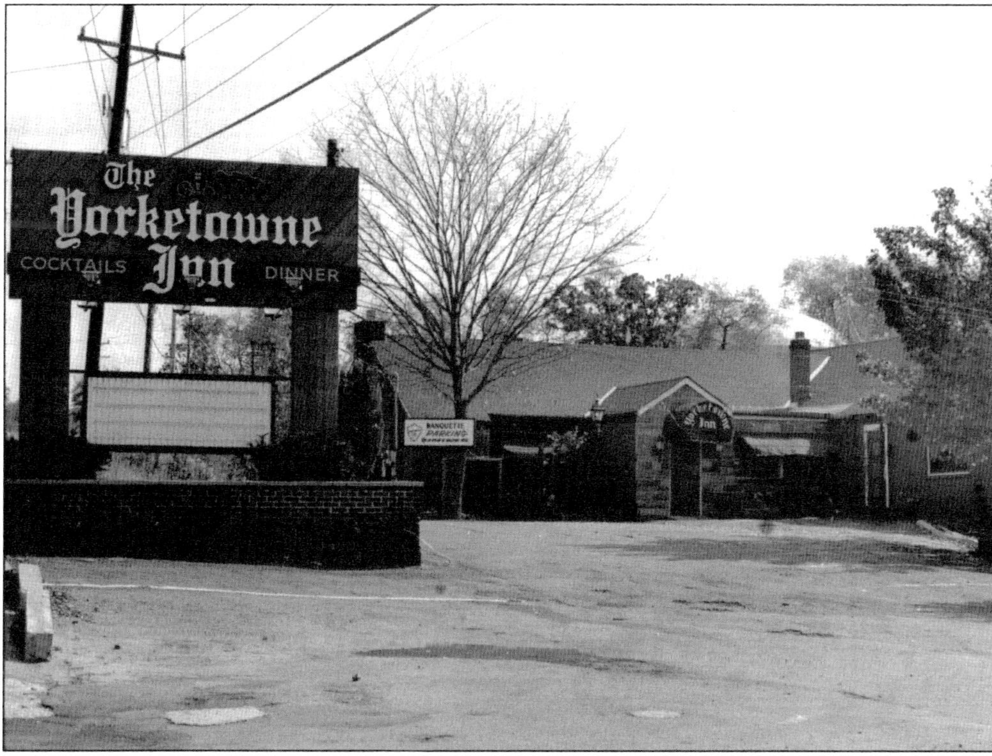

The Yorktowne Inn, located in the Logans Ferry neighborhood of Plum, is a prime example of one of the many restaurants and taverns locals frequented in the mid-20th century. The Cityview Tavern—also located in Logans Ferry—was a popular bar for locals. The community of Logans Ferry saw a lot of changes during the mid-20th century. When company-owned houses were sold off in the late 1940s, the community revised its name to Logans Ferry Heights, and a plan of community improvement was initiated. Roads were resurfaced, streetlights were installed, and Ostrosky's Market, one of the first stores in the community, was opened.

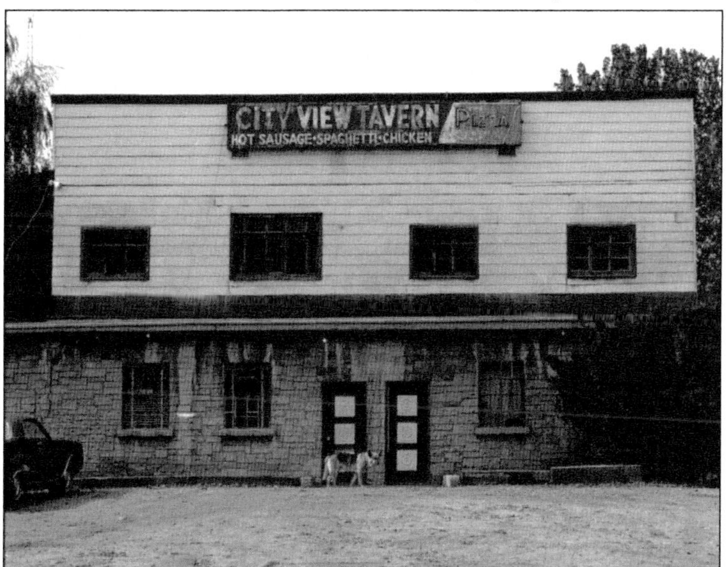

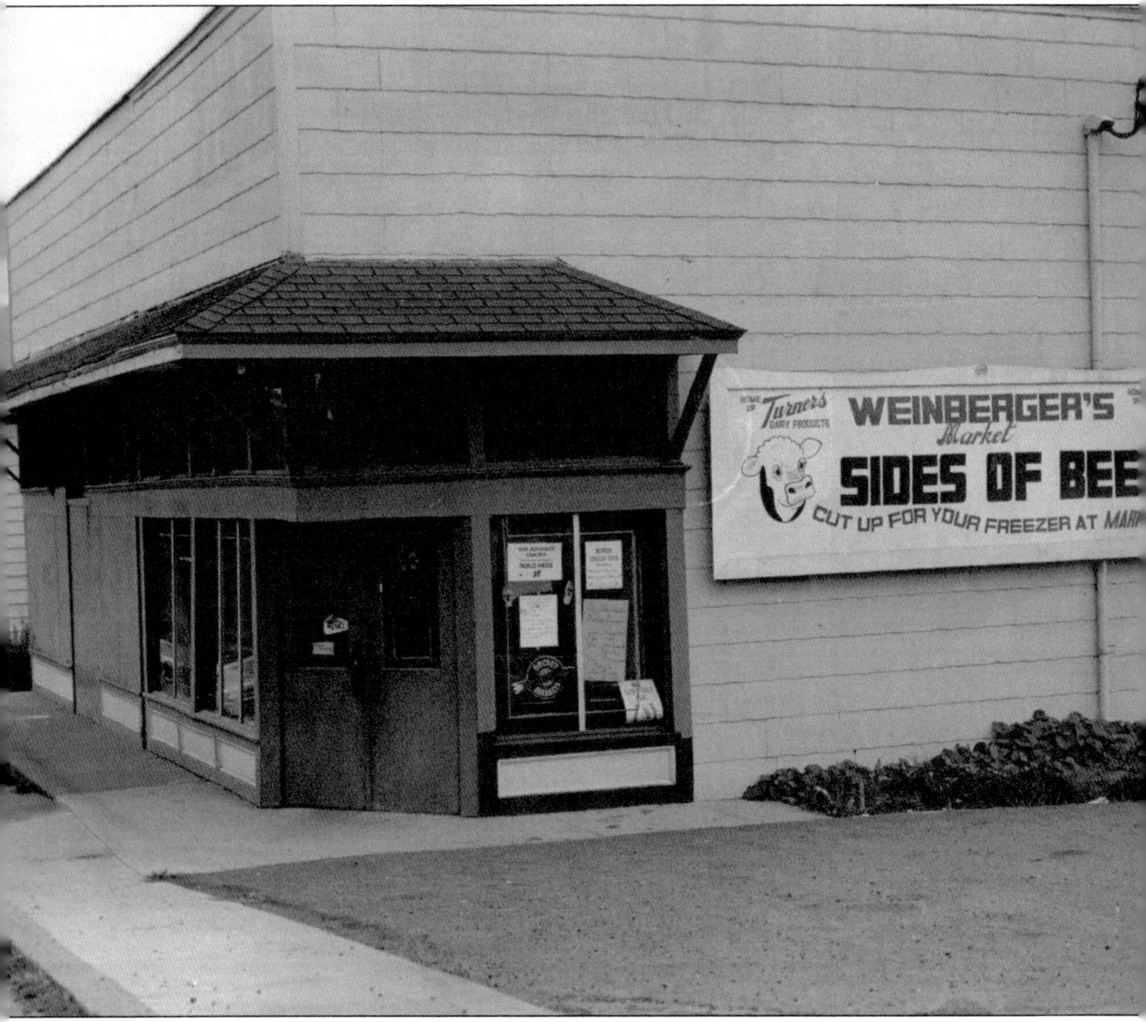

Weinberger's Market, in Renton, was one of many shops in the community center of Plum Borough. As Renton was home to the Renton Coal Mine, this store was in walking distance to many of the homes of the miners and their families. Customers were able to purchase groceries, put them on account, and pay when they received their paychecks. In addition to Weinberger's, there was the Renton Theatre, which had a dance hall above it. The dance hall was the scene of many organized parties and socials held by the 500 Club. Renton Theatre was located at the bottom of Renton Road near the entrance to the mine. Elizabeth Beckwith (a cousin of Renton Mine's founder, Walter Renton Calverly) operated the theater. The building burned down and was never rebuilt. There was also Renton chapel, which was served by ministers from Plum Creek Presbyterian Church.

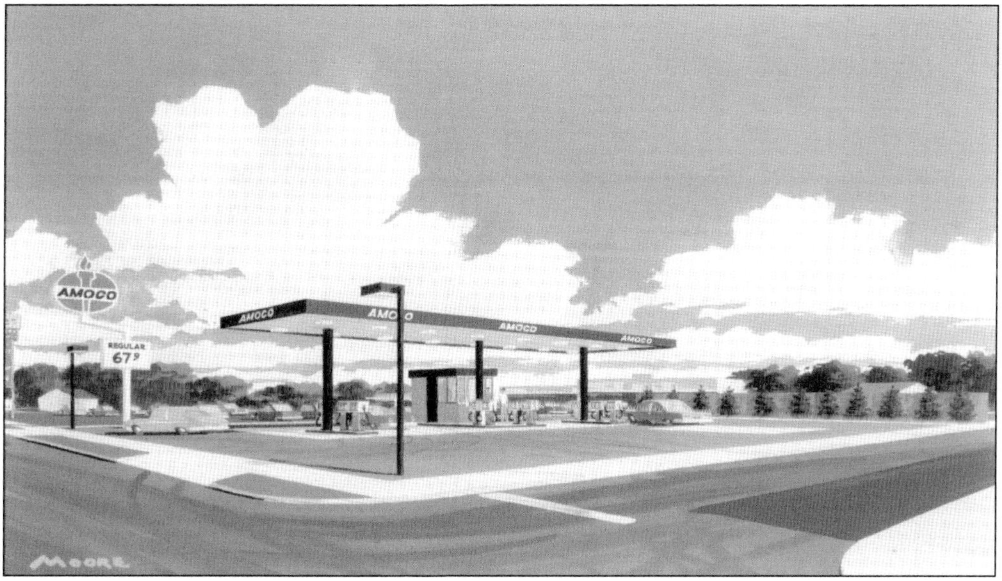

By the 1970s, Holiday Park had firmly established itself as part of the history of Plum. It had three schools, several small parks, and a growing commercial district along Golden Mile Highway. This artist's rendition depicts the Amoco station along this route. Notice the "high" price of gas—67.9¢!

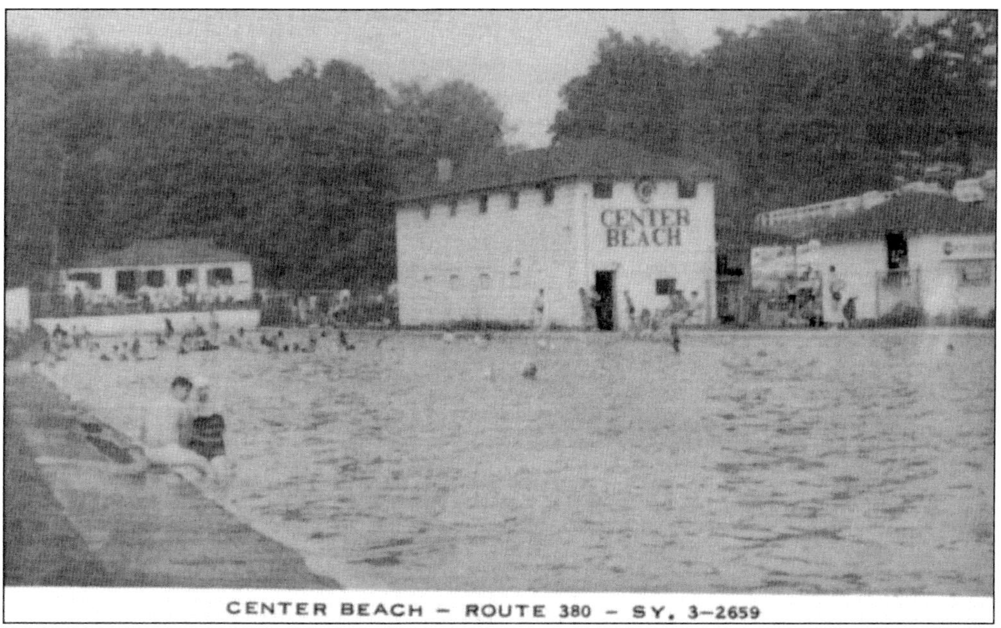

Another popular recreational spot for Plum residents was the pool known as Center Beach, which also included a picnic grove. It was located at the intersection of Center New Texas Road and Route 380 (near Center School). Other popular pools in eastern Allegheny County that date from this period include Kennywood Park in West Mifflin, Rainbow Gardens in modern-day White Oak, and Olympia Park in Versailles. Sadly, none of these pools still exist. (Courtesy of Gary Rogers.)

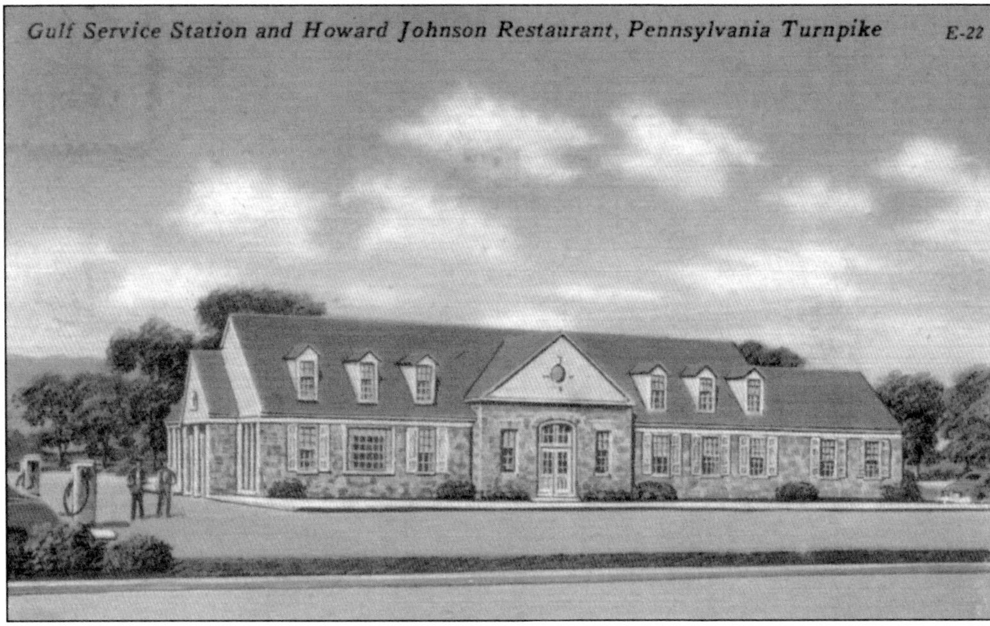

The Pennsylvania Turnpike (later known as Interstate 76) was a revolutionary concept in its day. Opened in 1940, over a decade before the Eisenhower administration began its Interstate-building program, the turnpike was the first "superhighway" in the United States. Shown above is the original Oakmont service plaza and below is the old Turnpike Bridge crossing the Allegheny River. Both structures were demolished and rebuilt in the first decade of the 21st century. (Both courtesy of Gary Rogers.)

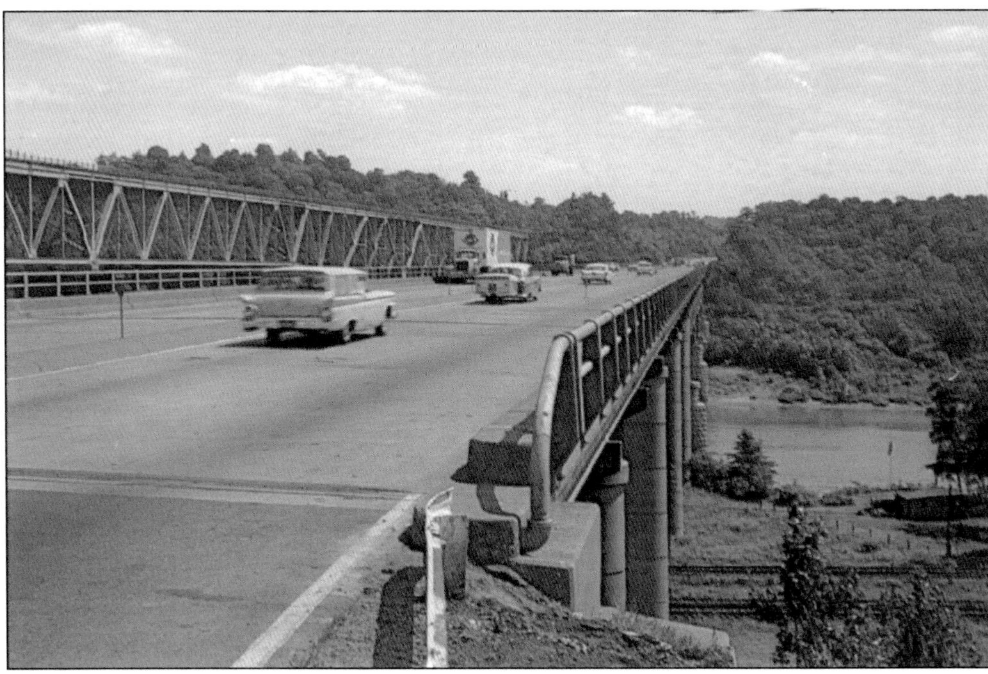

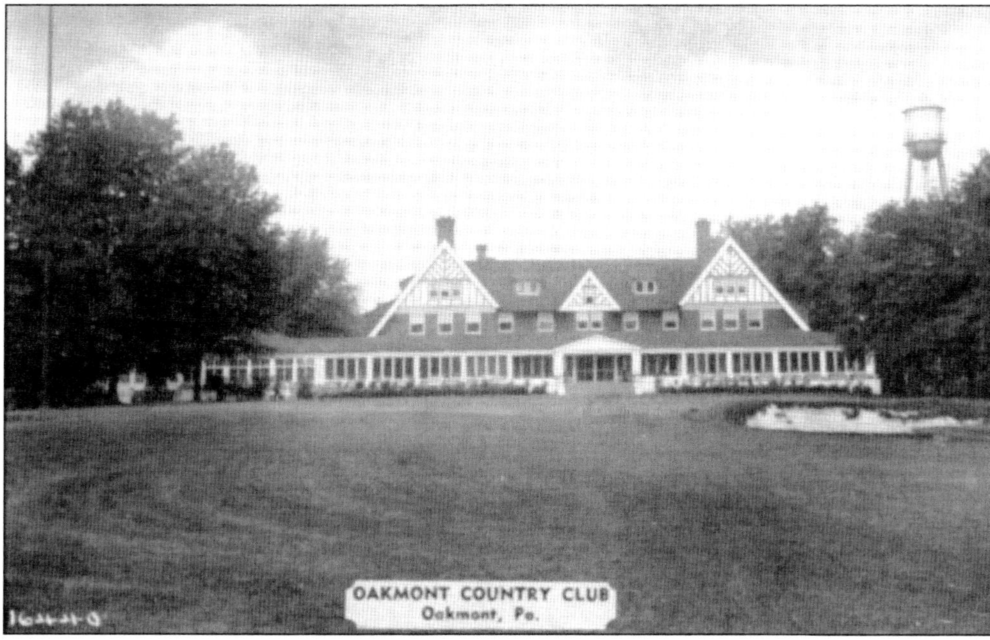

When one mentions Oakmont, golf often comes to mind. However, most of Oakmont Country Club lies within Plum Borough. In 1952, the residents of White Oak Level decided to break away from Plum Township and join Oakmont Borough. Oakmont Country Club caught wind of this and opted out of such a transition. These photographs, including one from right after its completion around 1903, display the clubhouse. Another golf course that existed in Plum was the Valley Heights Golf Course, which was open from 1923 to 1983. After its closure in late 1983, some of its turf was transported to Oakmont Country Club's nursery. (Both courtesy of Gary Rogers.)

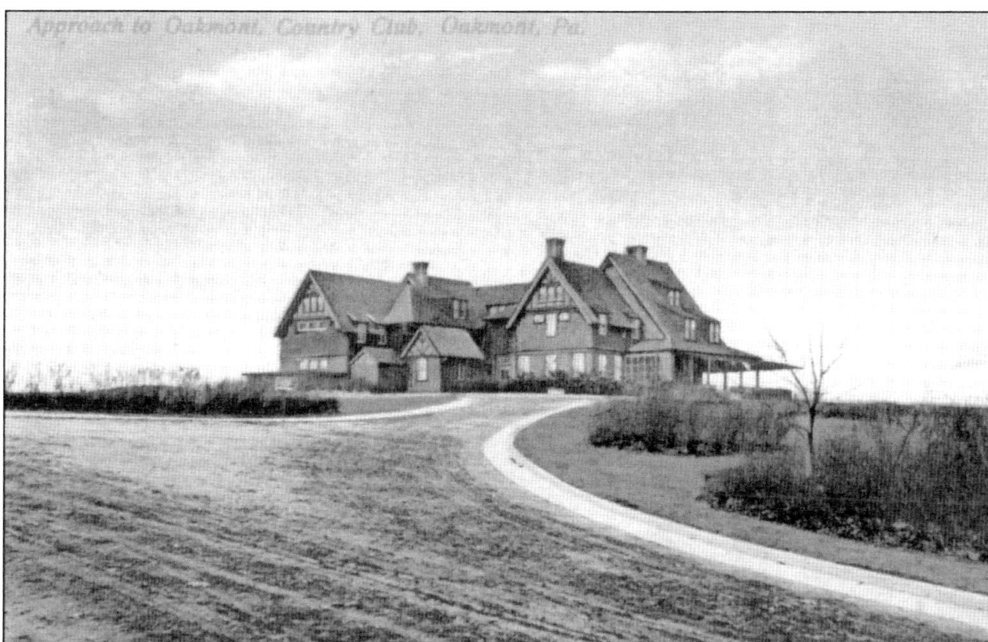

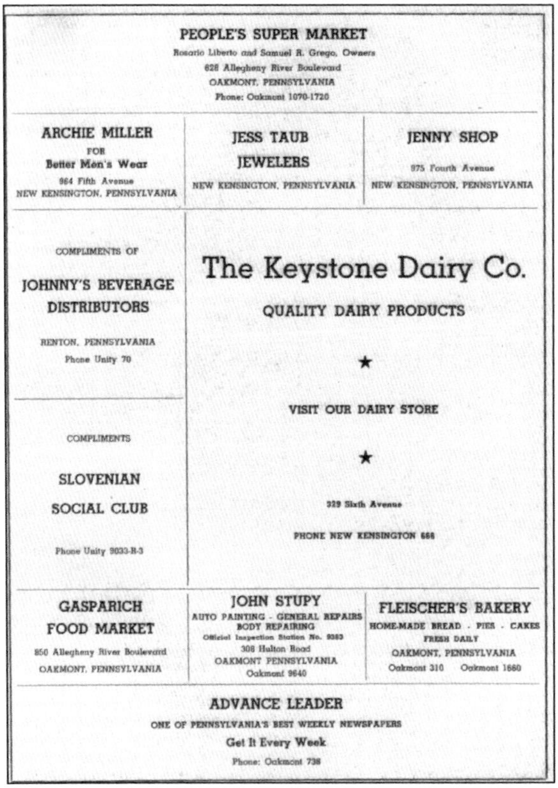

Then, as now, businesses took a keen interest in supporting local organizations. These advertisements were printed in the 1950 Plum Township High School *Criterion* yearbook. Businesses and social organizations throughout Plum and the surrounding areas had their advertisements printed in the yearbook, which was published annually by the senior class.

Plum was once home to a US Army Nike missile site. Nike site PI-25 opened in April 1955 and was situated on New Texas Road. It was in operation for five years before being closed in 1960. The command base was sold to the University of Pittsburgh for use as a research facility, which is shown here. The remainder of the property is the home of Adlai Stevenson Elementary School and A.E. Oblock Junior High School.

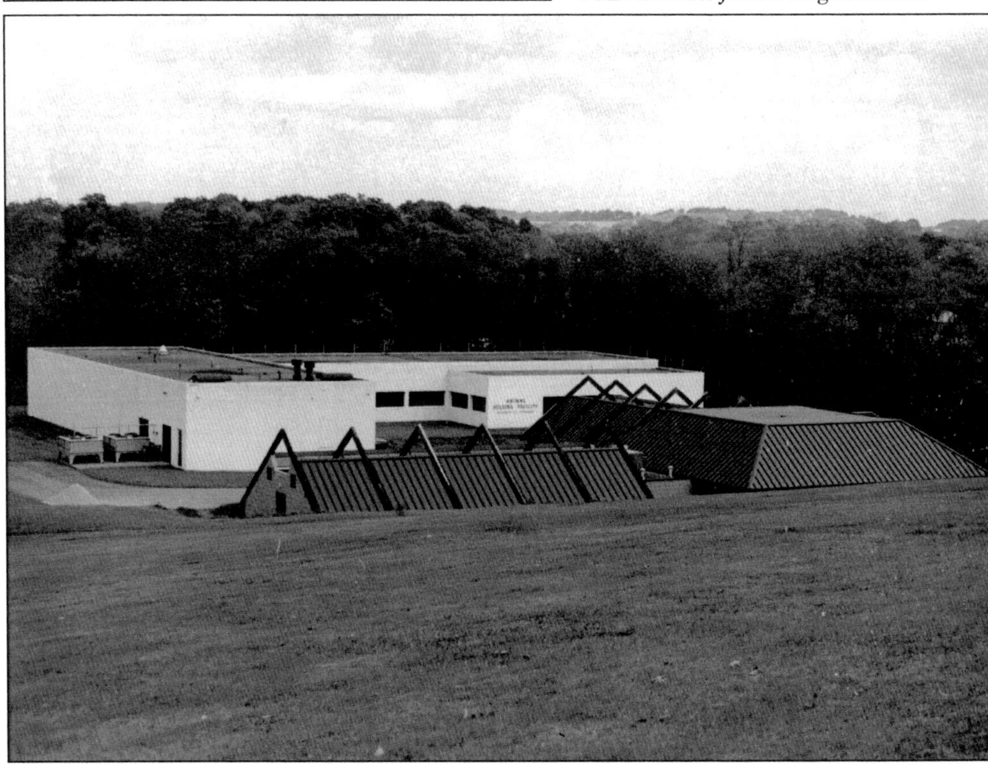

Four

Religion

Religion has been an important part of Plum's history since the town's founding. Many of the original church buildings no longer exist, and some congregations have dispersed or have been absorbed into other congregations. Some of these buildings include Olive Reformed Church, Laird Presbyterian Church, Davidson Chapel, and Renton Chapel.

Some local churches have histories going back almost as far as Plum's. The Presbyterian Church of Plum Creek dates to the late 18th century, Christ's Lutheran Church dates to 1784, and Unity United Presbyterian Church dates to 1833. Other churches, such as St. John the Baptist of Unity and St. Januarius of Renton, were founded as a result of the increased immigration of eastern Europeans to the region.

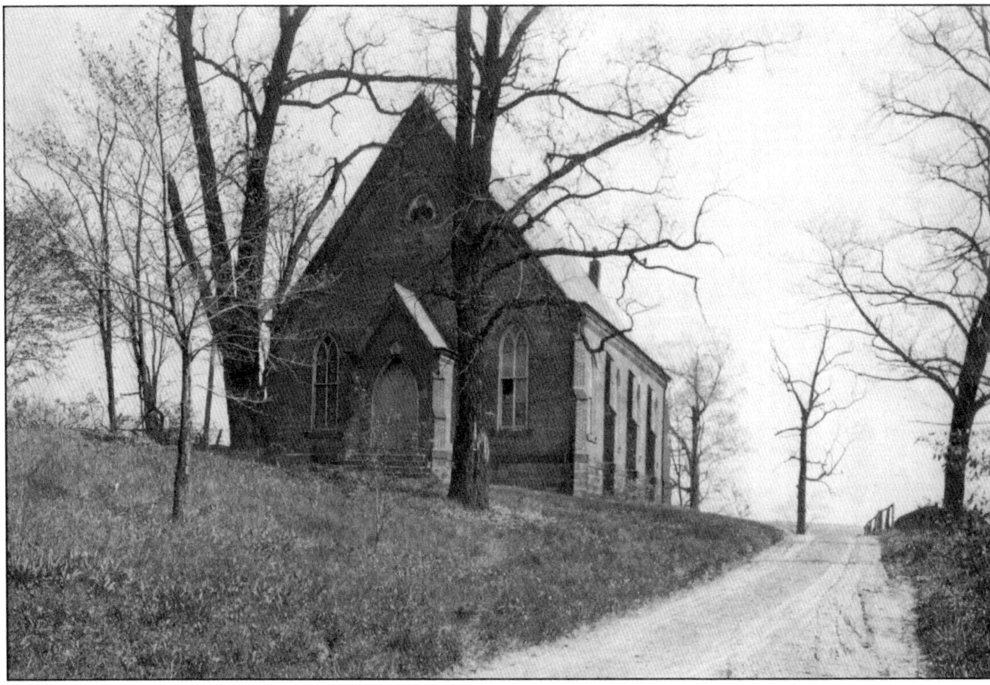

Laird Church, located at the corner of Saltsburg and New Texas Roads, was formed as a result of a split within Plum Creek's congregation. Some members chose to split away and stay in the old church building when a site for a new church was procured on Center New Texas Road. The new congregation became known as Laird Presbyterian Church and was named for Plum Creek's very first pastor, Rev. Francis Laird.

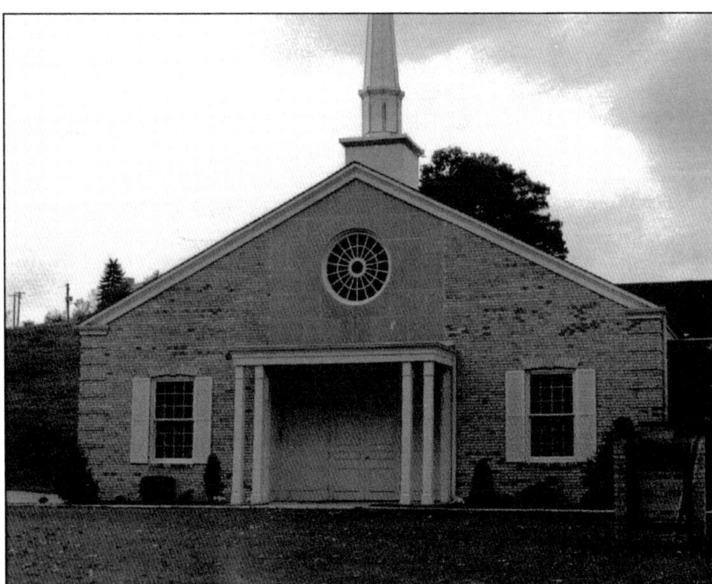

Construction of Plum Creek Presbyterian Church's newest sanctuary began November 25, 1962, and was completed in May 1964. By 1974, a new kitchen and the education wing were completed. In the 1890s, the congregation was fortunate enough to discover that their church was built over a productive natural-gas field. For several years, the church was able to draw some income from this.

Although the building used by Laird Church (which closed around 1916) no longer stands, Laird Cemetery can still be seen at the intersection of Saltsburg and New Texas Roads. The earliest recorded burial in this cemetery occurred in 1811; one of the last burials was Louella White in 1951. The cemetery is situated on land originally owned by William McJunkin; it is now maintained by the Allegheny County Parks and Recreation Department. The log-constructed Laird Church once sat directly across the street. The Plum High School Girls' Leaders Association donated the sign that stands at the front of the cemetery (right).

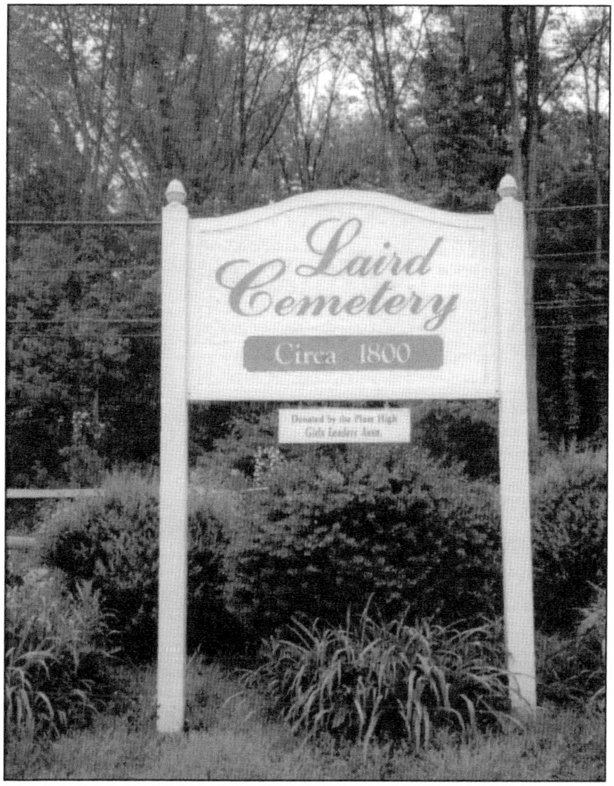

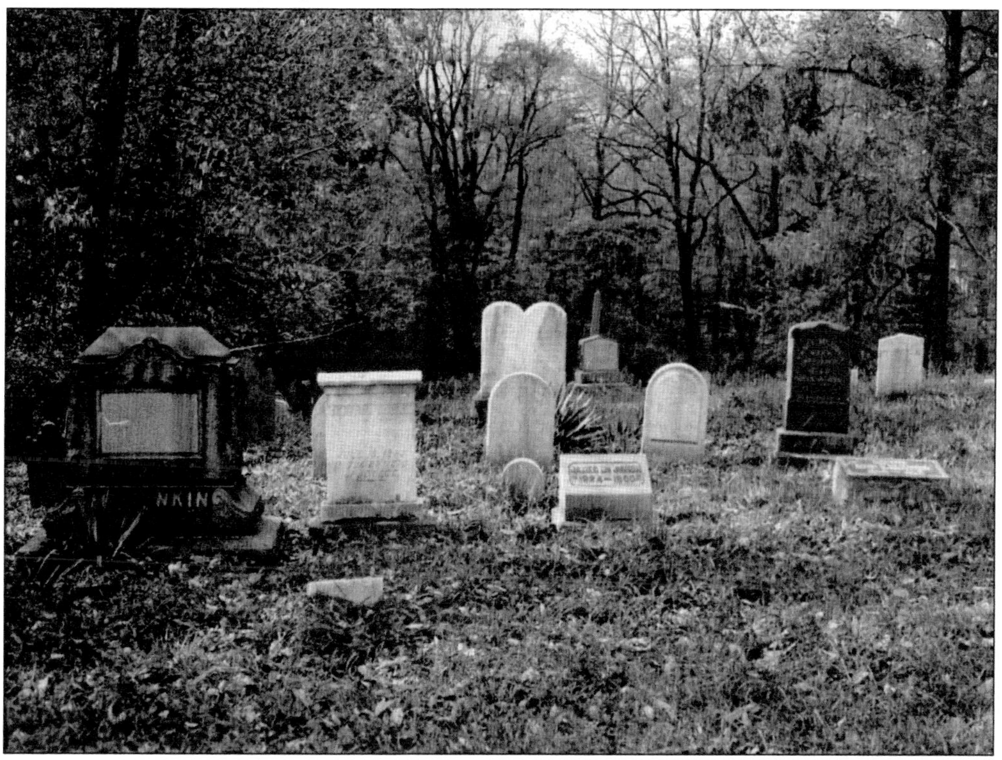

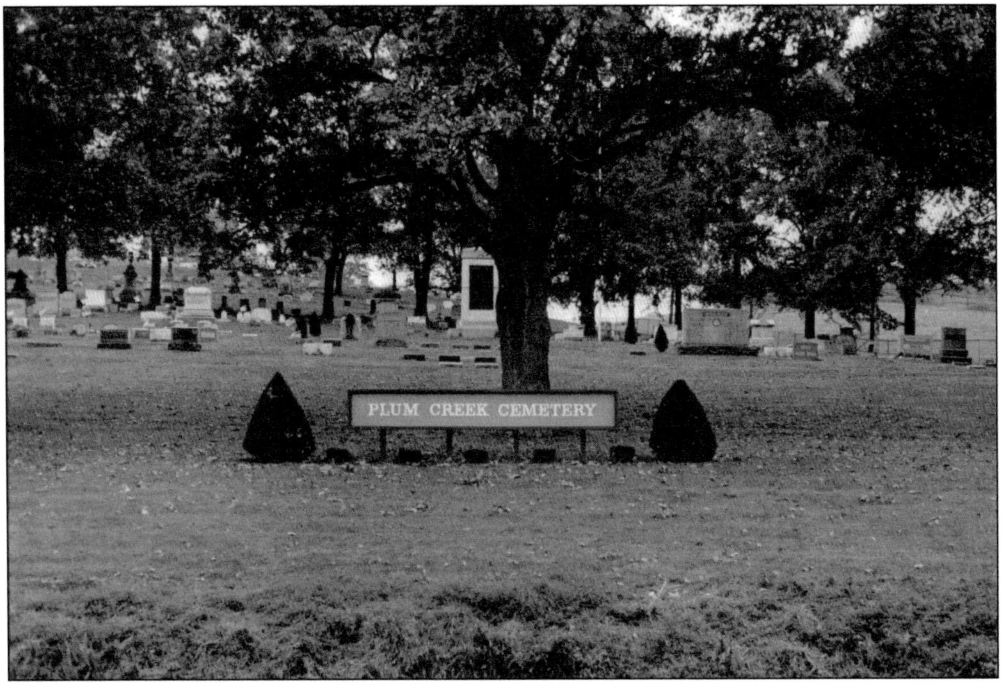

Plum Creek Cemetery, situated between New Texas and Center New Texas Roads, is the largest cemetery in the Borough. Originally owned by Plum Creek Presbyterian Church, the property was deeded to a non-profit organization on February 12, 1907.

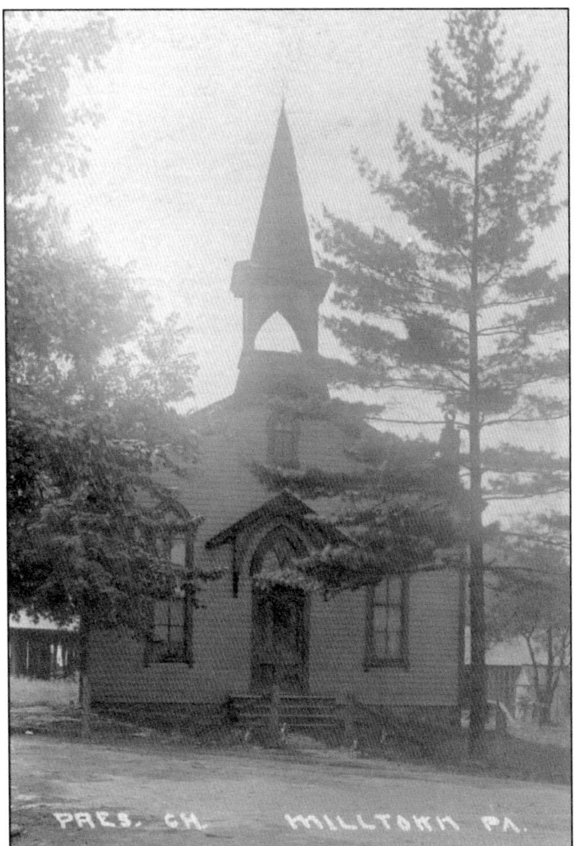

In 1849, a Sabbath school was founded by the Methodist church in Milltown. At some point in the 1870s, the school was abandoned by the Methodists, but the school carried on, basically independent of any outside connections. In 1876, Rev. John Kerr was invited to preach at Milltown, and a small chapel was built in the area. Kerr Presbyterian Church, as it became known, was officially organized on May 7, 1890. (Courtesy of Gary Rogers.)

Looking on as apple butter is prepared during one of the many events held at Kerr Presbyterian Church are, from left to right, Lois Repp, Mag Kuhn, Clemma Ciceske, Loretta Green, Mrs. Larick, unidentified, and Mrs. Alberti. Making apple butter was a major annual autumn event for the Ladies Aid Society of the church.

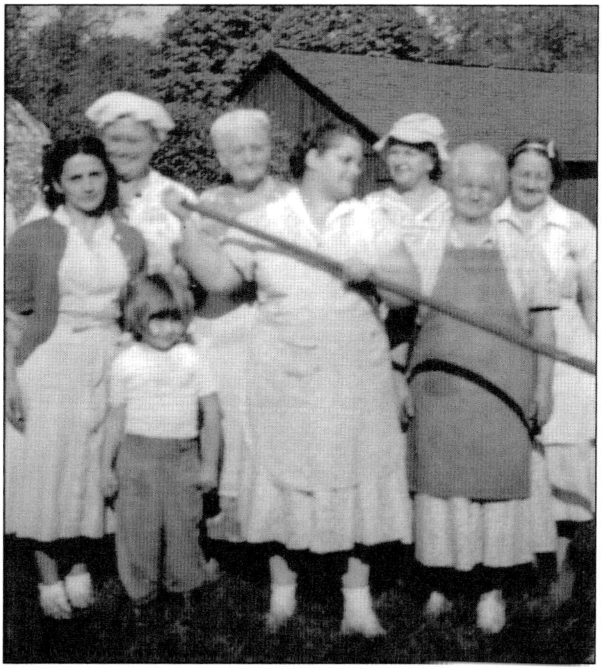

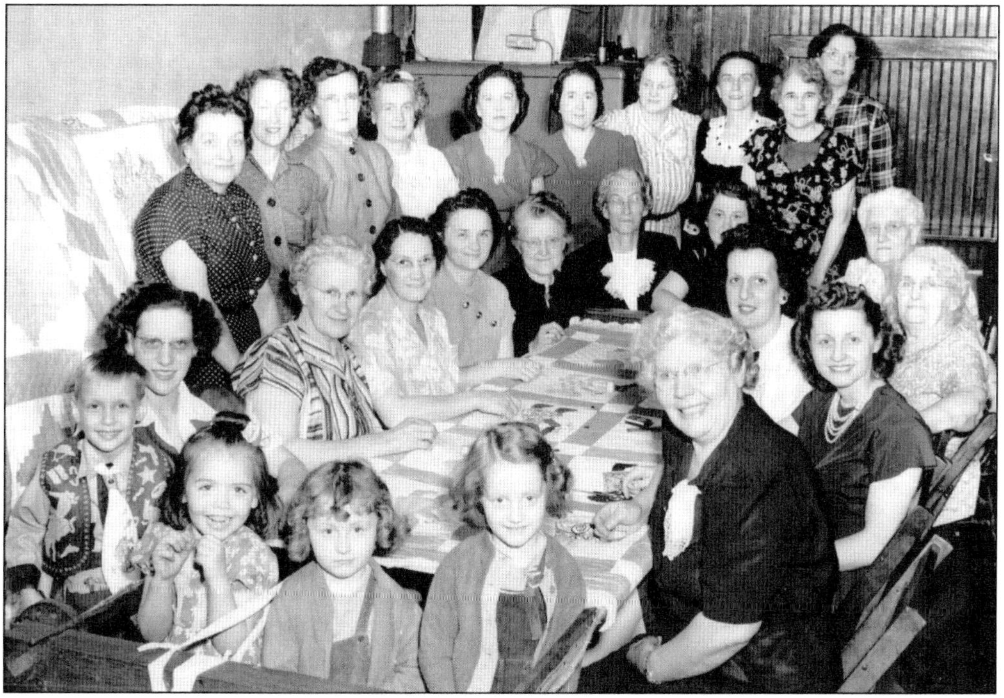

The Ladies Aid Society of Kerr Church gathers to have its photograph taken around 1948. Shown clockwise from left to right are (seated, from lower left) Grace Leonard (and her son), Clemma Ciceske, Loretta Green, Florence Richard, Stella Dible, Edna Wise, Janette Austin, Gayle Leroy, Annabelle Cook, Lizzie Bickerstaff, M. Kuhn, and Lyde Jeek; (standing) L. Foukes, Mabel Stephens, Margaret Mathius, Ida Cook, Lois Mullin, Jane Kuhn, A. Montgomery, Eleanor Skellive, Edna Mock, and Jane Kiser.

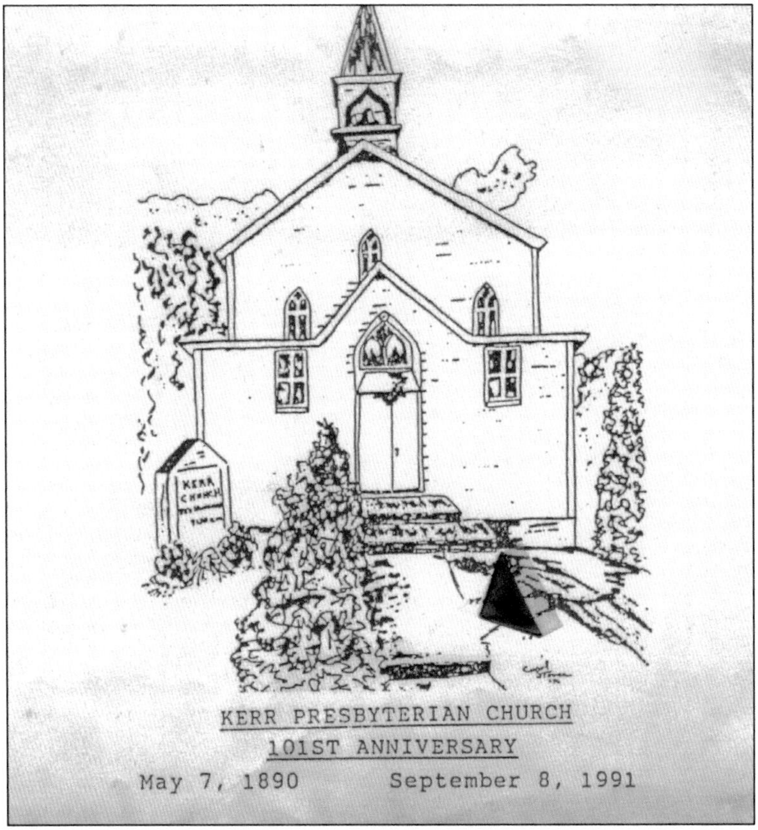

The sketch at left was drawn for the service on September 8, 1991, commemorating the 101st anniversary of Kerr Presbyterian Church. Below is a photograph of the interior of the sanctuary. The first chapel was built in 1877 on land that was conveyed to the First Presbyterian Church of Verona in 1881. On June 24, the property was conveyed to a board of trustees that led the congregation to submit a petition to the Presbytery of Blairsville in 1890. This petition led to the founding of Kerr Presbyterian Church in 1891.

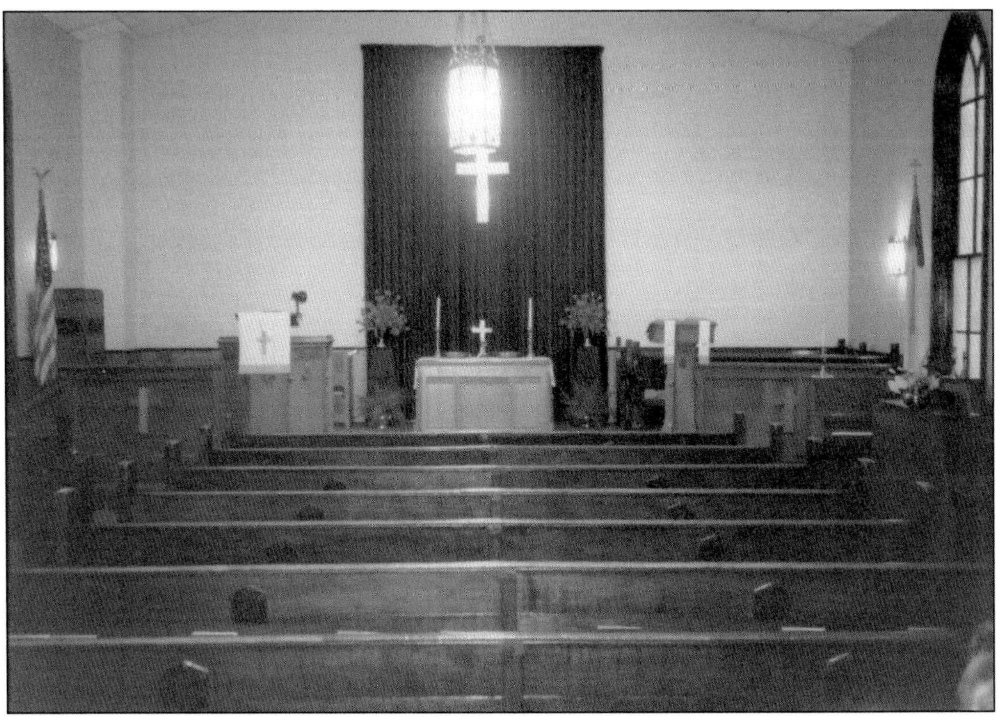

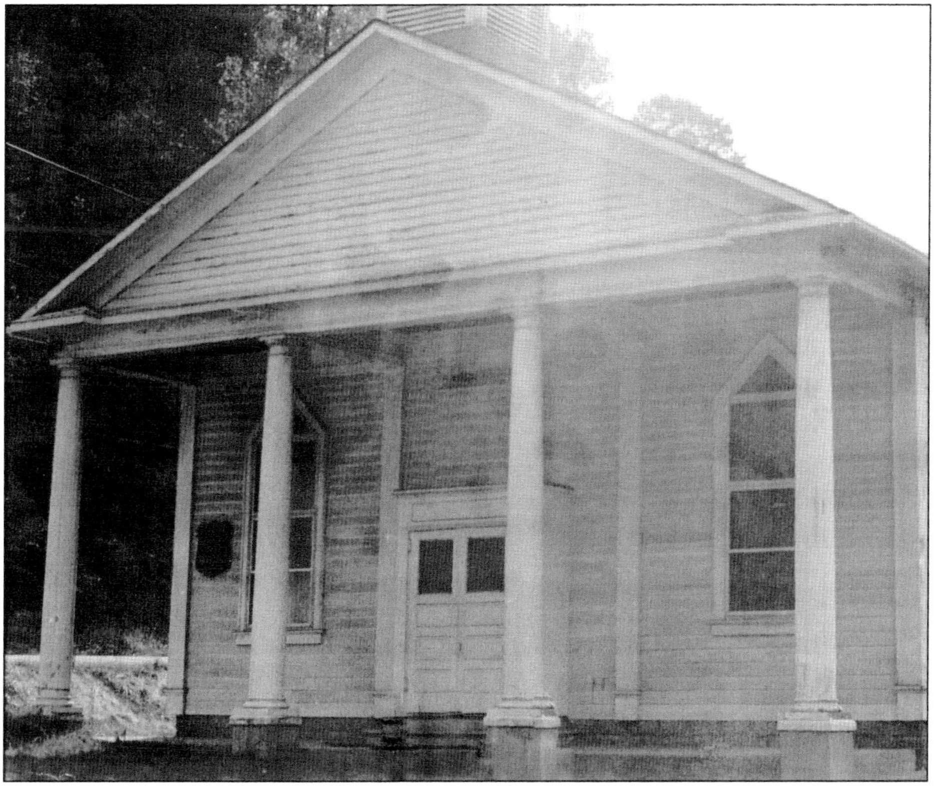

The land that came to be known as Logans Ferry was first deeded to John Little in 1769. The second owner, John W. Woods, sold the land to Alexander Logan. Alexander's son Hugh donated land for Logans Ferry Church, which was built in 1856. The church fell under the care of the Presbytery of Blairsville of what was then the Associate Reformed Presbyterian Church of America. The congregation was officially organized on December 7, 1857. The Presbytery of Blairsville felt that the church should have an official beginning date of 1856 as that was the year that the church was built. The postcard on which this photograph is printed shows a postmark of 1909.

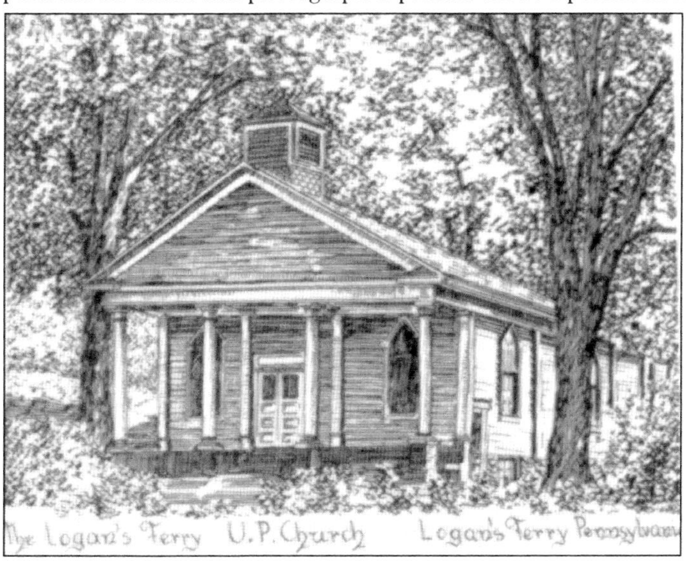

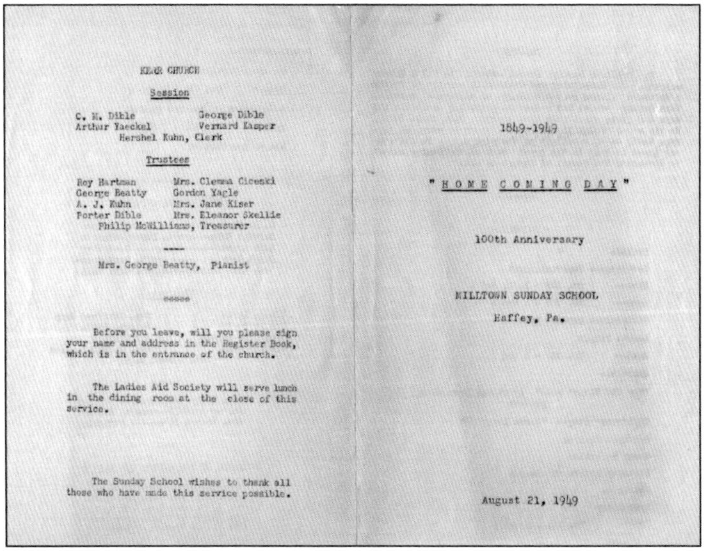

KERR CHURCH

Session

C. M. Dible   George Dible
Arthur Yaeckel   Vernard Kasper
Hershel Kuhn, Clerk

Trustees

Roy Hartman   Mrs. Clemma Cicoski
George Beatty   Gordon Yagle
A. J. Kuhn   Mrs. Jane Kiser
Porter Dible   Mrs. Eleanor Skellie
Philip McWilliams, Treasurer

Mrs. George Beatty, Pianist

Before you leave, will you please sign your name and address in the Register Book, which is in the entrance of the church.

The Ladies Aid Society will serve lunch in the dining room at the close of this service.

The Sunday School wishes to thank all those who have made this service possible.

1849-1949

"HOME COMING DAY"

100th Anniversary

MILLTOWN SUNDAY SCHOOL

Haffey, Pa.

August 21, 1949

This pamphlet is from the 100th-anniversary service of the Milltown Sunday school on August 21, 1949. After being incorporated into the Presbyterian Church of the United States in 1891, the congregation of Kerr Presbyterian Church grew slowly, but the Sabbath school continued to be strong and active. In 1914, Kerr Church called its first full-time minister, Rev. Thomas Ewing Thompson.

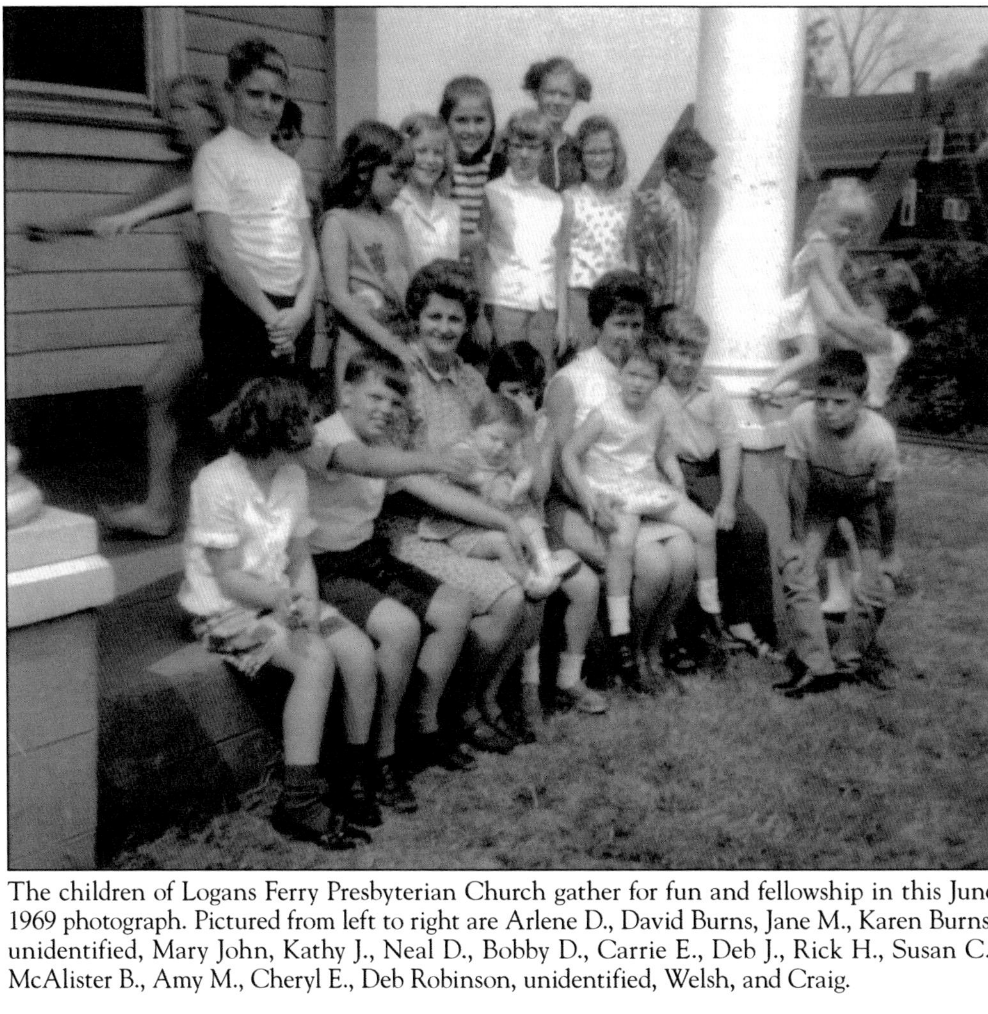

The children of Logans Ferry Presbyterian Church gather for fun and fellowship in this June 1969 photograph. Pictured from left to right are Arlene D., David Burns, Jane M., Karen Burns, unidentified, Mary John, Kathy J., Neal D., Bobby D., Carrie E., Deb J., Rick H., Susan C., McAlister B., Amy M., Cheryl E., Deb Robinson, unidentified, Welsh, and Craig.

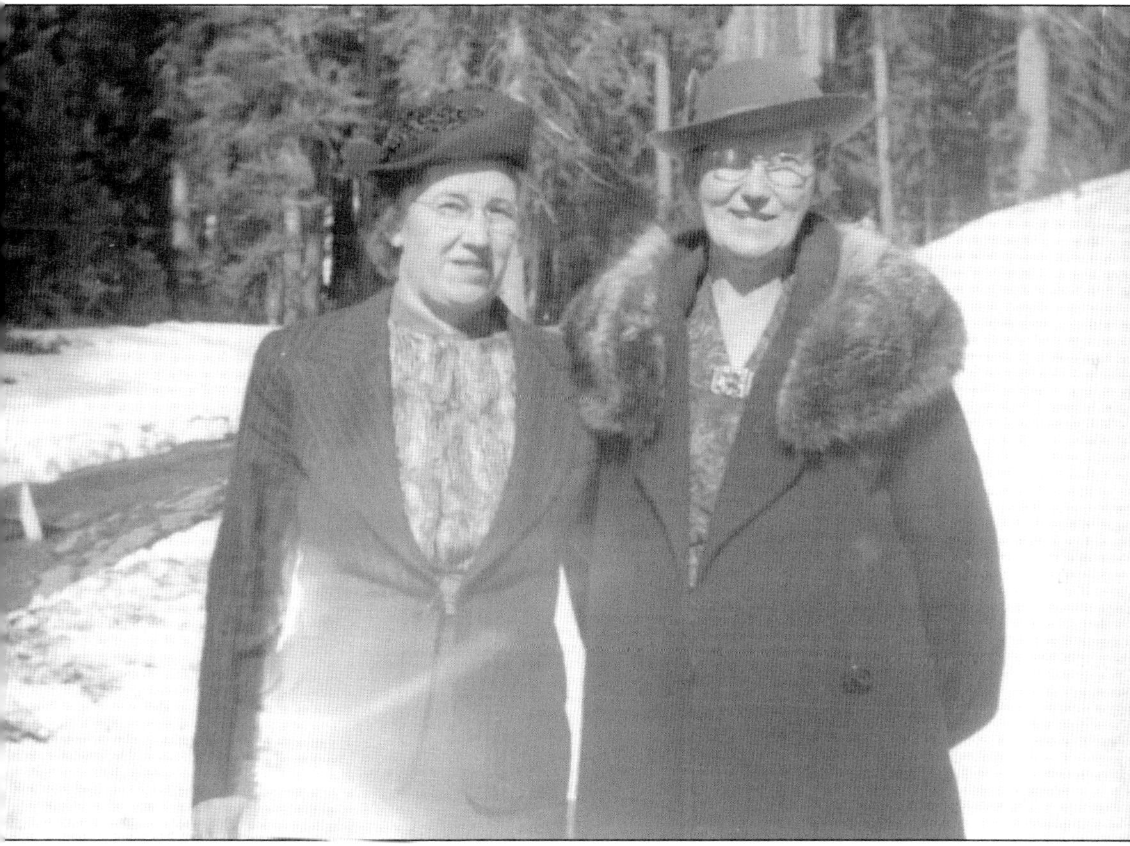

Two fellow congregants pose in their Sunday best on a cold winter morning in front of Logans Ferry Presbyterian Church. The original church building that these parishioners worshipped in served the congregation for 124 years. In 1856, Hugh J. Logan Sr.—owner of much of the land that would become known as Logans Ferry—donated a parcel of land as a site for the people to construct a church. During the autumn of 1856, the original church building was constructed. The church originally entered into the Associate Reformed Presbyterian Church of North America via the Presbytery of Blairsville. (In 1858, the Associate and Associate Reformed Presbyterian Churches came together to form the United Presbyterian Church.) In 1980, the recently dissolved Parnassus Presbyterian Church building in New Kensington was for sale. Logans Ferry purchased the Parnassus building and worshipped there for the first time on February 3, 1980. Unfortunately, the original church building no longer exists.

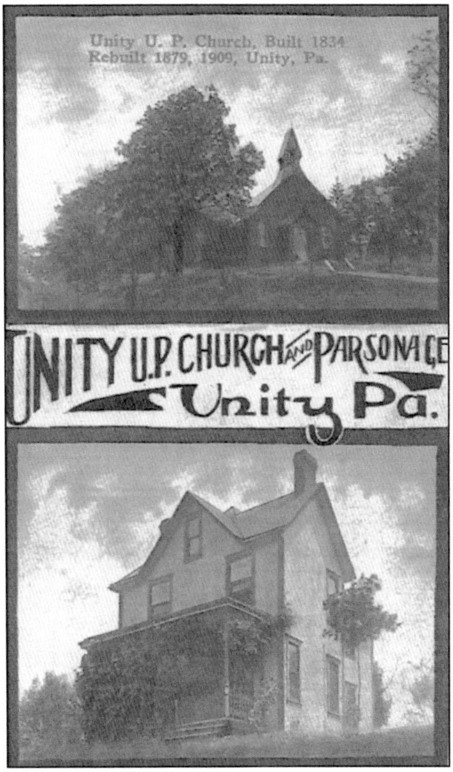

This postcard image displays Unity United Presbyterian Church's parsonage and church building. The church began as Unity Associate Reformed Church on April 2, 1833, under no formal organization. The original church building was completed in the fall of 1836. The current parsonage, built around 1932, replaced an old wood-frame structure, and the current church building was dedicated on January 13, 1957.

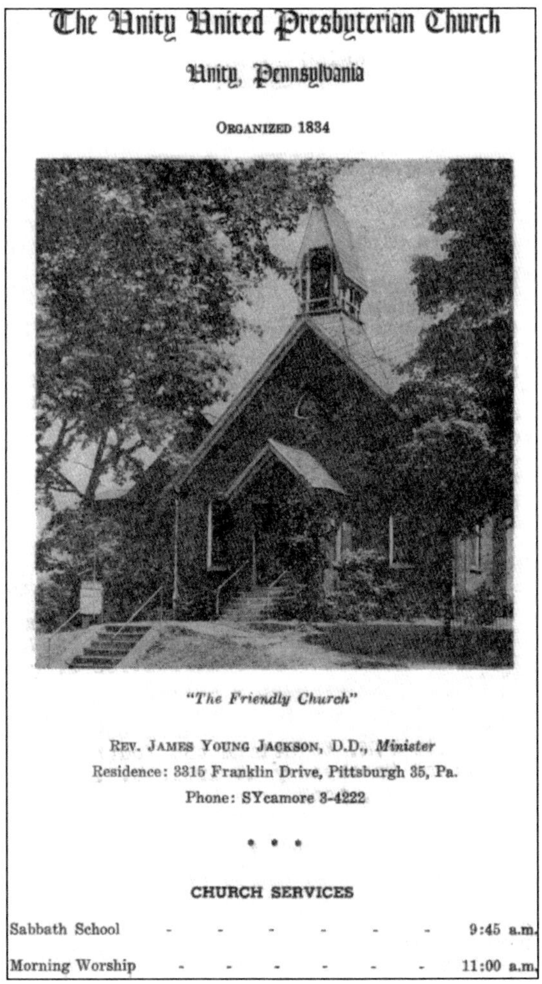
The Unity United Presbyterian Church

Unity, Pennsylvania

ORGANIZED 1834

"The Friendly Church"

REV. JAMES YOUNG JACKSON, D.D., *Minister*
Residence: 3315 Franklin Drive, Pittsburgh 35, Pa.
Phone: SYcamore 8-4222

• • •

CHURCH SERVICES

Sabbath School - - - - - - - 9:45 a.m.
Morning Worship - - - - - - 11:00 a.m.

Unity United Presbyterian Church prided itself as being "the Friendly Church." Shown is a bulletin cover from Sunday, October 28, 1956. The steeple, along with a lower entrance and Colonial-style façade, were added in the 1960s. In 1982, memorial windows from the old redbrick structure were renovated and installed in the current building.

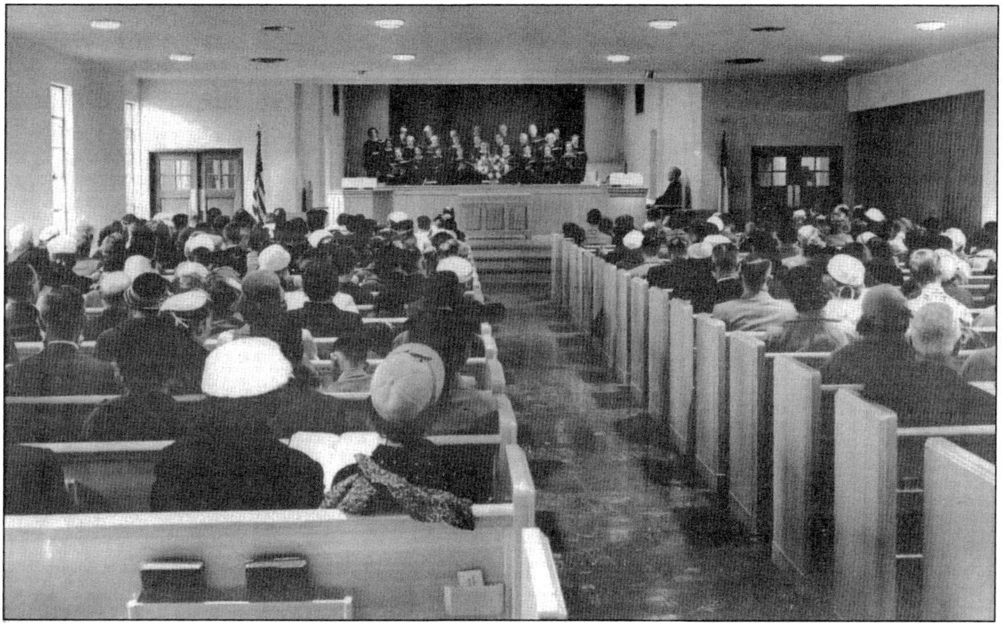

Parishioners pack the sanctuary of the new Unity United Presbyterian Church building for its first service, which was held on Sunday, January 6, 1957. The new building was officially dedicated on Sunday, January 13, 1957. It was under Rev. Dr. J.Y. Jackson's leadership that the new church building program was initiated. Reverend Jackson began his tenure at Unity Church in 1947.

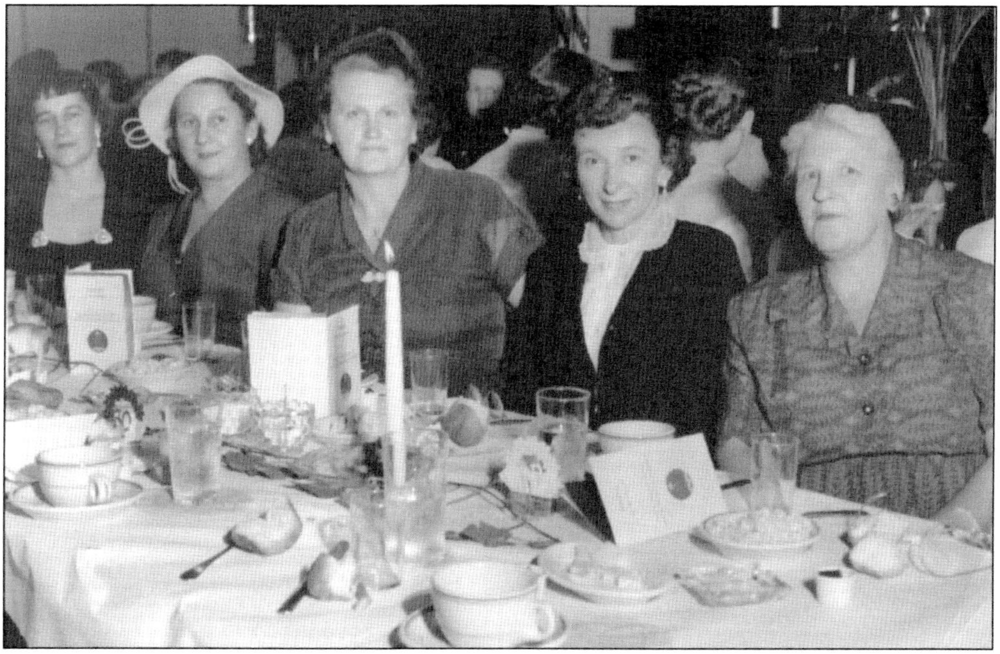

Members of St. John the Baptist Parish attend a meeting of the Catholic Daughters of America in Tarentum, sometime around 1959. The Catholic Daughters of America was founded in 1903 by John E. Carberry and several other Knights of Columbus in Utica, New York. The society takes pride in being a "charitable, benevolent, and patriotic sorority for Catholic ladies." (Courtesy of St. John the Baptist Parish.)

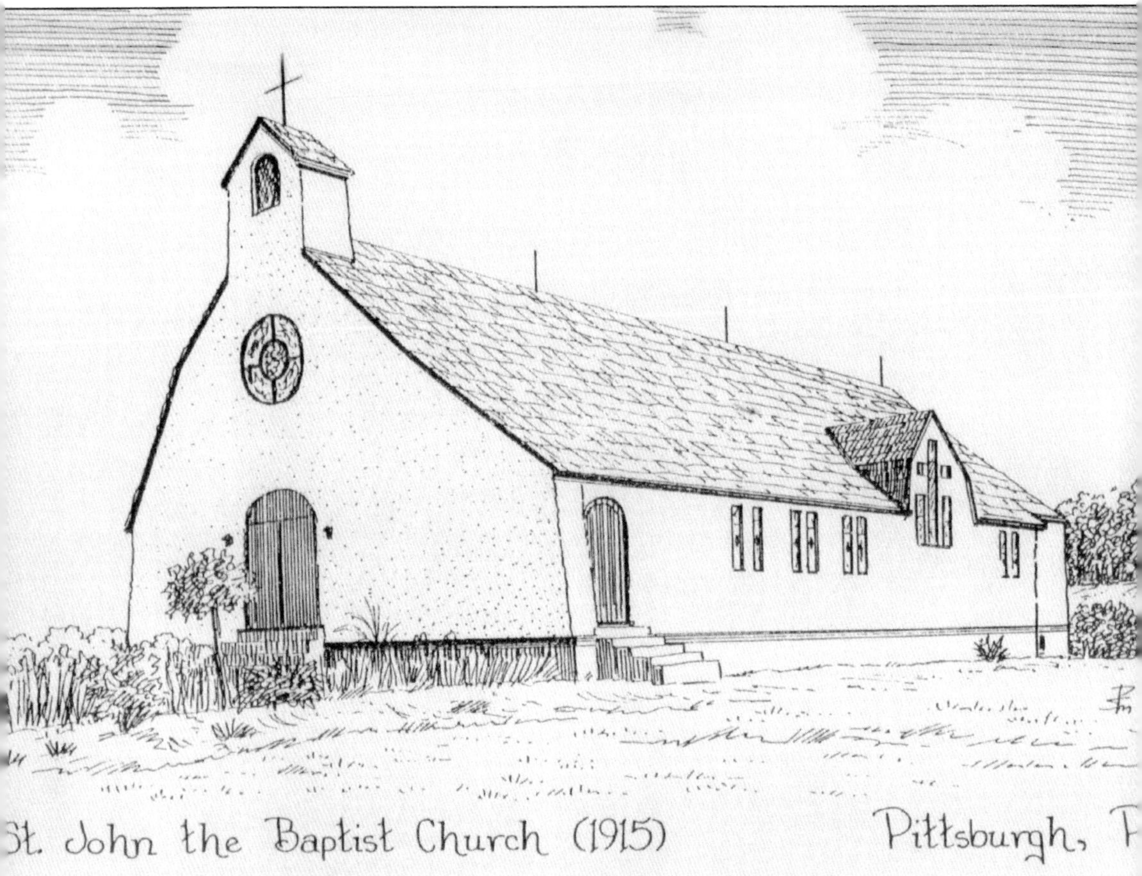

Slovaks were one of the many ethnicities that were part of the great influx of US immigrants around the turn of the 20th century. Many Slovaks settled in the communities of North Bessemer and Unity. Lake Erie Railroad, Union Railroad, and Portland Cement Company were three of the larger employers that these Slovak immigrants worked for. The Slovak people of Plum had very limited choices when it came to where they felt comfortable worshipping. They could go to the primarily English-speaking parish of St. Joseph in Verona, or make the long trek to Braddock (home to Slovak Catholic, Lutheran, and Calvinist congregations). Rev. Adalbert Kazincy of St. Michael's in Braddock offered his assistance and located a Father Moravec, who agreed to minister to the Slovak Catholics of Plum. By 1915, St. John's was able to procure a parcel of land. Construction of the church building began in 1917, and it was dedicated on July 14, 1918. (Courtesy of St. John the Baptist Parish.)

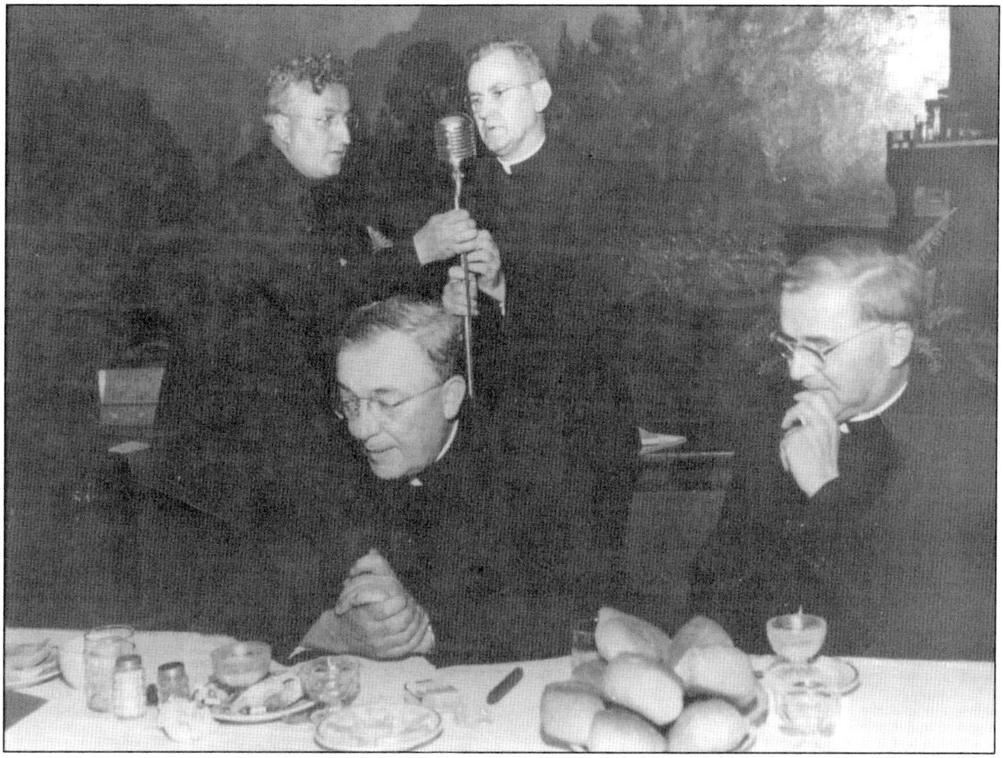

Since its inception, the leadership of St. John the Baptist was active in propelling the church through the 20th century. Father Quilter, who was instrumental in the building of the first church, was replaced by Father Michael Fialko in 1933. Father Fialko and Monsignor Koshner are shown above at a church dinner in 1955. Father Raynak took charge of St. John's in 1955, and under his leadership a new sanctuary (below) and school were built. The church continued to grow in numbers, and even more room was needed. Land was secured from the Molchan and Brunner families in order to expand the church parking lot and build a convent. (Both courtesy of St. John the Baptist Parish.)

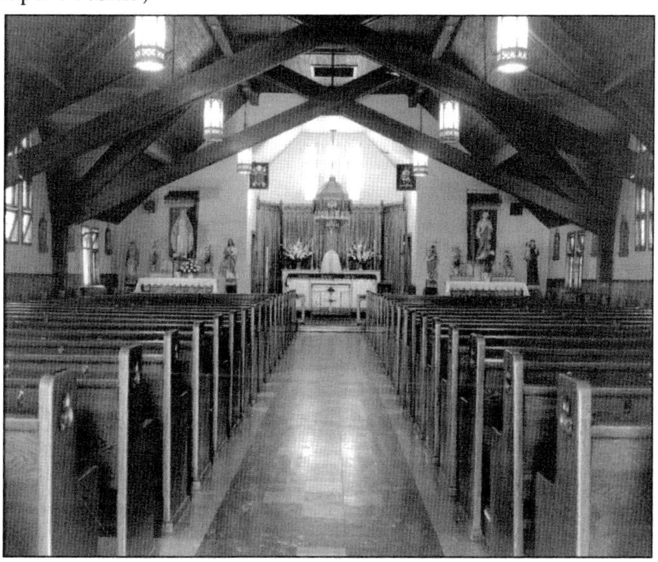

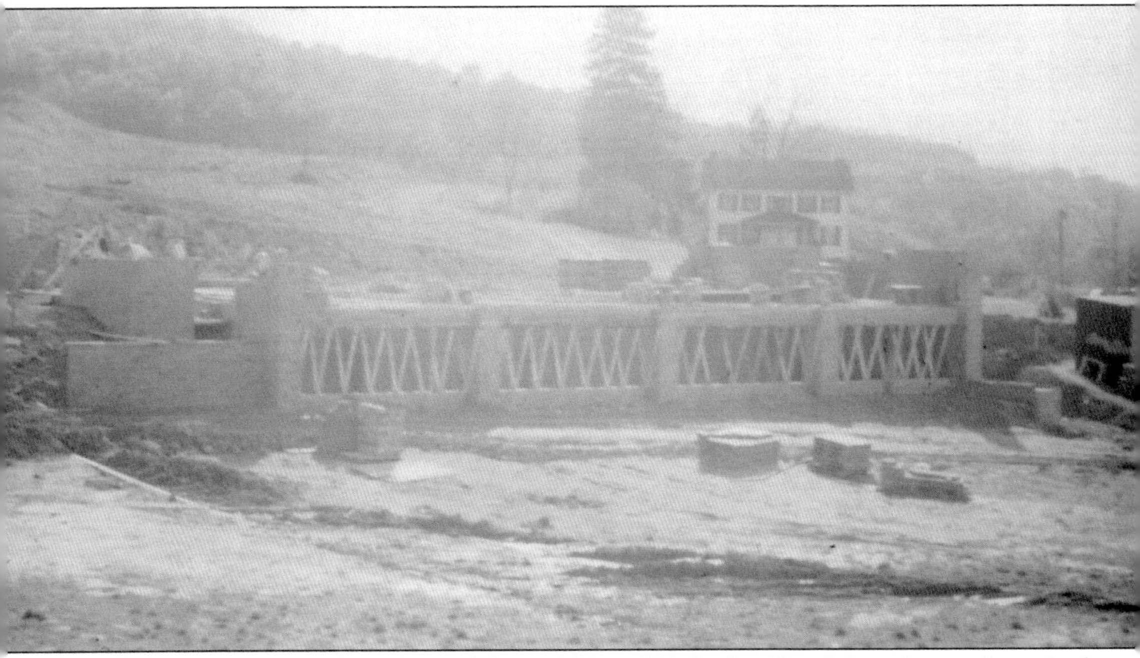

The congregation now known as Holiday Park United Methodist Church has a history dating back to before the Civil War. The present congregation was formed as part of a merger of the Sardis Methodist Church and Holiday Park Evangelical United Brethren Church. Sardis Methodist Church began around 1850 when Duncan and Marjorie Keith Sr. deeded one-quarter acre of land to the trustees of the Methodist church for conducting church services. The Holiday Park Evangelical United Brethren Church, pictured, is of more recent origin. It began as a mission in 1959 and held its first service, attended by 24 people, in the Dice family's farmhouse (which can be seen in the background). In 1961, Orin Sampson gave nine acres situated across the street from the Dice farmhouse. Construction of the education building began there on July 23, 1961. The cornerstone was laid on November 12, 1961, and construction was completed on September 9, 1962. (Courtesy of Holiday Park United Methodist Church.)

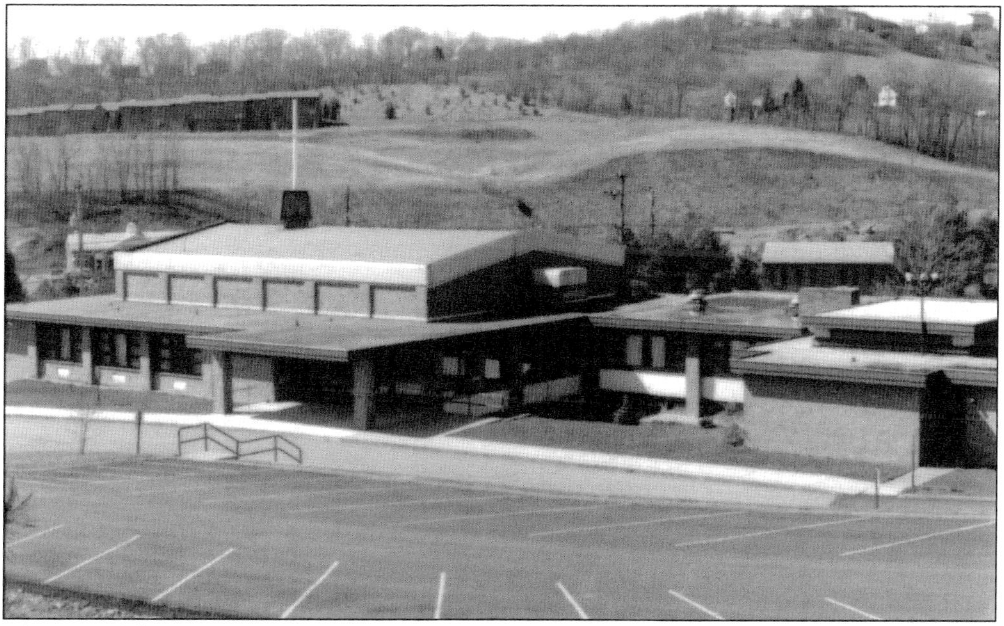

The Sardis Methodist Church and Holiday Park Evangelical United Brethren Church remained separate entities until 1967. At this time, it became apparent that the Methodist church and United Brethren church would unite. A decision was made to unite these two congregations prior to the official national union that took place on April 23, 1968. The Holiday Park site was chosen as the permanent site for the united congregation. The first combined service was held October 1, 1967. (Courtesy of Holiday Park United Methodist Church.)

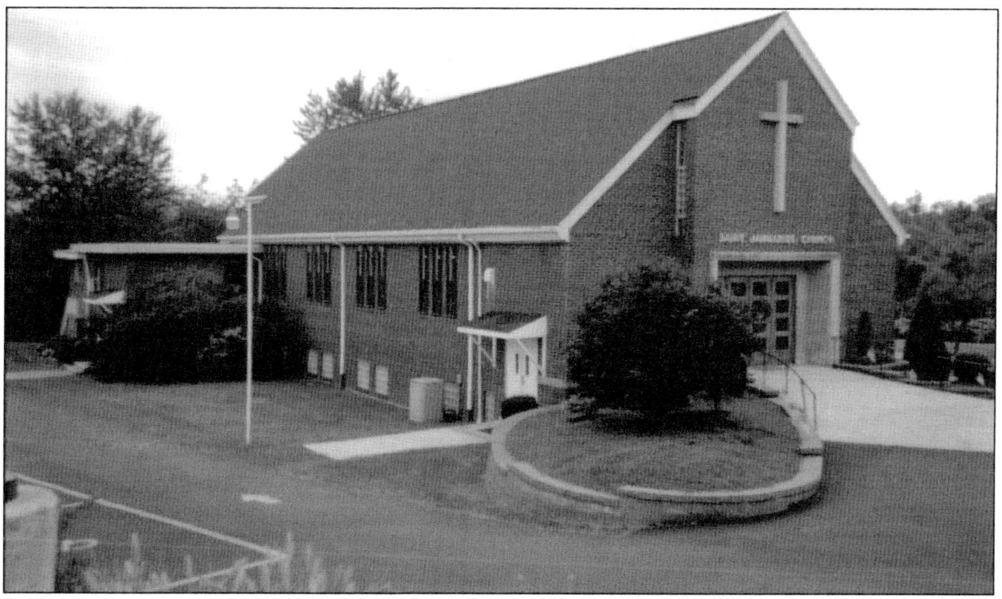

St. Januarius Roman Catholic Church in Renton began as a mission of St. John the Baptist Parish on March 11, 1920. Father Quilter served as the first pastor to St. Januarius, and the congregation worshipped in the Renton company store. It was not until a capital campaign was initiated in 1950 that the funds were procured to build a permanent church. Mass was celebrated in the new building on November 30, 1952, by Fr. Arthur Garbin.

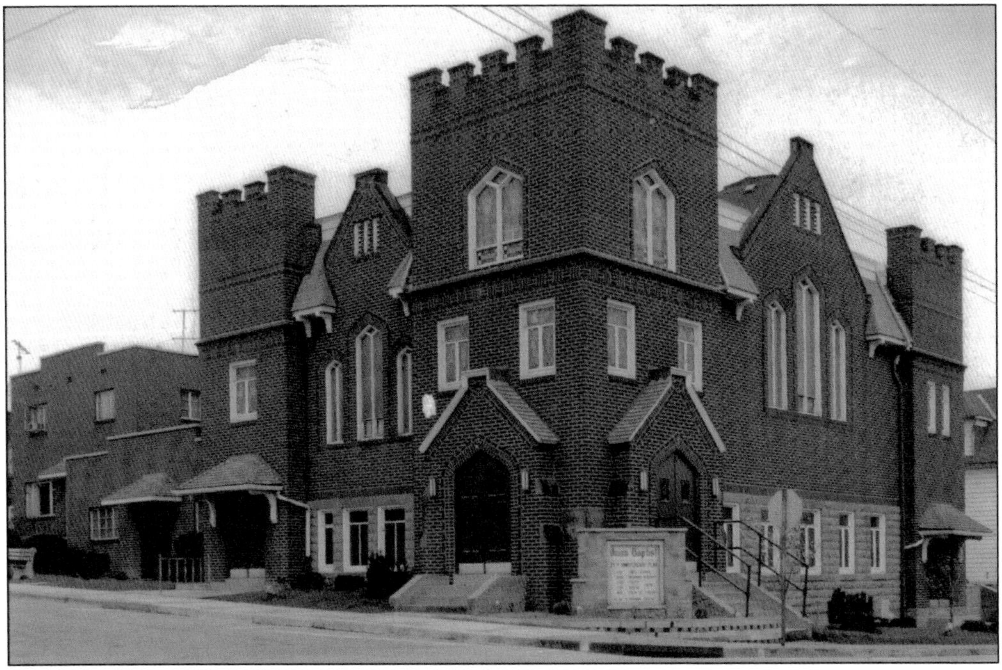

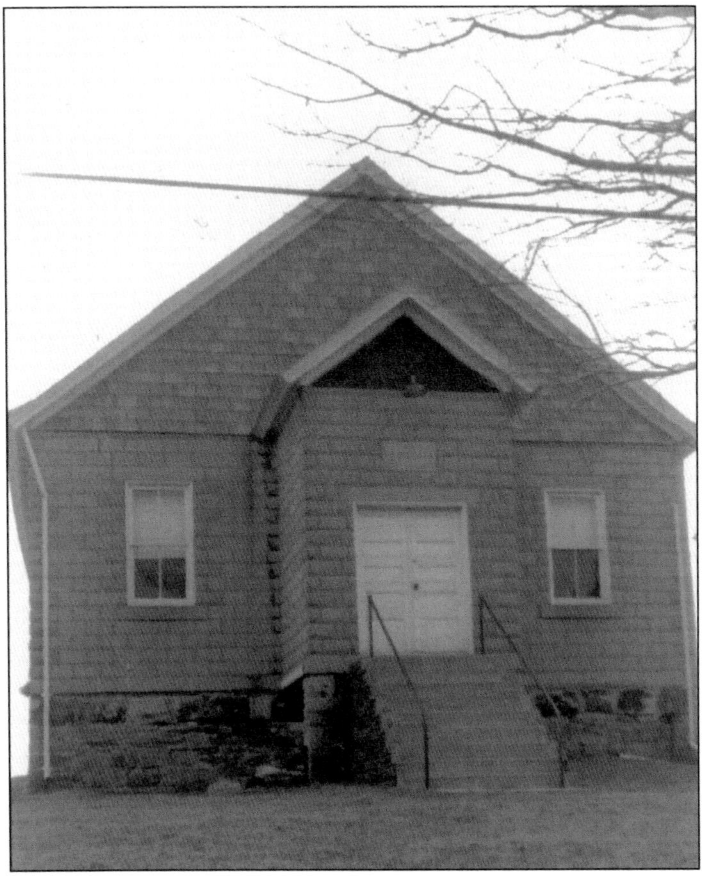

One of the most notable residential booms occurred in Holiday Park. Around 1959, the members of Union Baptist Church of Arnold, Pennsylvania (above) sought to set up a new mission. This mission manifested itself as a new congregation for the people of Holiday Park. By October 1959, permission was granted for use of the old Olive Reformed Church on Ridge Road (left) as a site for Sunday afternoon services. By 1960, morning services were initiated. Rev. Dale Chaddock conducted 9:30 a.m. services at the Holiday Park site and then hurried back to the mother church for the 11 a.m. service. (Both courtesy of Holiday Park Baptist Church.)

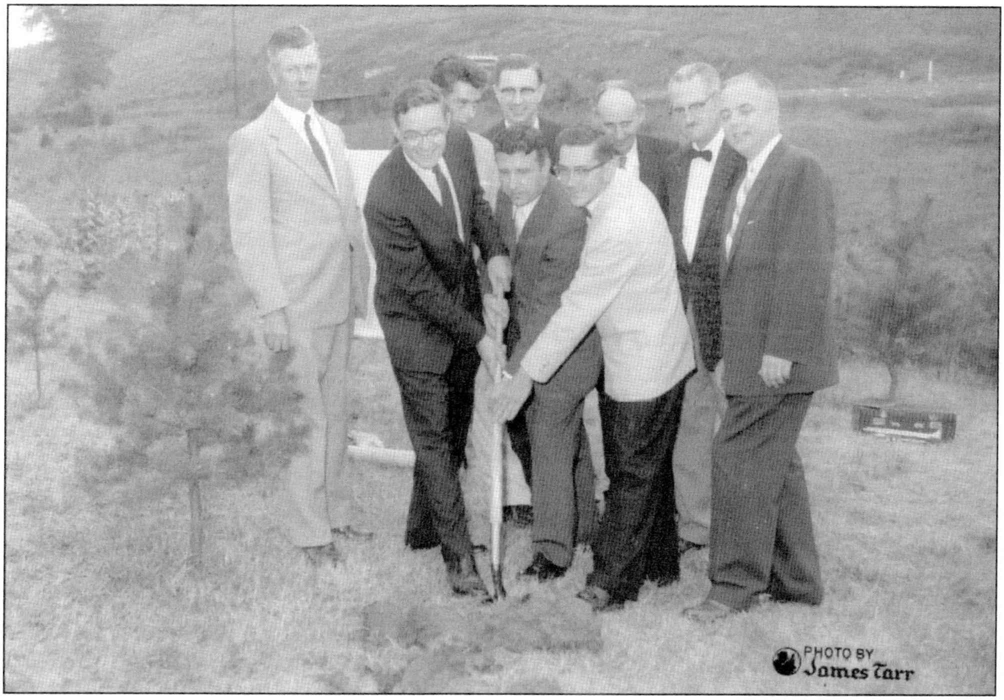

Holiday Park Baptist Church was officially organized on June 2, 1960. Reverend Chaddock was called to be the first full-time pastor of the new congregation. A five-acre tract of land was purchased off of Hialeah Drive near Route 286. The ground breaking ceremony was held on September 1, 1960, and is shown above. Amongst those participating was Reverend Chaddock and members of the board of trustees, including Larry Talmage, David Guenther, Stanley Guenther, and Stanley Zetts. The photograph below shows the interior of the completed sanctuary. (Both courtesy of Holiday Park Baptist Church.)

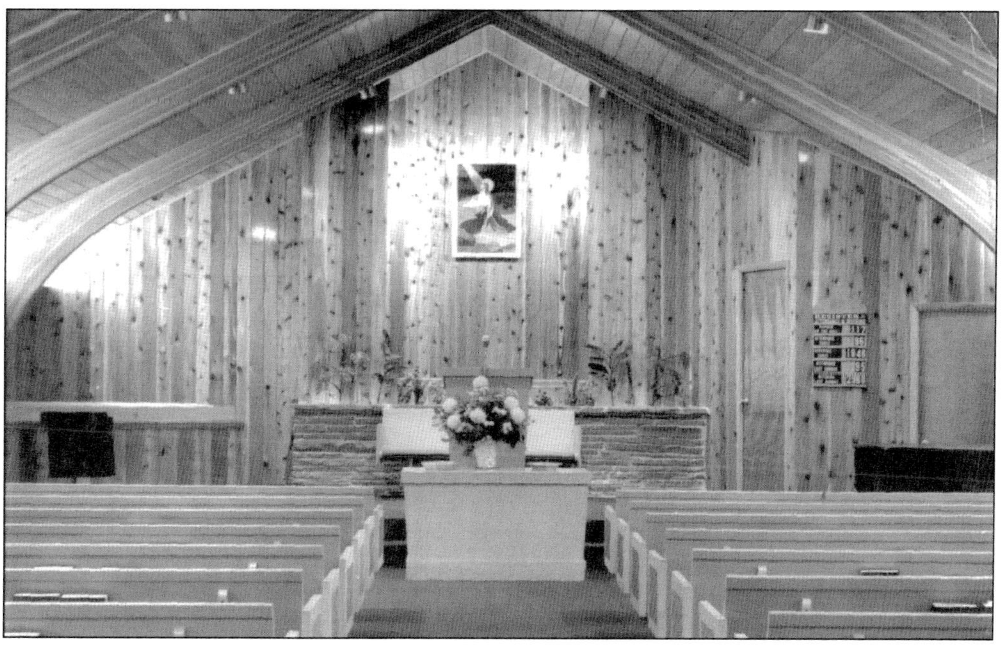

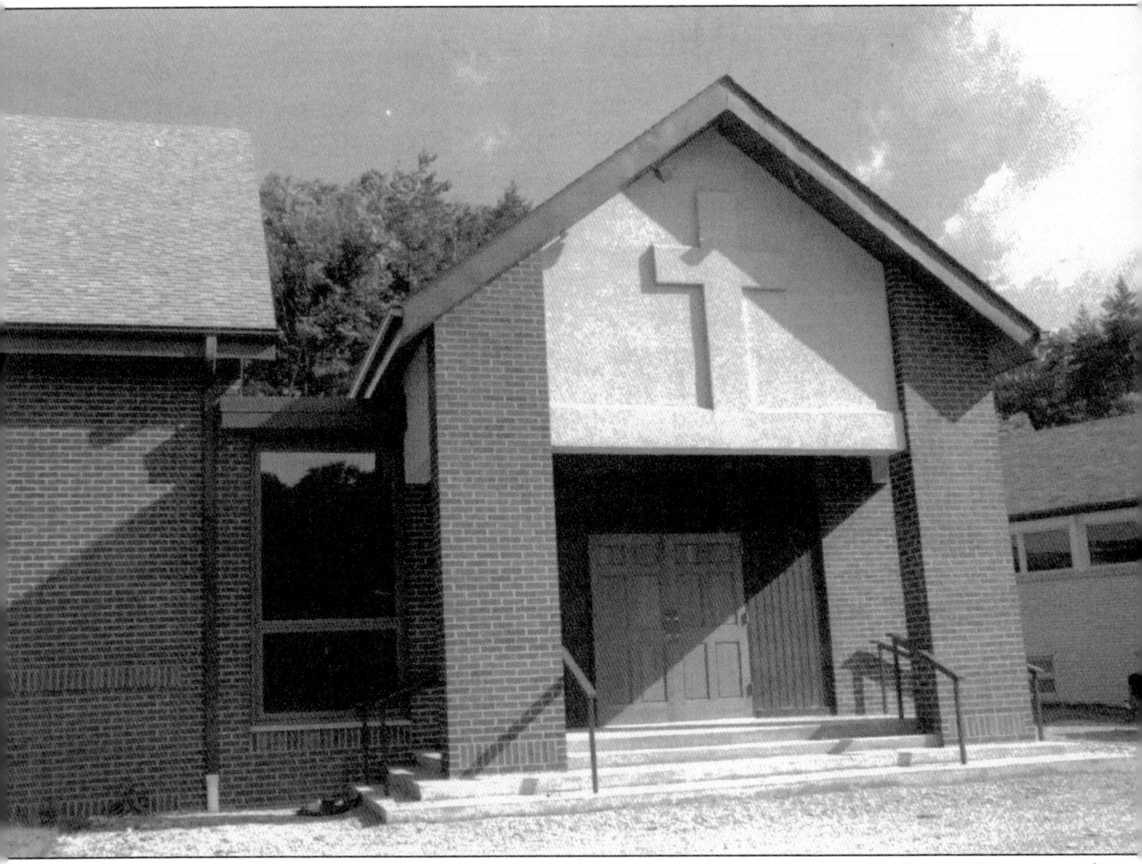

By the 1980s, Holiday Park Baptist Church had seen several years of substantial growth and found the need to expand. By 1986, the planning phase for a new church building was underway. A contractor was hired in 1987, and in the autumn of 1988, parishioners of Holiday Park Baptist Church were able to occupy their new building. The old sanctuary was converted into classroom space. By the 1980s, the Holiday Park area had five churches, three banks, a fire department, a YMCA and two YMCA pools, a bowling alley, two shopping centers, and a sub–post office that was housed inside a drug store. (Courtesy of Holiday Park Baptist Church.)

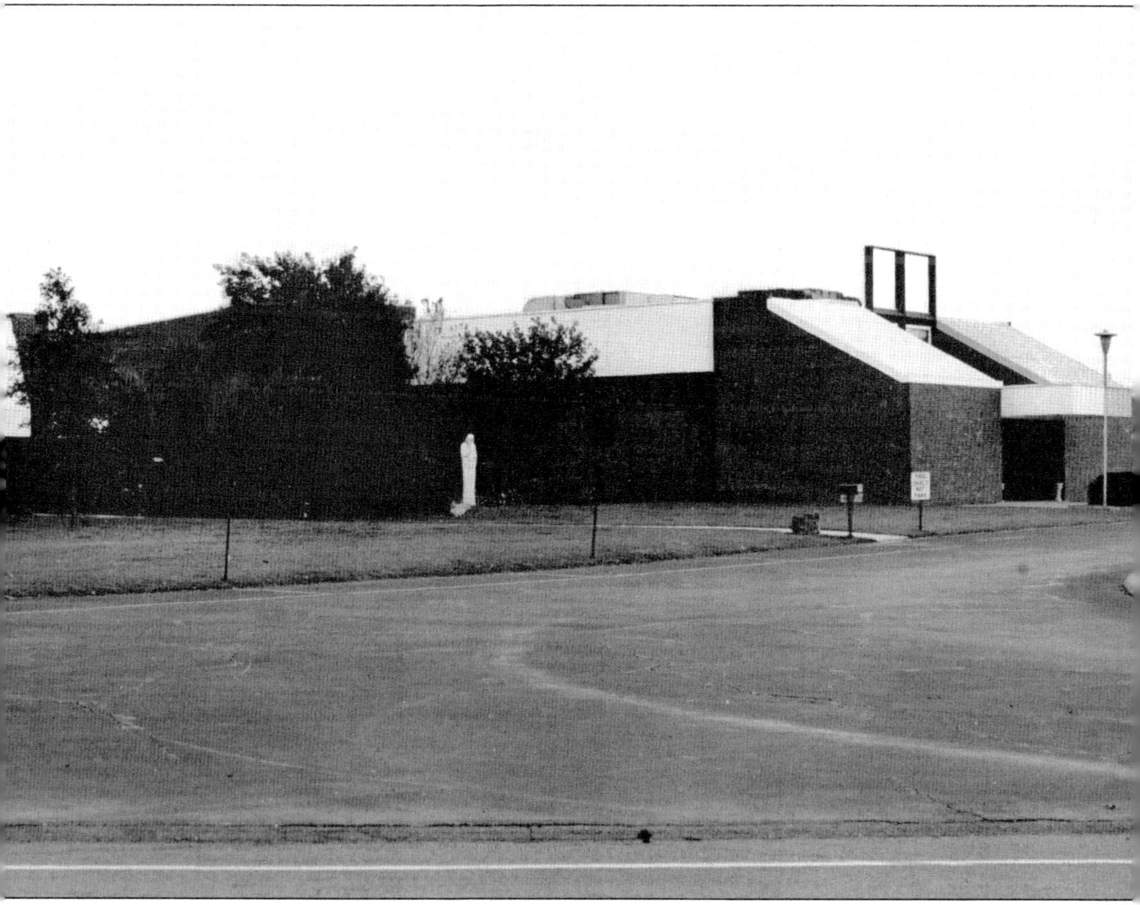

A need to minister to the Catholic population of Holiday Park and Woodlawn Estates was brought to the attention of Bishop John Wright of the Catholic Diocese of Pittsburgh, and on June 10, 1968, the community saw the establishment of Mary, Cause of Our Joy (Our Lady of Joy) Parish. Fr. Francis V. Marchukonis was appointed its first pastor. Sunday masses, for the first three years, were celebrated in the auditorium at Our Lady of Mercy Academy in Monroeville. Construction of the first rectory, located farther down O'Block Road from the site of the proposed church building, began in June 1968. The garage of this rectory was converted into a chapel for weekday masses, baptisms, and confessions. From its inception in 1968 through 1988, the church's population rose from 760 families to 1,342 families.

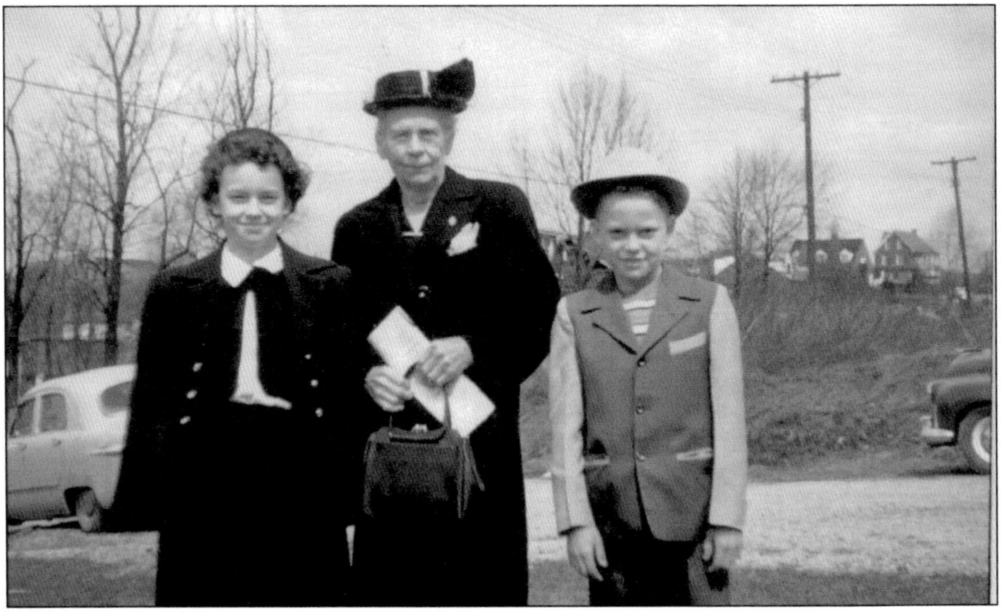

Here are some of the parishioners of Bethel United Presbyterian Church (located along Beatty Road in neighboring Monroeville). Bethel Church dates to the 19th century and members from several old local families have been members, including the Carpenters. Above, Martha Carpenter—aunt of Isabella and Eleanor Carpenter—stands between her grandniece Louise and grandnephew Jimmie Stewart. Martha was the sister of Edgar Heron Carpenter and William Murry Carpenter. Below, Emma Carpenter—Isabella and Eleanor's mother—is shown smiling happily. Emma (née Brodmerkel) was married to William Murry Carpenter. These photographs were taken by Earl H. Seitz Sr.

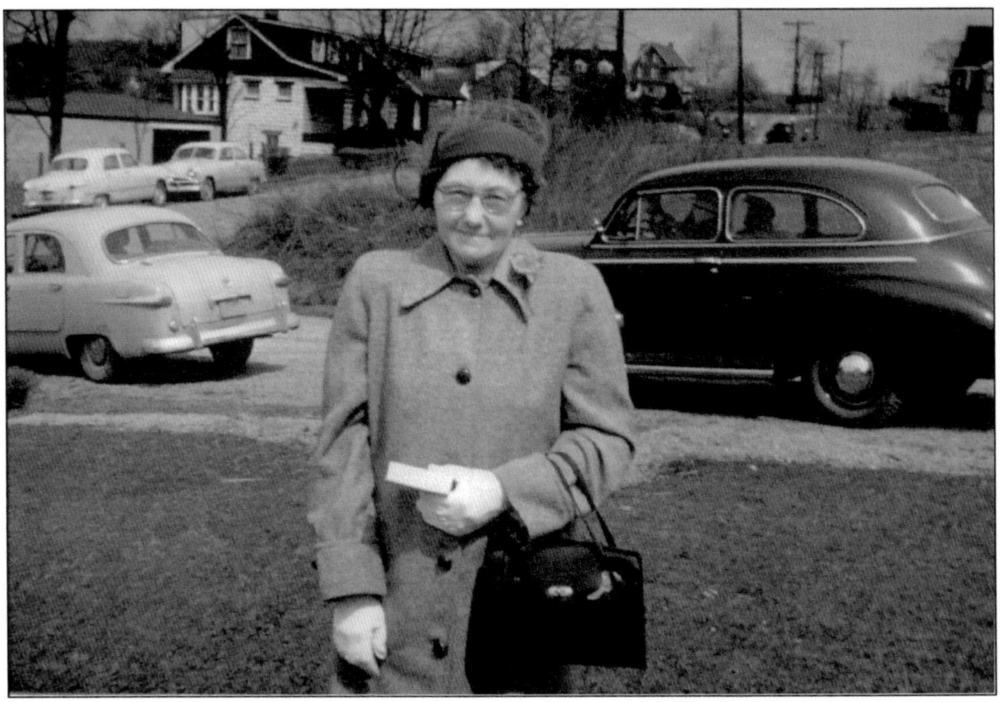

Five

Schools

The education system of today is much different than what children had access to over a century ago. The facilities in Plum were very basic. Families who could afford to do so would often send their children over the Appalachians in order to attend schools "back east." There were very few families who could afford this arrangement.

One of the first schoolhouses built in Plum was erected around 1806. It was a log structure located near Plum Creek Presbyterian Church. By 1889, Plum was home to nine one-room schools. They had an average enrollment of 25 to 30 students in grades one through eight (though sometimes not every grade had students in it). During this era, there would be a bench with a bucket on it in the back of the classroom. One of the boys in the school would fetch fresh water each morning from a nearby spring, creek, or well. It was also the boys' responsibility to carry coal in a bucket to fuel the fire for the school's pot-bellied stove. The coal stove certainly came in handy during the chilly Pennsylvania winters. Children often had to walk up to a mile on their way to school. If the weather was deemed too inclement for the children to walk, one of the fathers would take them via horse-drawn sleigh or sled.

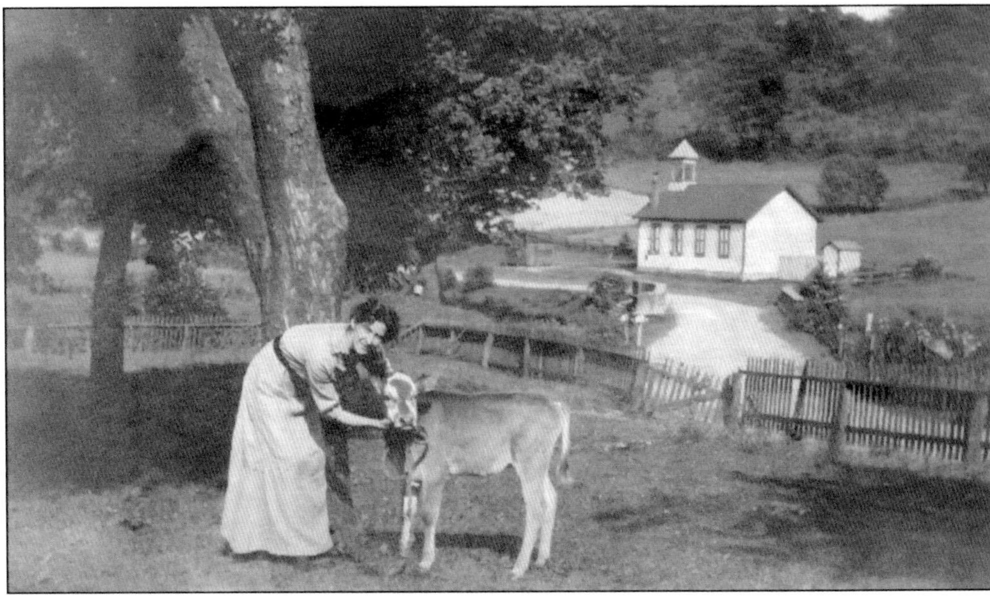

In this photograph, taken around the turn of the 20th century, an unidentified woman poses on a farm across Milltown Road from Franklin School. Franklin, along with Lincoln, Madison, New Texas, Jackson, Center, VanBuren, Freemont, Kossuth, and McMath, was one of the one-room schoolhouses in the area in 1889. Franklin was built in 1875.

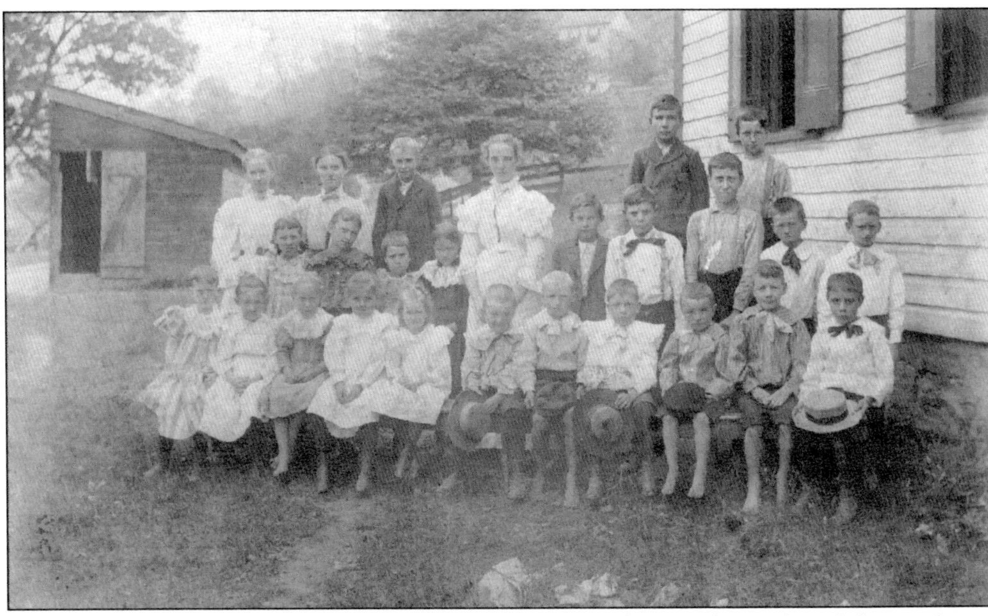

This picture of Franklin School students was taken around 1895. Shown from left to right are (first row) Kathryn Kerr, unidentified, Helen McKelvey, Ethel Ripp, unidentified, Harry Ripp, Johnny Triselitel, Parker Dible, Will Dible, and Johnny Kuhn; (second row) Katie Kuhn, Celie Lipold, Margaret Hartman, unidentified, Harry Ciceske, Charlie Kuhn, George Hess, Howard McKelvey, and John Kerr; (third row) Ella Hess, Rose Hess, unidentified, teacher Sophie Reiter, Judd Brady, and John Yourd.

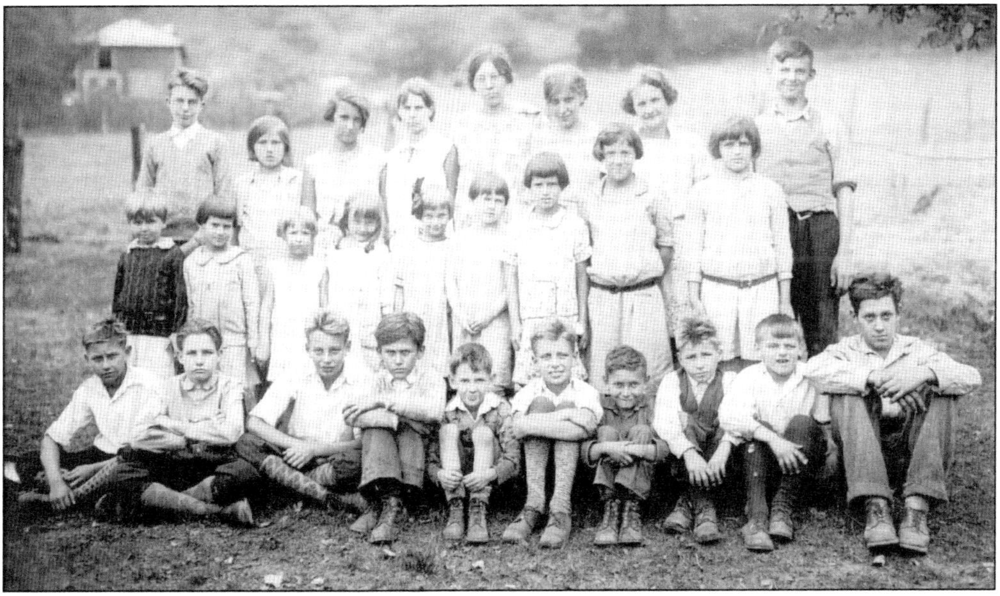

This photograph of Franklin School students was taken on Tuesday, October 7, 1930. When Franklin School was opened in the 1870s, one-room schoolhouses ruled the day. The schools were constructed of wood and averaged a population of 25 to 30 students in the first through eighth grades. Especially in the early days, not every grade had a student.

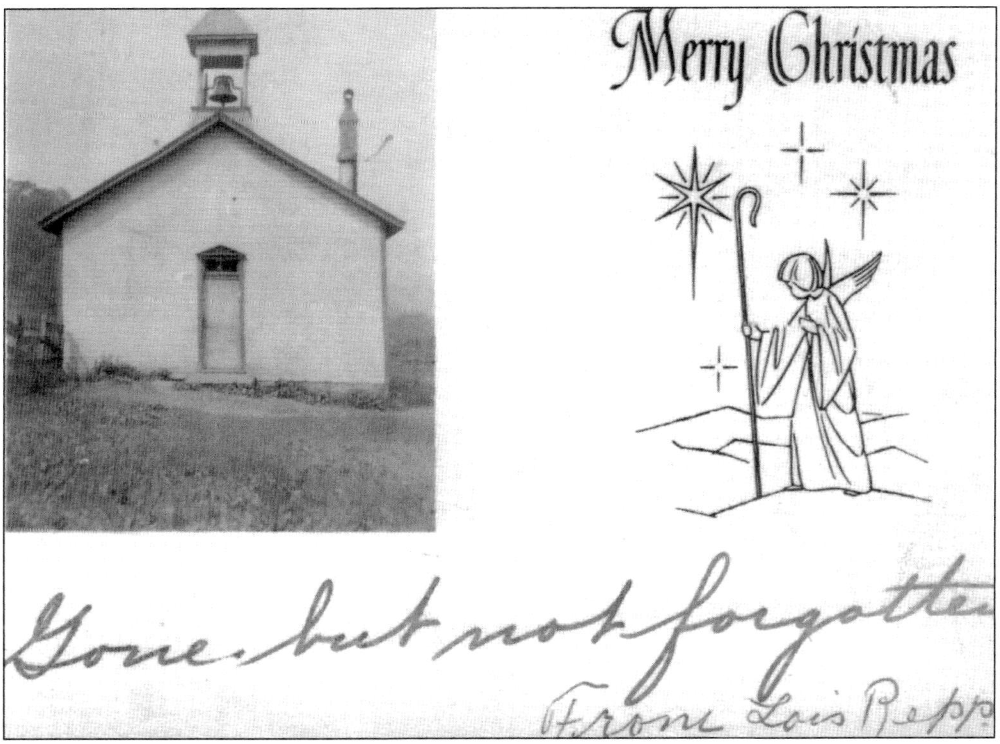

This Christmas card displays a picture of Franklin School as it was in 1938. The quote at the bottom of the card, written by Franklin School alum Lois Repp—"Gone but not forgotten"—shows the fondness former students hold for their school.

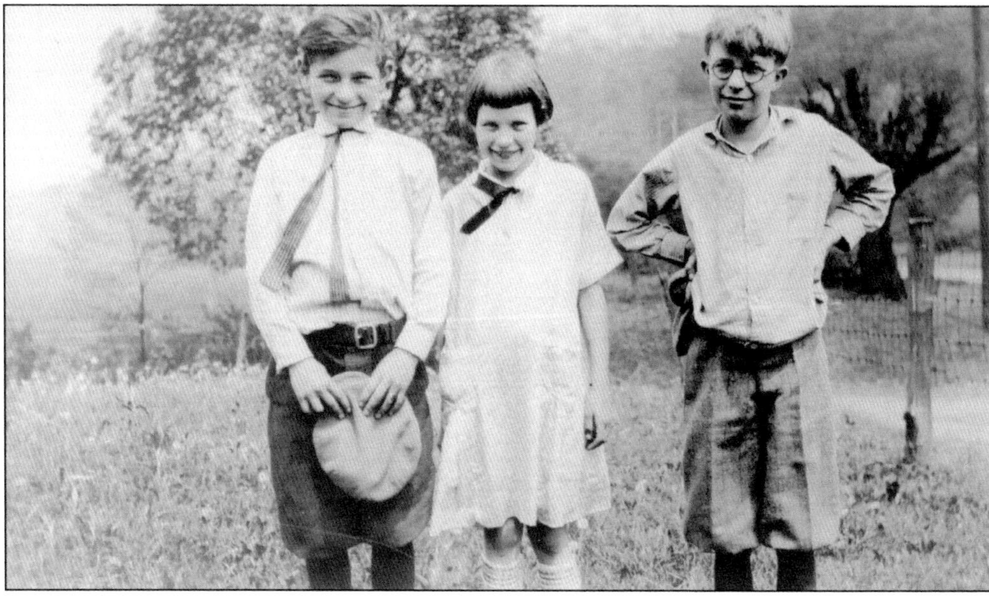

Some time in the 1920s, George Lichtenfels, William Ciceske, and Lois Ciceske posed for this picture. They were all students of Franklin School. Shown below is a report card for the last reporting period of the 1927–1928 school year at Franklin.

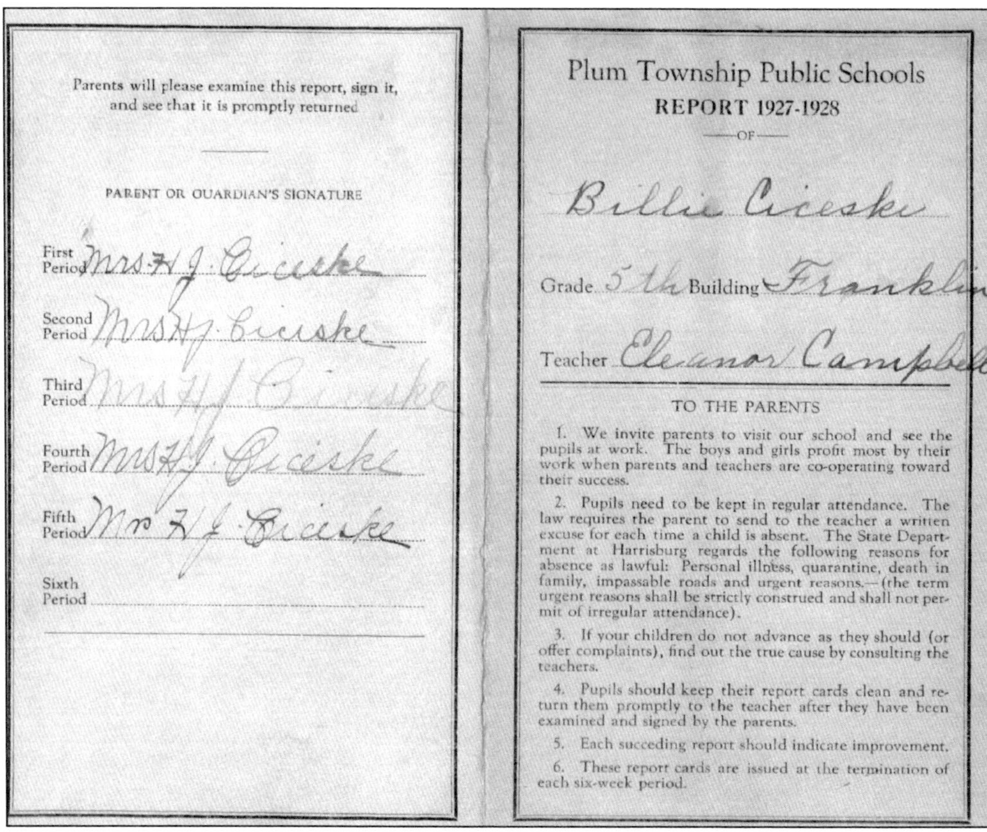

Parents will please examine this report, sign it, and see that it is promptly returned

PARENT OR GUARDIAN'S SIGNATURE

First Period Mrs H J Ciceske

Second Period Mrs H J Ciceske

Third Period Mrs H J Ciceske

Fourth Period Mrs H J Ciceske

Fifth Period Mrs H J Ciceske

Sixth Period

Plum Township Public Schools

REPORT 1927-1928

—OF—

Billie Ciceske

Grade 5th Building Franklin

Teacher Eleanor Campbell

TO THE PARENTS

1. We invite parents to visit our school and see the pupils at work. The boys and girls profit most by their work when parents and teachers are co-operating toward their success.

2. Pupils need to be kept in regular attendance. The law requires the parent to send to the teacher a written excuse for each time a child is absent. The State Department at Harrisburg regards the following reasons for absence as lawful: Personal illness, quarantine, death in family, impassable roads and urgent reasons.—(the term urgent reasons shall be strictly construed and shall not permit of irregular attendance).

3. If your children do not advance as they should (or offer complaints), find out the true cause by consulting the teachers.

4. Pupils should keep their report cards clean and return them promptly to the teacher after they have been examined and signed by the parents.

5. Each succeding report should indicate improvement.

6. These report cards are issued at the termination of each six-week period.

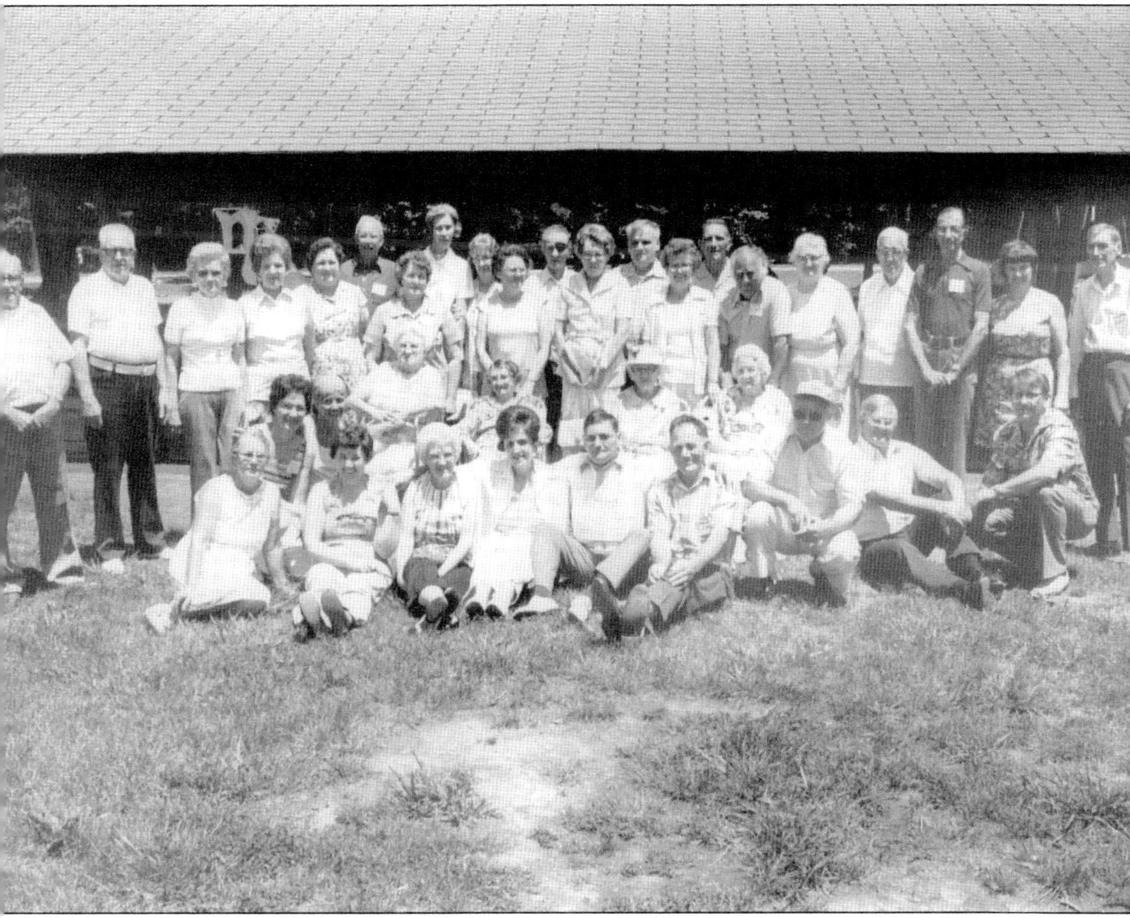

The members of the various "classes" of Franklin School kept in touch for many years after "graduation" and even had reunions from time to time. This picture is from the 1976 Franklin School Reunion, held in Penn Hills Park on June 26 of that year. Pictured in this photo are, from left to right, (first row) Thelma Ritter Legates, Margaret Lesko Boyce, Edna Wise Mock, Alice Parlak, John Lesko, and Charles Ritter; (second row) Edna Kirch Berger, Helen Lesko Rodgers, Clara (nee Kiser), Anna Mink, Katie (nee Kuhn), Mabel Repp Ferguson, Arthur Ritter, Harold Ritter, and Mike Lesko; (third row) Fred Hartman, Clyde Wise, Margaret Blasko Marudin, Dorothy Parlak Fiala, Ruth Kirch Gromley, Genevieve Merryman, Isabelle Kirchartz, "Teacher" Dorothy Cass, Ann Kozusko, Pete Ritter, Anna Duran, Curtis Wise, Bill Ciceske, Jean Farneth, and Clifford Repp; (fourth row) Henry Kelly, Lois Ciceske, Helen Kelly Booth, Leland Horner, Mike Parlak, and Gerald Kirch.

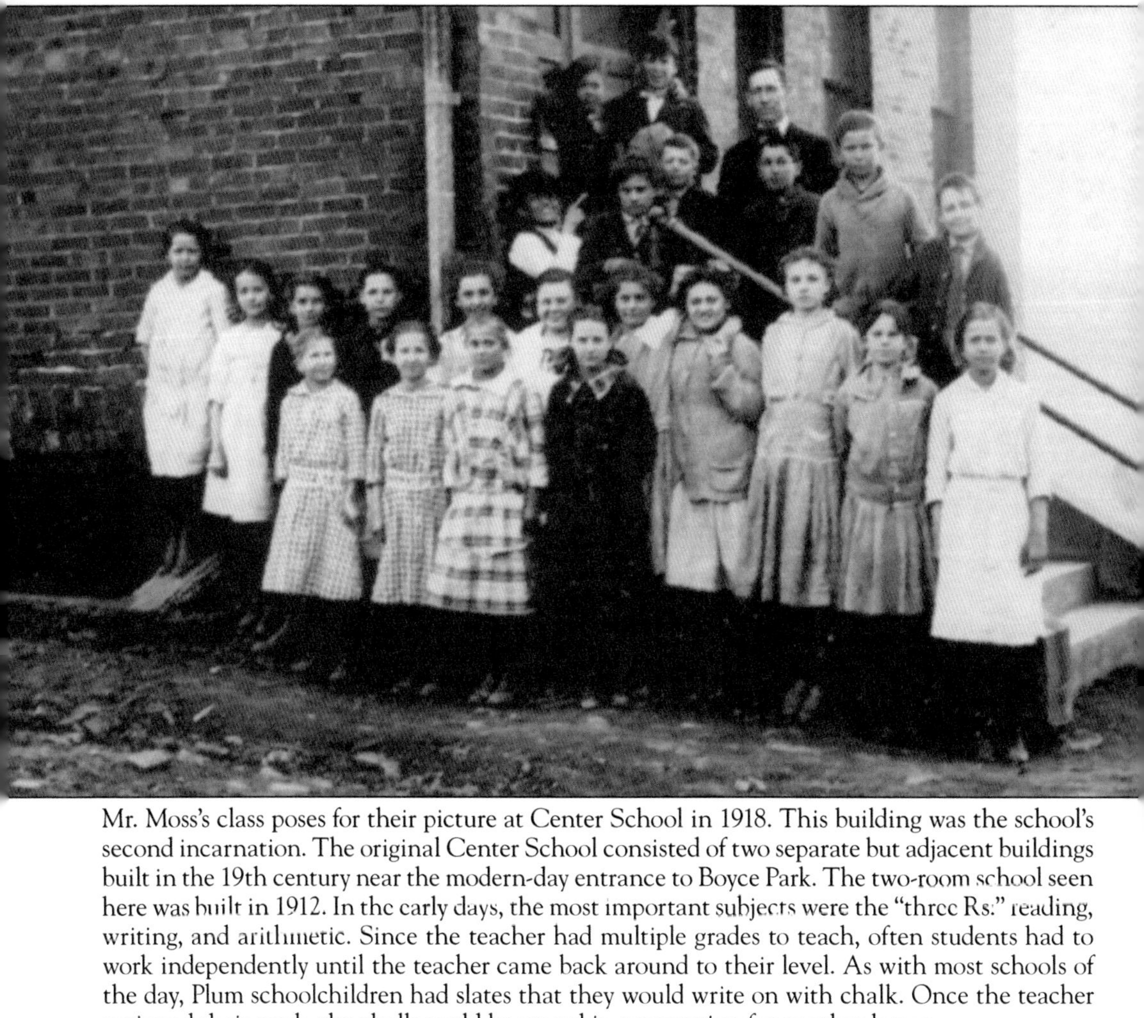

Mr. Moss's class poses for their picture at Center School in 1918. This building was the school's second incarnation. The original Center School consisted of two separate but adjacent buildings built in the 19th century near the modern-day entrance to Boyce Park. The two-room school seen here was built in 1912. In the early days, the most important subjects were the "three Rs:" reading, writing, and arithmetic. Since the teacher had multiple grades to teach, often students had to work independently until the teacher came back around to their level. As with most schools of the day, Plum schoolchildren had slates that they would write on with chalk. Once the teacher reviewed their work, the chalk could be erased in preparation for another lesson.

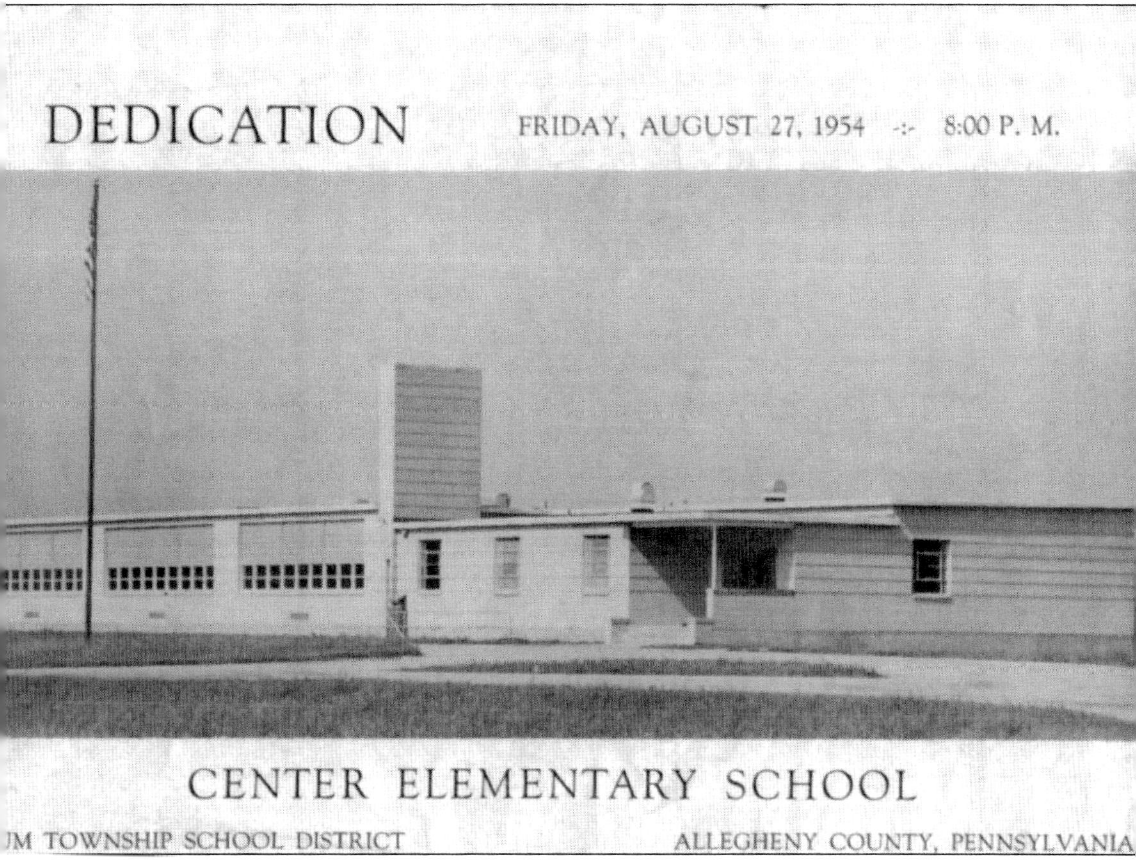

The new Center Elementary School's dedication took place on Friday, August 27, 1954. The total cost for construction of the building was $260,000. Built on 16 acres, the original building had seven classrooms and a heating and cooling system that could handle an additional six classrooms "when the need [arose]"—according to the dedication ceremony program. Nine classrooms were later added. The rear of the building houses a playground. Center School was not the only school that had multiple incarnations. Stewart School was built in 1938 at the intersection of Webster and Greensburg Roads. Originally, the school had three classrooms with two grades in each. A fourth room was used for music classes. Stewart School was not used during the 1966–1967 and 1967–1968 school years. When the school was used again in 1968, two classrooms, a library, and a cafeteria had been added.

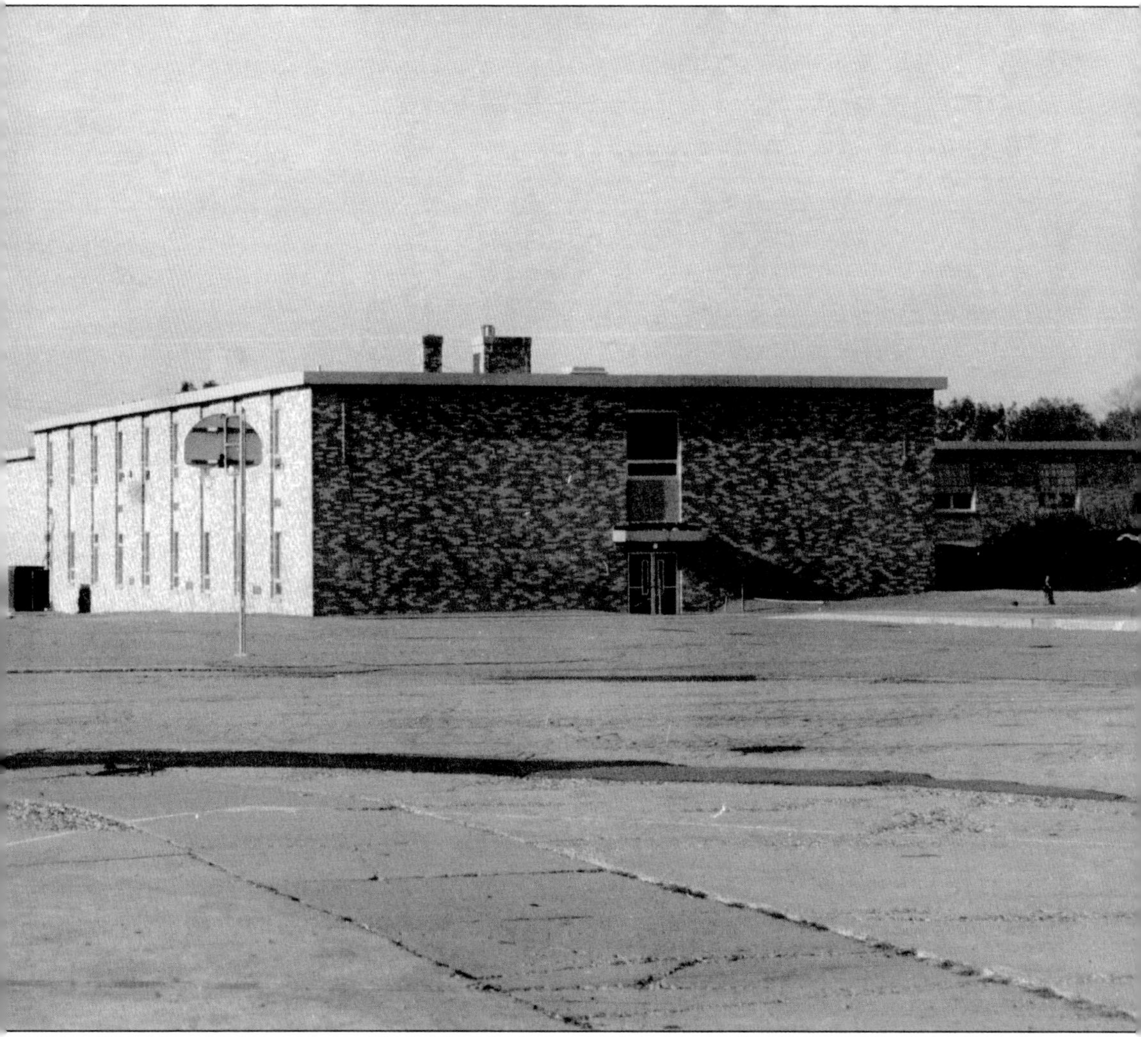

Adlai Stevenson Elementary School is located in the Holiday Park area of Plum Borough. Its campus is joined with that of A.E. Oblock Junior High School. The land where Adlai Stevenson and Oblock Schools sit was once a Nike missile site. This site was operated by soldiers of the Army 1st Missile Battalion. The command center and base houses were located at the intersection of New Texas Road and Lindsay Lane, and the launch site was located across the valley on the hill at the top of Presque Isle Drive in Holiday Park. The site was armed with 30 Ajax MIM-3 missiles and 12 missile launchers. These missiles had a range of 26 miles. Each summer, the public was invited to an open house, and the missiles were brought to the surface for display. The silos still exist under the school and are used as storage space.

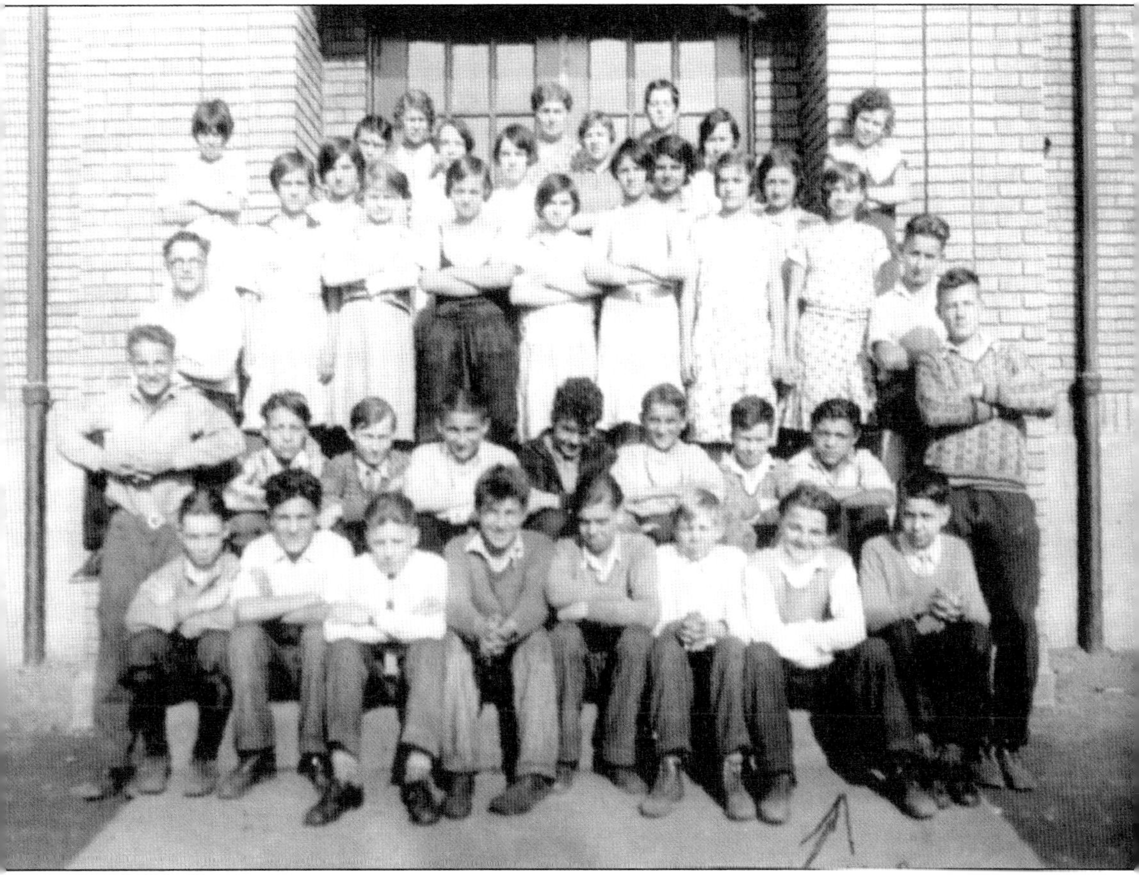

Harding School was built in the early 1920s. Around this time, many of the smaller, one-room schools were closed in favor of consolidated, multi-grade buildings. The closed schools included Freemont, Unity, New Texas, Center, McKinley, and Lincoln. Pictured is the 1931 eighth-grade class of Harding School. Other consolidated schools included Renton (built in 1918), Logans Ferry (built in 1922), and Stewart (built in 1938).

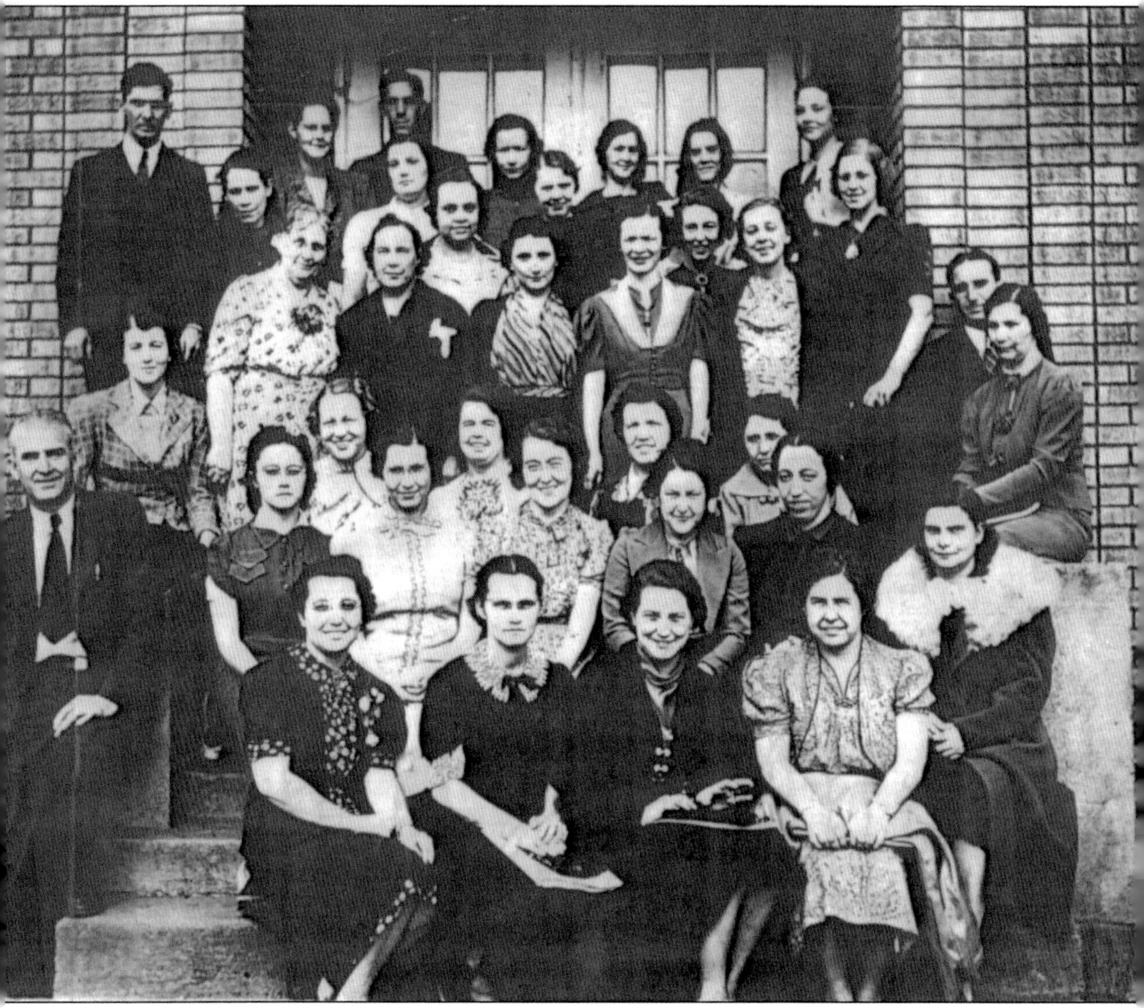

This Plum Township School District teachers' meeting was held at Harding School on September 30, 1938. Among those pictured are Guy R. Smith, Rose Alberta, Cora Brookes, Stella Steiner, Elizabeth Gould, Ethel Retler, Lindy McJunkin, Edit Elliott, Ann Brunner, Miss Newell, Belle Starr, Dorothy Clements, Edna ?, Betty McJunkin, Grace Gould, Miss Doak, Helen Murphy, Mrs. Hamilton, Ms. Skullen, Emma Alberts, unidentified, Helen Matthews, Bill Hornbeck, John ?, Marion Frack, Florence Nesbit, Elaine Roos, Majorie McMahon, Pearl Manning, Miss Thalker, Lucy McLaughlin, Bob Frack, Virginia Davidson, Miss Perrine, Miss Williams, and Ann Metro. This meeting occurred two years before the opening of Plum School District's high school.

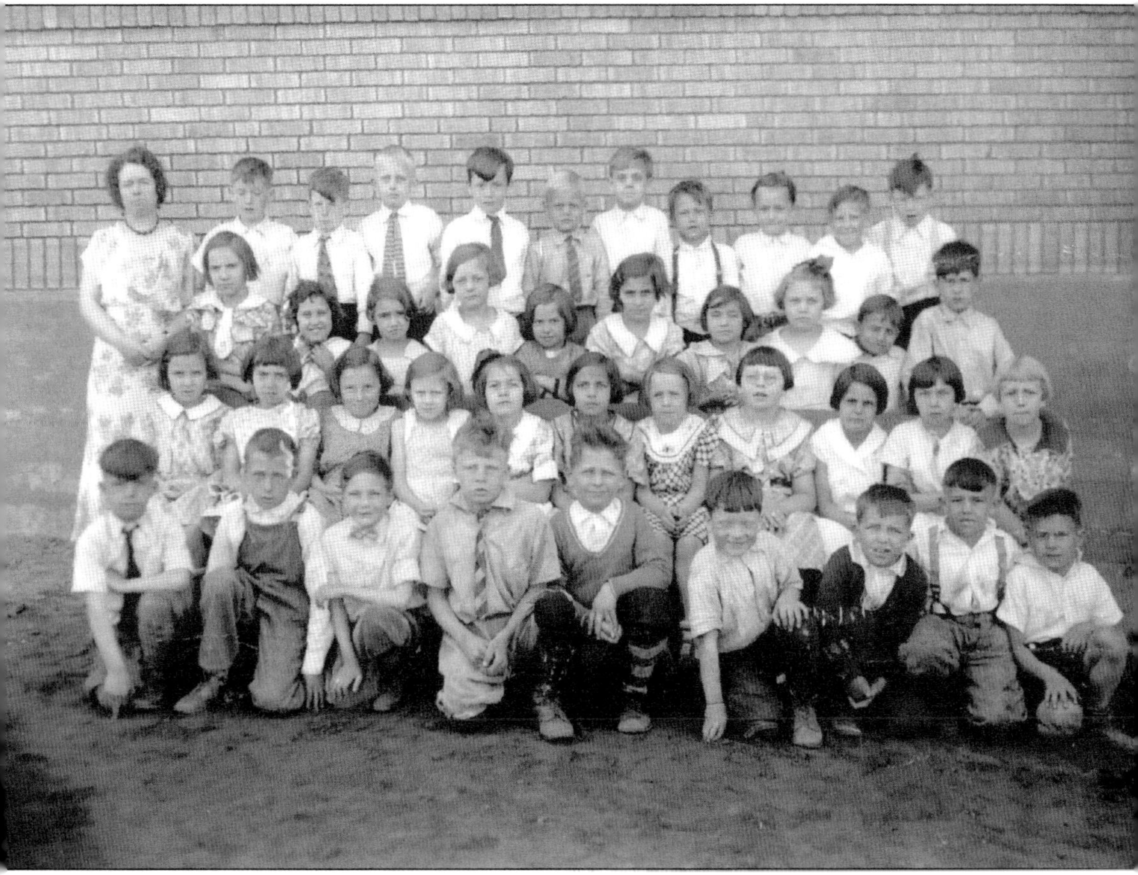

This picture shows a Harding School class posing with their teacher. When Harding School opened, many of the one-room schools were being phased out. Initially, Harding School had grades one through eight, but it was later reduced to grades one through five. It was also around this time that transportation for students became a major issue. Transportation to and from school obviously had evolved over the years. It was during the 1930s that the school district–sponsored transportation of students was introduced. Plum Township School District submitted bids to various bus operators, and McCoy Brothers in Center won. They continued to provide bus service to local students for many years until the business closed.

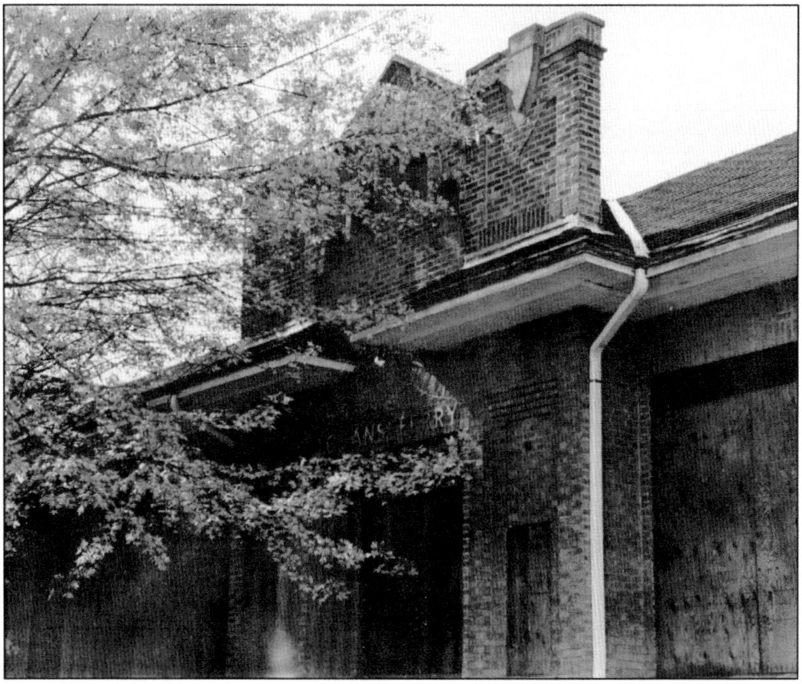

Logans Ferry School had seen better days when these pictures was taken. Built around 1920, the school initially had eight classrooms; a cafeteria and two more classrooms were added later. Not far from Logans Ferry—along Route 366 on the county border—was Stewart School. It was a joint school: students from both Allegheny and Westmoreland Counties attended. The original redbrick school was converted into a residence upon the completion of the yellow-brick school building in 1938. Another school located near Logans Ferry was the Van Buren School. It was at the bottom of Logans Ferry Hill, near New Kensington.

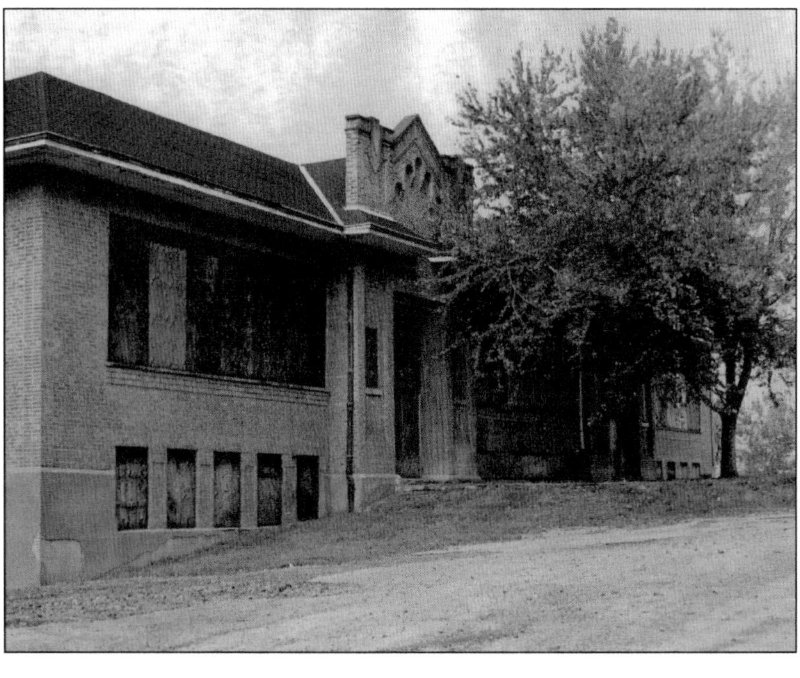

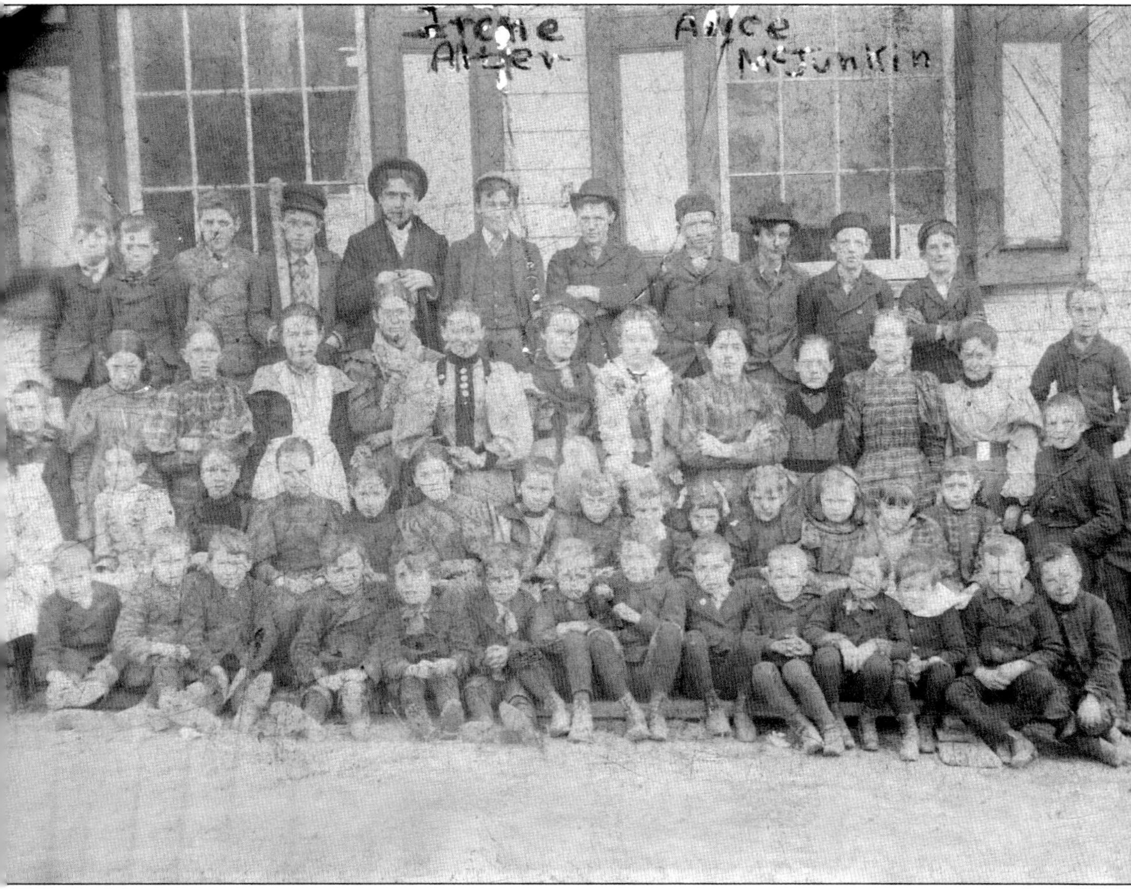

This late-19th-century photograph shows the 52 students who were taught at the New Texas School by teacher Mary Clements. The school's regular teacher, Gray Monroe, was fighting in the Spanish-American War during this time. Mary Clements is sixth from the left in the third row. Children from several of Plum's oldest families attended New Texas at this time, including the Armstrongs, Davidsons, and McJunkins. Through the early 1900s, Plum had been serviced by over 15 schools, though all were not in existence at the same time. These schools included two different Center Schools (the third not being built until 1954), Franklin School, Freemont School, Jackson School, Kossuth School, Lincoln School, McKinley School, McMath School, New Texas School, Stewart School, Unity School, Van Buren School, Webster School, and White Oak Levels School.

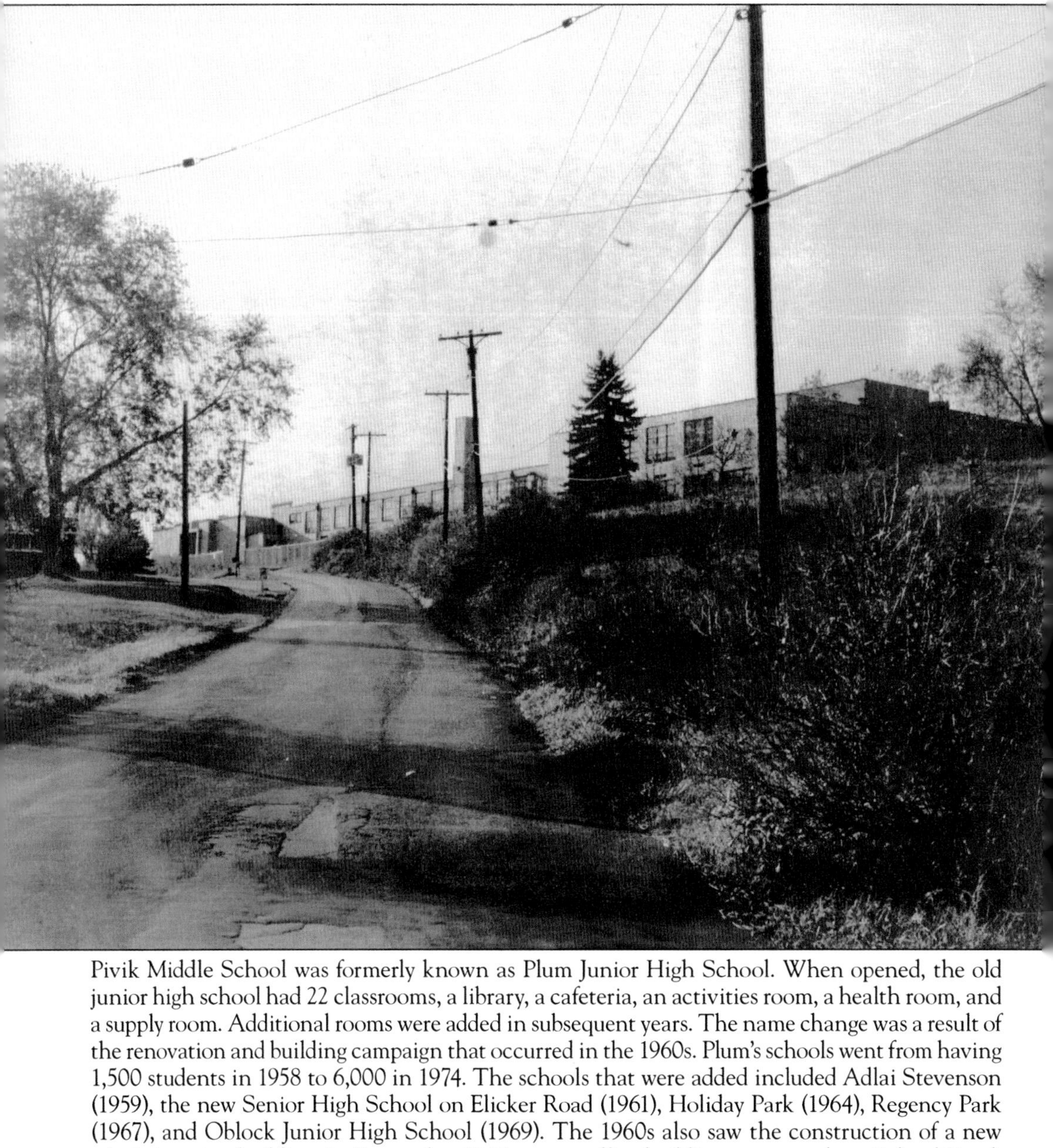

Pivik Middle School was formerly known as Plum Junior High School. When opened, the old junior high school had 22 classrooms, a library, a cafeteria, an activities room, a health room, and a supply room. Additional rooms were added in subsequent years. The name change was a result of the renovation and building campaign that occurred in the 1960s. Plum's schools went from having 1,500 students in 1958 to 6,000 in 1974. The schools that were added included Adlai Stevenson (1959), the new Senior High School on Elicker Road (1961), Holiday Park (1964), Regency Park (1967), and Oblock Junior High School (1969). The 1960s also saw the construction of a new administration building. In September 1968, a new office building went up along School Road. Most of the school district offices moved into this building.

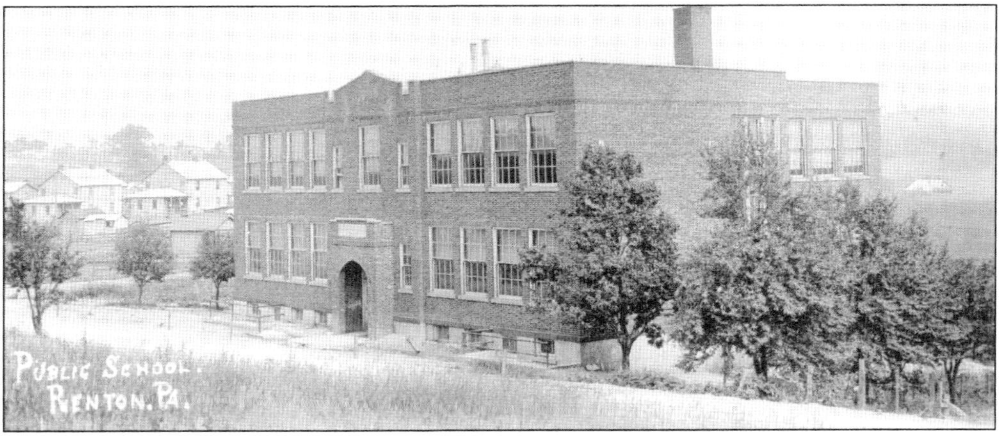

Built in 1918, Renton School was one of the first "modern" schools in Plum. It was built not long after the establishment of Renton Mine and the surrounding company town. During the Great Depression, Renton School hosted a soup kitchen. (Courtesy of Gary Rogers.)

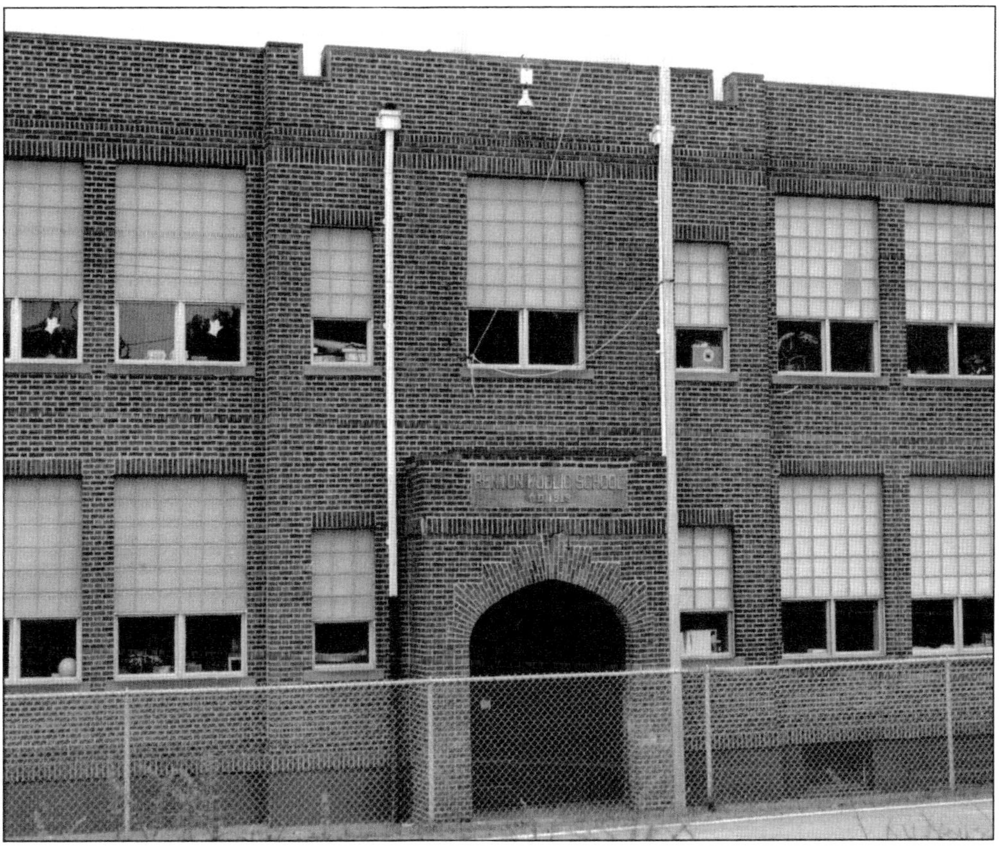

Renton School, the first of the consolidated one-room schoolhouses built in Plum, went on to serve the surrounding community through the 1980s, after which it was closed and eventually demolished. Currently, a nursing home sits on the old Renton School property.

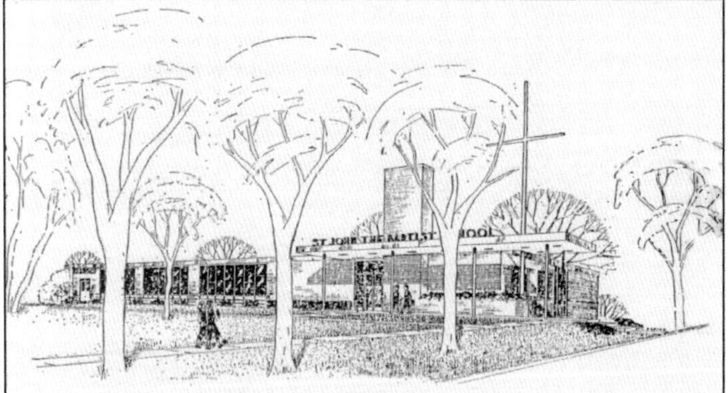

St. John the Baptist School

PLUM BOROUGH

UNITY, PENNSYLVANIA

DEDICATED ON
SEPTEMBER 2, 1959
ADDITION TO SCHOOL
DEDICATED JANUARY, 1964

St. John the Baptist School was dedicated on September 2, 1959, by then-Bishop Wright. An addition was built and dedicated around 1964. The ground breaking ceremony, shown below, was held on June 22, 1958. Around this time, the topic of school district mergers was being discussed in the state legislature. The mandate finally came in 1963, and it was proposed that the school districts of Plum and Oakmont merge. Plum was opposed to this plan. Plum School District presented its position to the Allegheny County School Board and the Commonwealth of Pennsylvania and was allowed to remain a separate entity. (Both courtesy of St. John the Baptist Parish.)

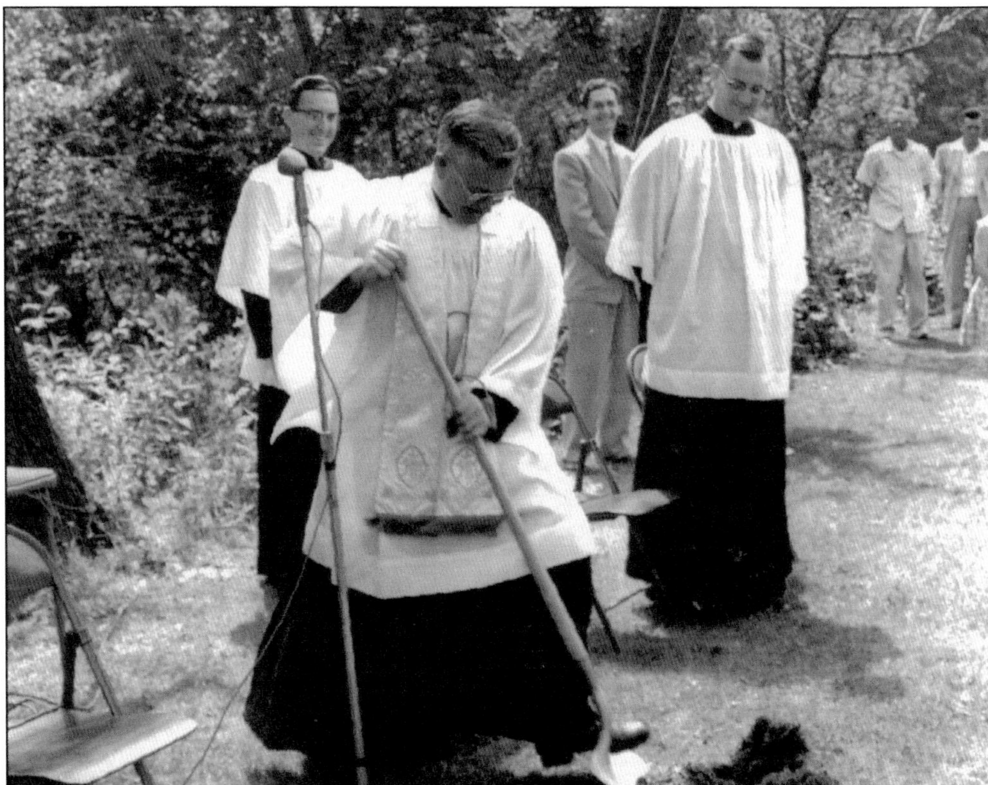

This old postcard shows Unity School, built around the turn of the 20th century. As a two-story building, it was an unusual construction because one-story schools were still popular. Each floor had one classroom. When Harding School opened in 1924, Unity was slowly phased out. The building was torn down in 1952, and the People's Bank of Unity was built in its place. (Courtesy of Gary Rogers.)

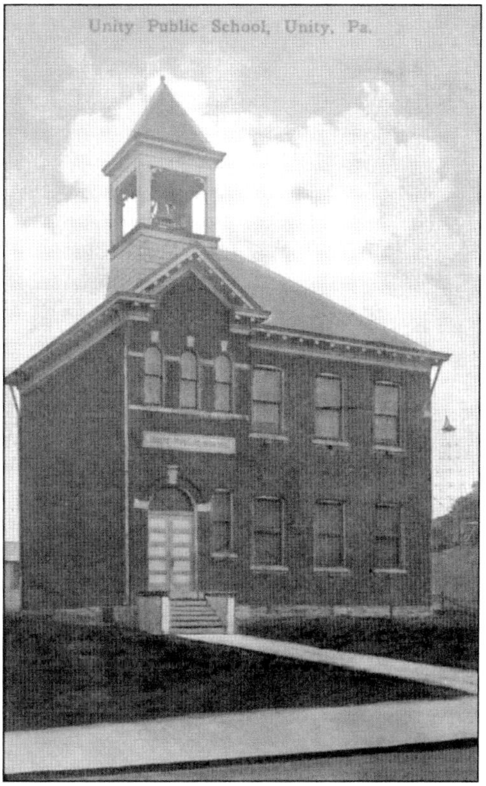

Prior to Plum High School's opening at the start of the 1939–1940 school year, students were given the option of attending high schools in other districts—including New Kensington, Verona, Oakmont, Penn Hills, Turtle Creek's Union High, and Wilkinsburg. Guy R. Smith, supervising principal until his retirement in 1950, was instrumental in opening Plum Township High School, which was formally dedicated in October 1940.

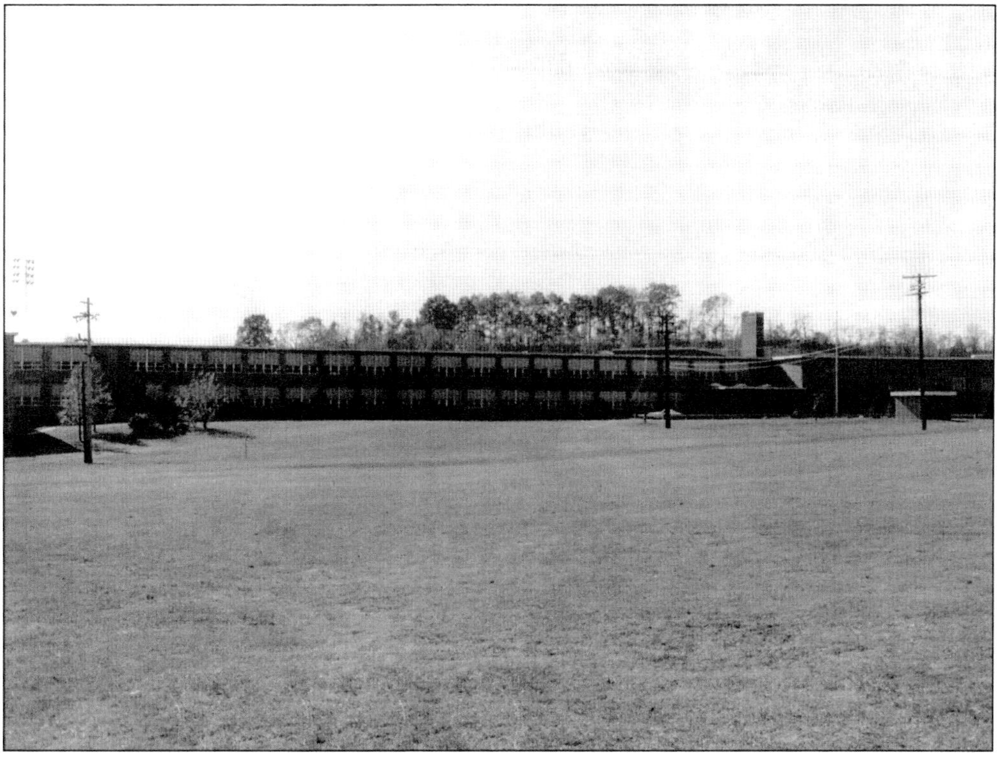

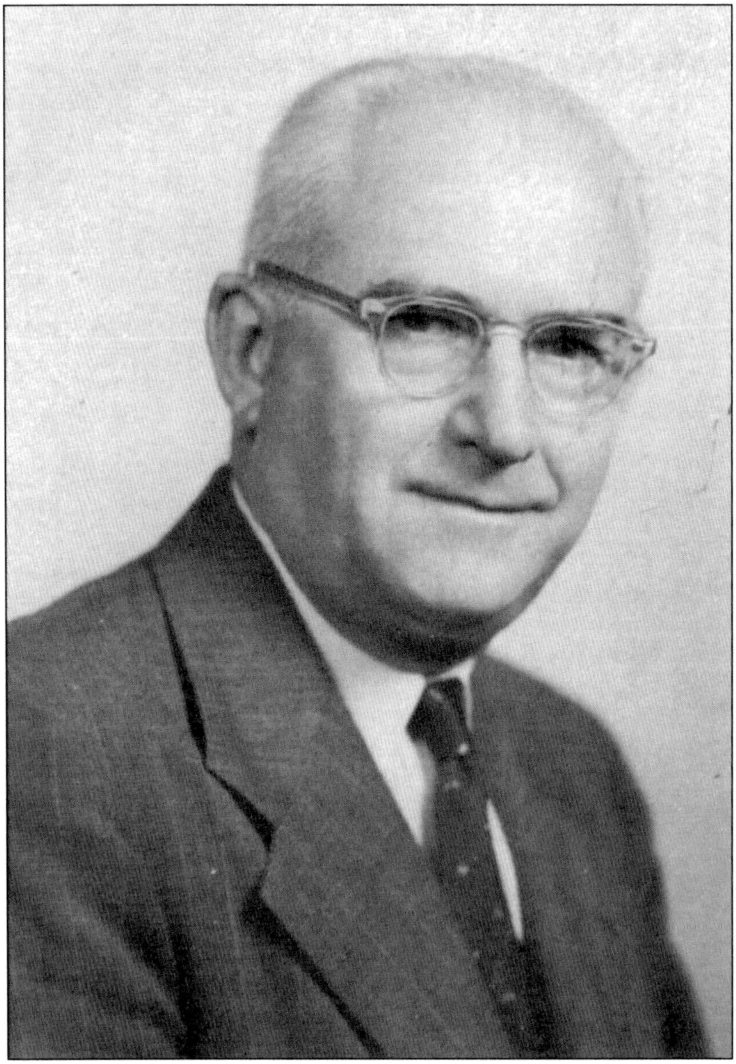

Guy R. Smith served as supervising principal from 1919 to 1950. When he first began his teaching career in Plum in 1906, teachers were paid $35 a month. At the beginning of his tenure as supervising principal, there were 21 teachers and a district dotted with one-room schoolhouses.

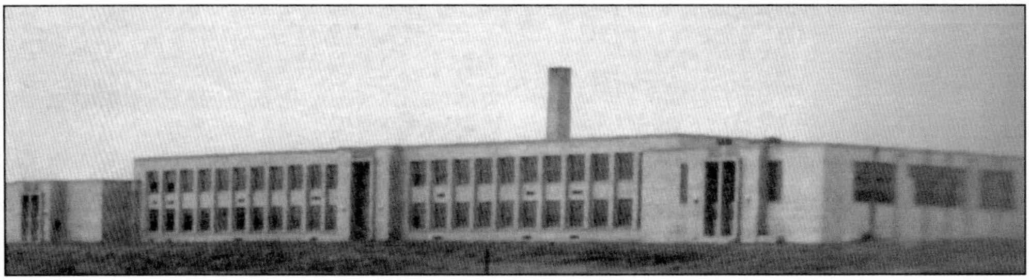

This shows Plum Township High School as it appeared in 1941. Plum outgrew its beloved high school within two decades. When the new Plum Borough Senior High School was dedicated on April 18, 1961, the old high school became Plum Borough Junior High School. The new high school sits on a 42-acre site.

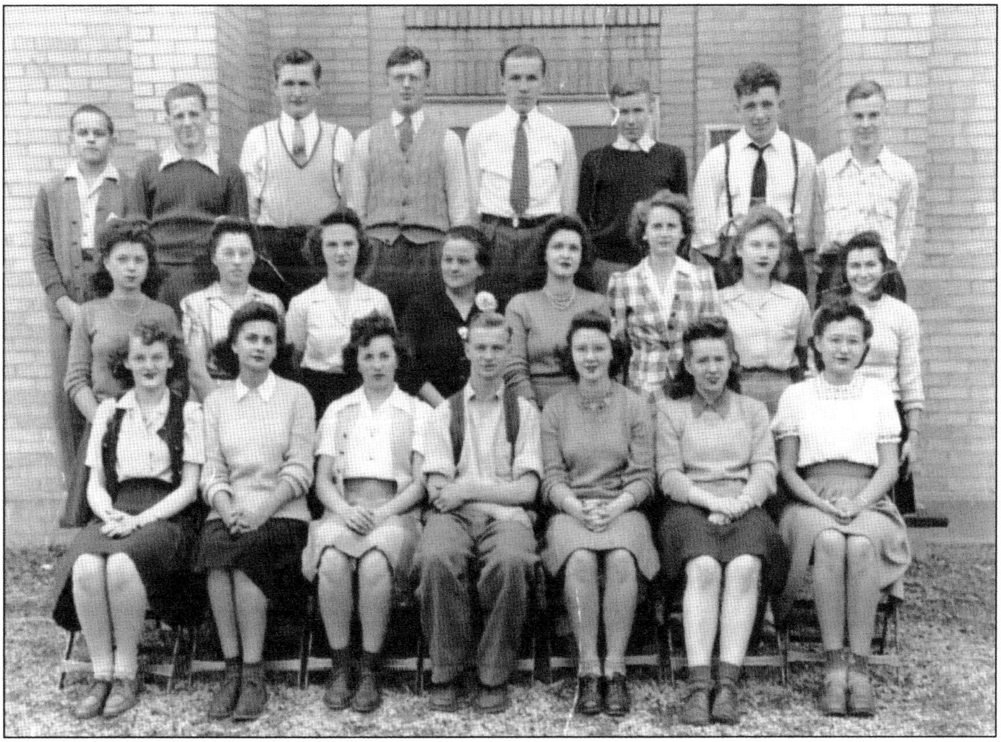

Pictured here is the 1943–1944 Plum High School Wildlife Club. Having a high school within the community opened a wealth of extracurricular activities to the students of Plum. Prior to the existence of Plum Township High School, high school-aged students had the opportunity to attend secondary schools in neighboring towns, such as Penn Hills or Murrysville. In addition to the Wildlife Club, students who attended Plum High School during the mid-1940s could join a variety of other clubs, including the Airplane Club, Stage Crew, Future Farmers of America, and the Literary Circle.

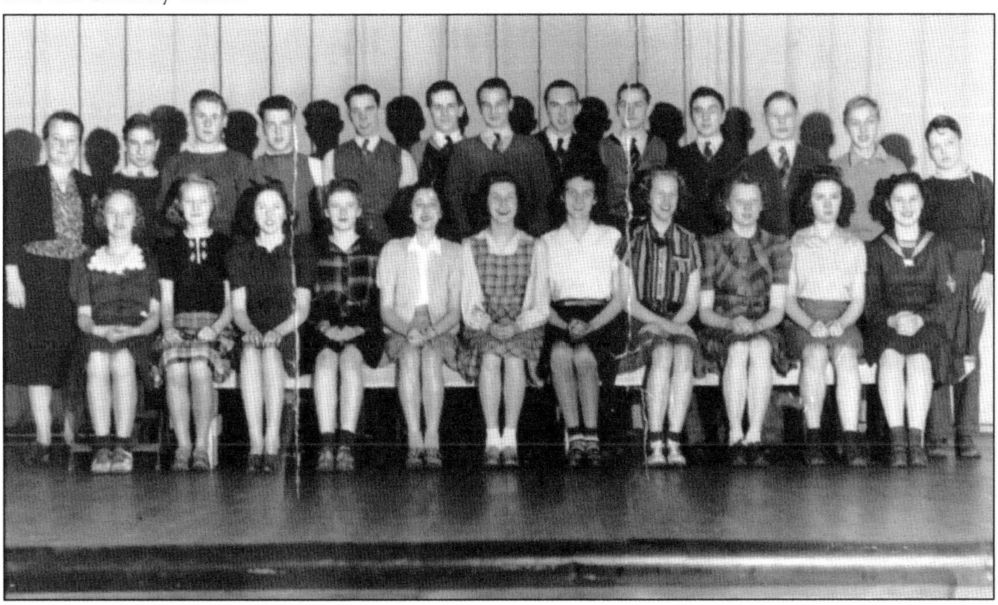

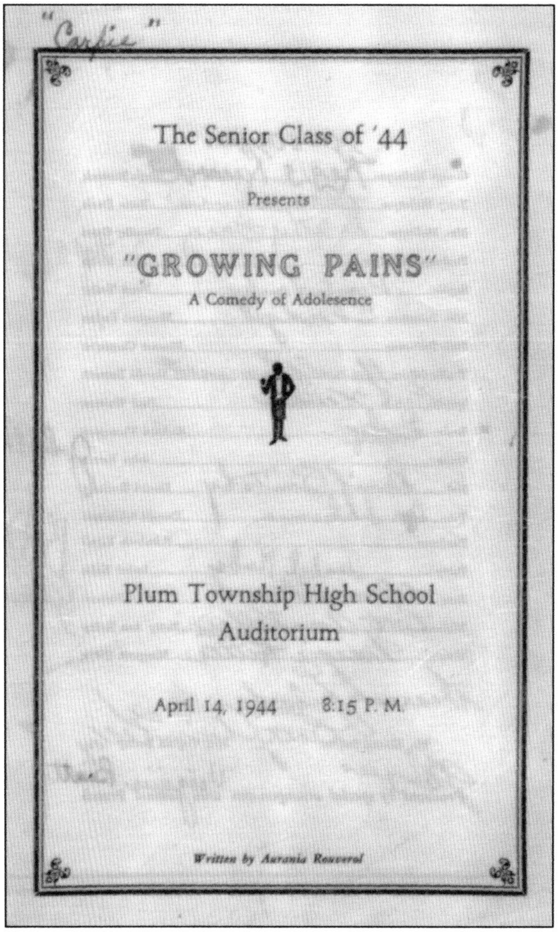
The Senior Class of '44

Presents

"GROWING PAINS"

A Comedy of Adolescence

Plum Township High School
Auditorium

April 14, 1944 8:15 P. M.

Written by Aurania Rouverol

Growing Pains: A Comedy of Adolescence was Plum Township High School's play in 1944, and the title seems appropriate for a turbulent period such as the 1940s. By 1943, the number of Plum alumni joining the ranks of the US military was 97. Commencement speeches reflected the primary preoccupation of the time, including the salutation by Albert Bentz titled "Plum Township High School and the War."

Members and sponsors of the student council of Plum Senior High School's class of 1941 included, from left to right, (sitting) I. Muffley, J. Eiler, J. Jameroone, B. Davidson, B. Davis, and R. Subic; (standing) D. Ayrst, B. Williams, P. Wekluk, Mr. Pero, P. Truby, Miss McJunkin, J. Elliot, G. Waugaman, and P. Waikus. The president was Betty Davidson, and the three vice presidents were Betty Davis, Rose Subic, and John Jameroone. Pero and McJunkin were the faculty sponsors.

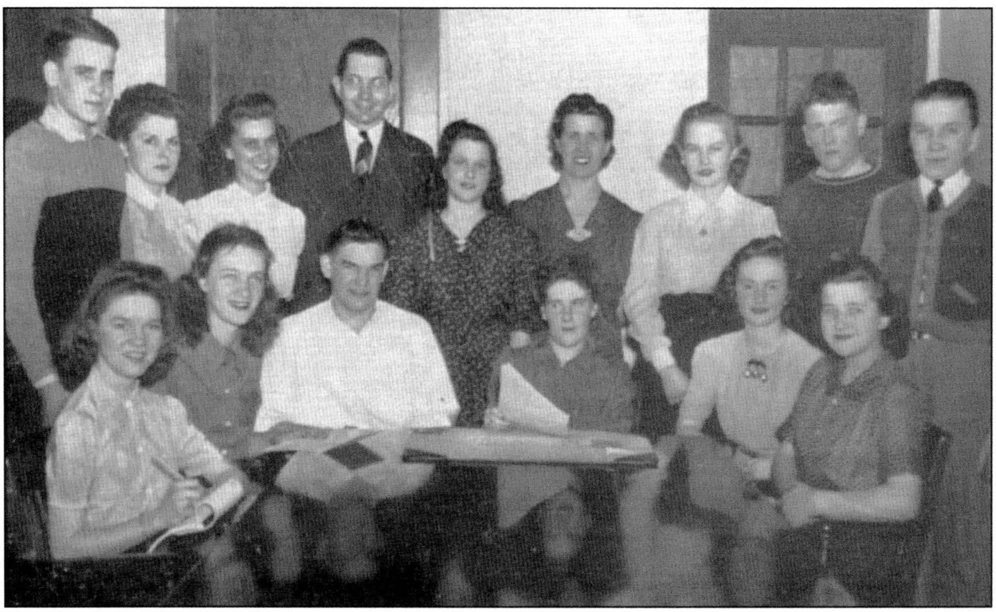

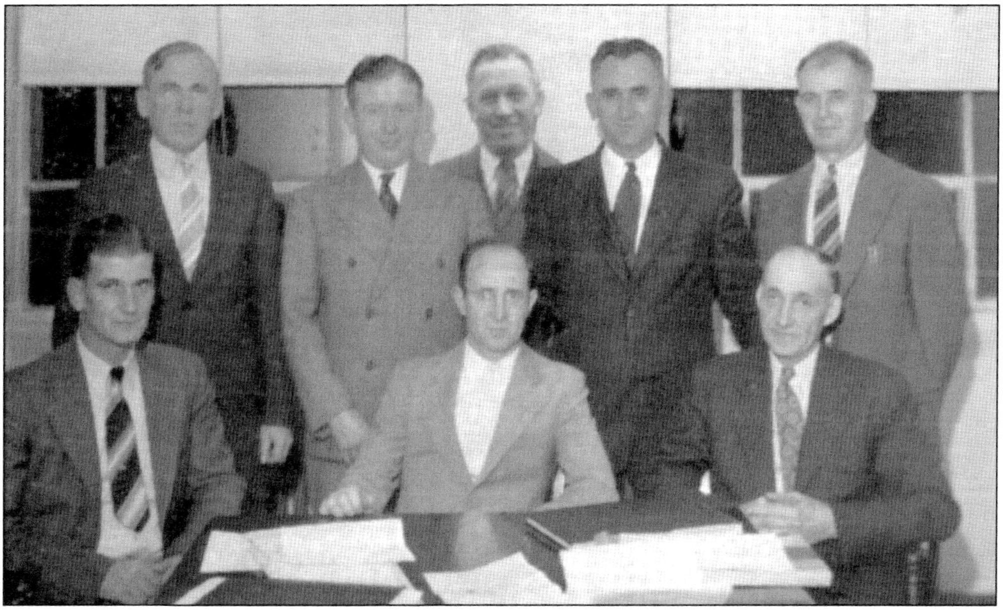

In addition to a supervising principal, Plum Township School District was administered by a board of education. Pictured here is the board in 1941. The members are, from left to right, (seated) Herbert P. Kerr, G.N. Truby, and Oliver M. Thompson; (standing) President C.N. Hays, John Kalik, Harry Muholland, Joseph Thomas, and secretary C.W. Christy.

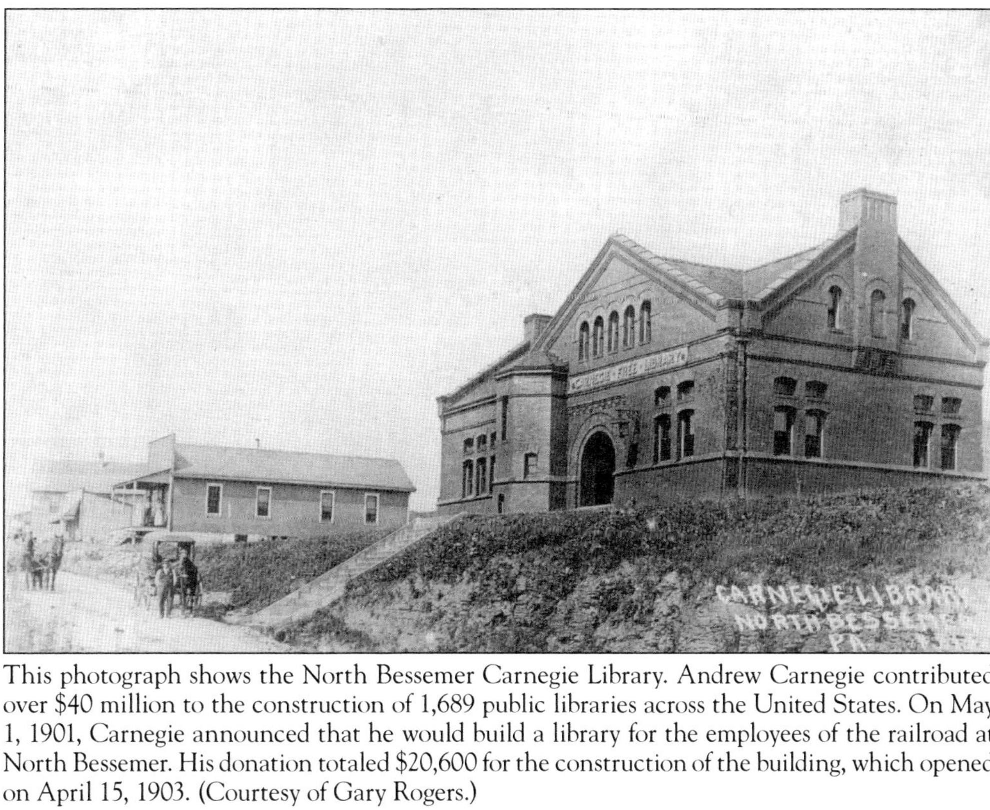

This photograph shows the North Bessemer Carnegie Library. Andrew Carnegie contributed over $40 million to the construction of 1,689 public libraries across the United States. On May 1, 1901, Carnegie announced that he would build a library for the employees of the railroad at North Bessemer. His donation totaled $20,600 for the construction of the building, which opened on April 15, 1903. (Courtesy of Gary Rogers.)

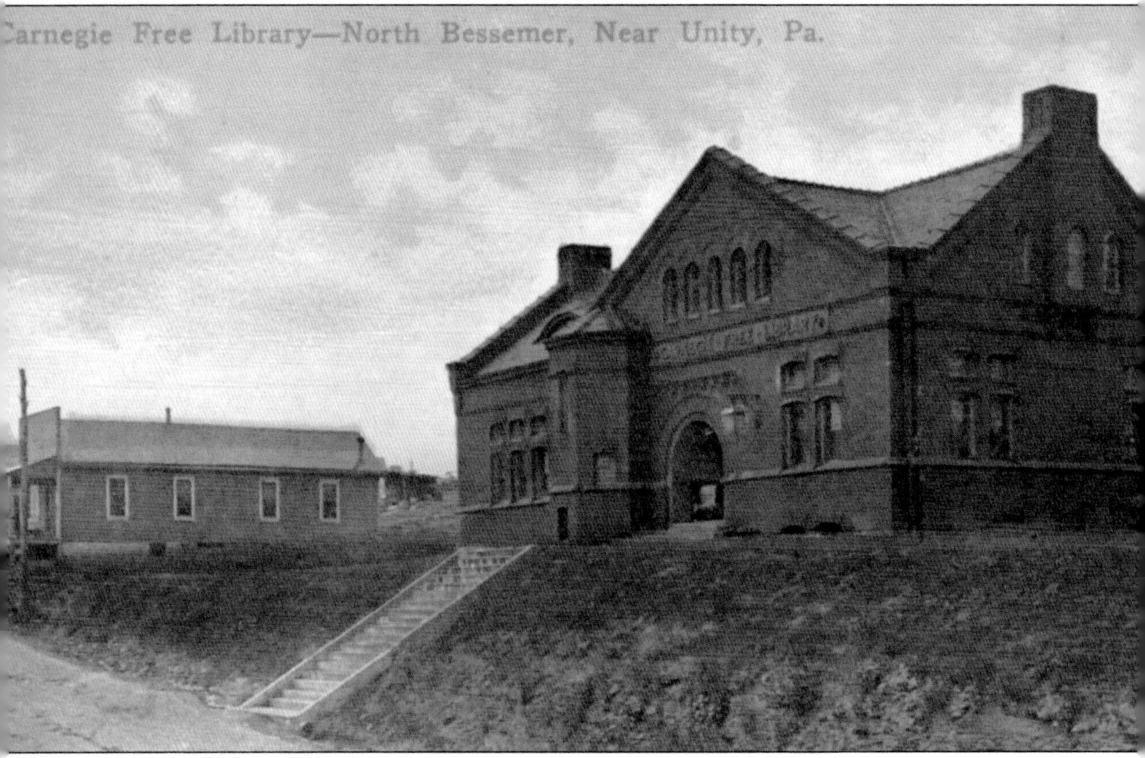

Unfortunately, the Carnegie Library of North Bessemer no longer exists. In 1958, the building was in major need of renovation, as was the neighboring North Bessemer Hotel. The Bessemer and Lake Erie Railroad made the decision to raze the library and hotel. The railroad chose to build a new dormitory for railroad employees on the site of the library. (Courtesy of Gary Rogers.)

Six

Government

Three months after the founding of Allegheny County on September 24, 1788, Plum Township was established. Along with Versailles, St. Clair, Pitt, Marshall, Elizabeth, and Moon, Plum constituted one of the original seven townships of Allegheny County. After some secessions of land by Patton (Monroeville), Verona, and Oakmont, Plum decreased to its present size of 28.88 square miles. It still remains the largest borough in Allegheny County and the second largest in the state of Pennsylvania.

Some of the earliest surviving records (around 1906) of the Plum Township Board of Supervisors show that meetings were conducted in supervisors' homes and later in the New Texas School. Prior to Plum becoming a borough in 1956, two Plum neighborhoods sought to secede from the township. White Oak Level (of which Oakmont Country Club is part) succeeded in joining the borough of Oakmont; however, the country club opted out of the secession plans and most of its land remains within Plum. The community of East Oakmont also wished to become a part of Oakmont, but Plum leaders quickly applied for borough status for the town and prevented the secession. (Under state law, neighborhoods are allowed to secede from a township to a borough but may not secede from one borough to another).

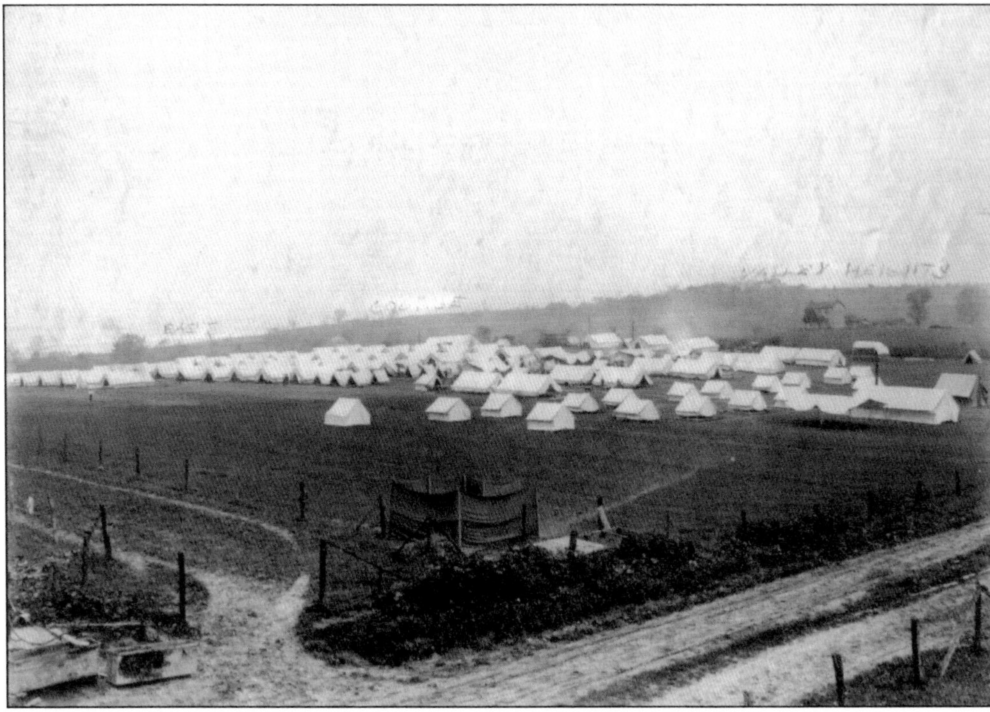

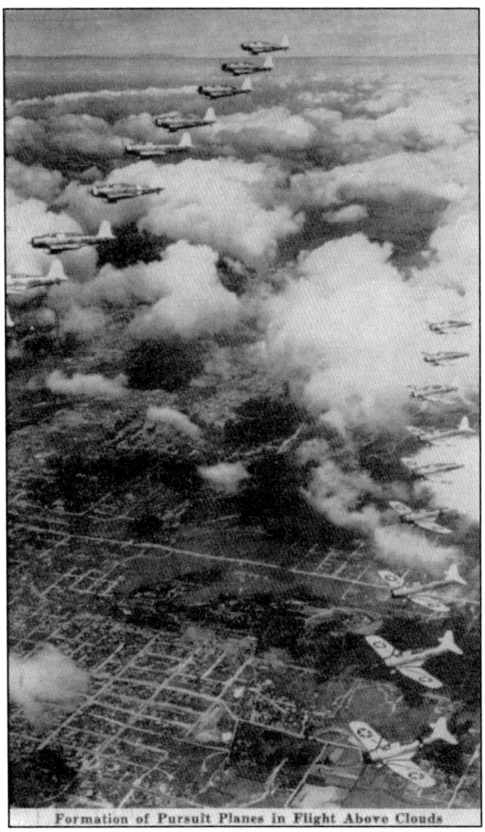

During World War I, the Powell Farm in East Oakmont was home to Camp Gaillard. Camp Gaillard was home to the training camp of the 15th Engineers. The 15th departed their training camp on July 5, 1917. They headed first for England and then France, where they landed on July 20, 1917.

Plum was no stranger to having its sons and daughters serve their country. This postcard was sent to Eleanor Carpenter by then-Pfc. Robert McJunkin.

During World War II, many natives of Plum answered the call to serve. Here, Walter Wallace McJunkin poses for his US Navy photograph. Walter, a member of the third-generation of American-born McJunkins, was one of the seven children born to James and Mable Board McJunkin. The autograph in the lower-right corner reads, "My Love, Wallace."

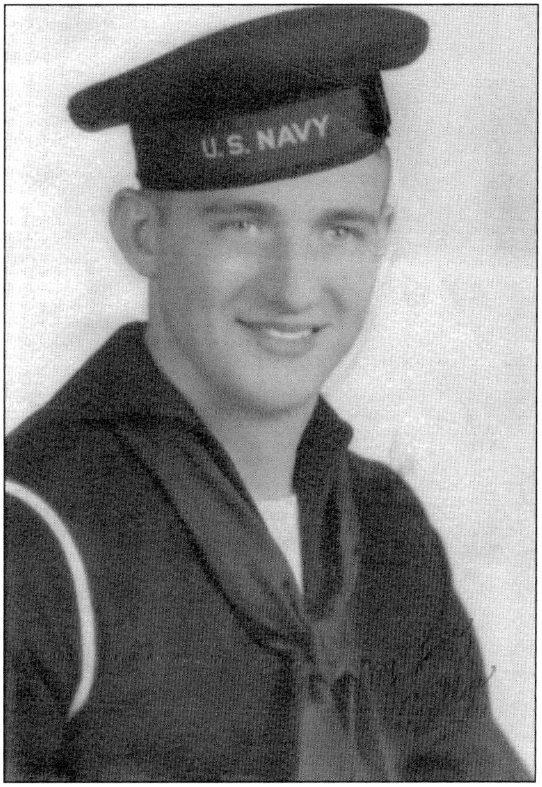

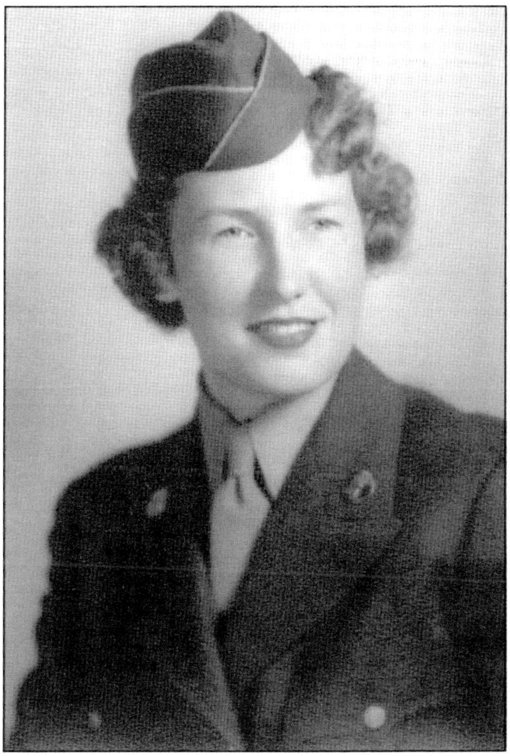

Plum native Isabella Stewart poses proudly for her military photograph. Another local soldier, Oakmont native Pvt. Robert Campbell, was stationed at Pearl Harbor on the fateful day of December 7, 1941. In early January of 1942, Oakmont hosted a week of prayer, holding church services each night for a week in remembrance of those lost on that "day which will live in infamy."

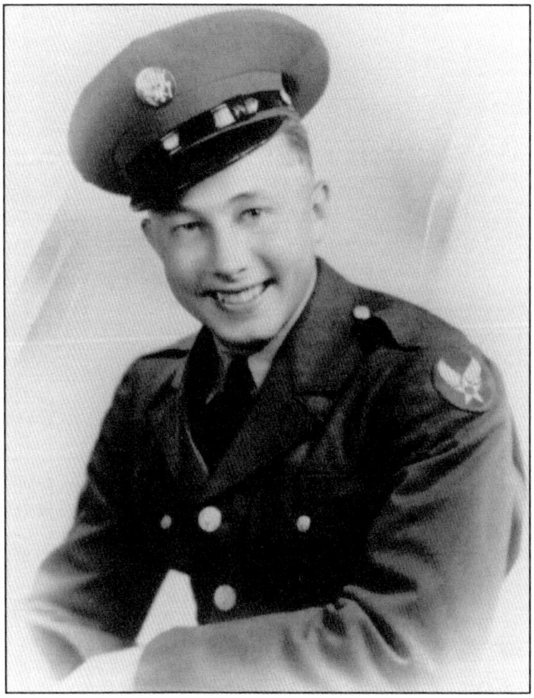

Every community saw young citizens join the armed forces during World War II. Robert C. Klingensmith of New Kensington served in the Army and went on to obtain the rank of Sergeant. He was not the only member of his family to serve his country; in addition to several cousins, his grandfather, George Brodmerkel Sr., served in the Union army during the Civil War.

Pictured here is Plum's Municipal Building on New Texas Road. Plum officially made the transition from township status to borough status in 1956. This was done primarily to prevent any further loss of territory to surrounding municipalities.

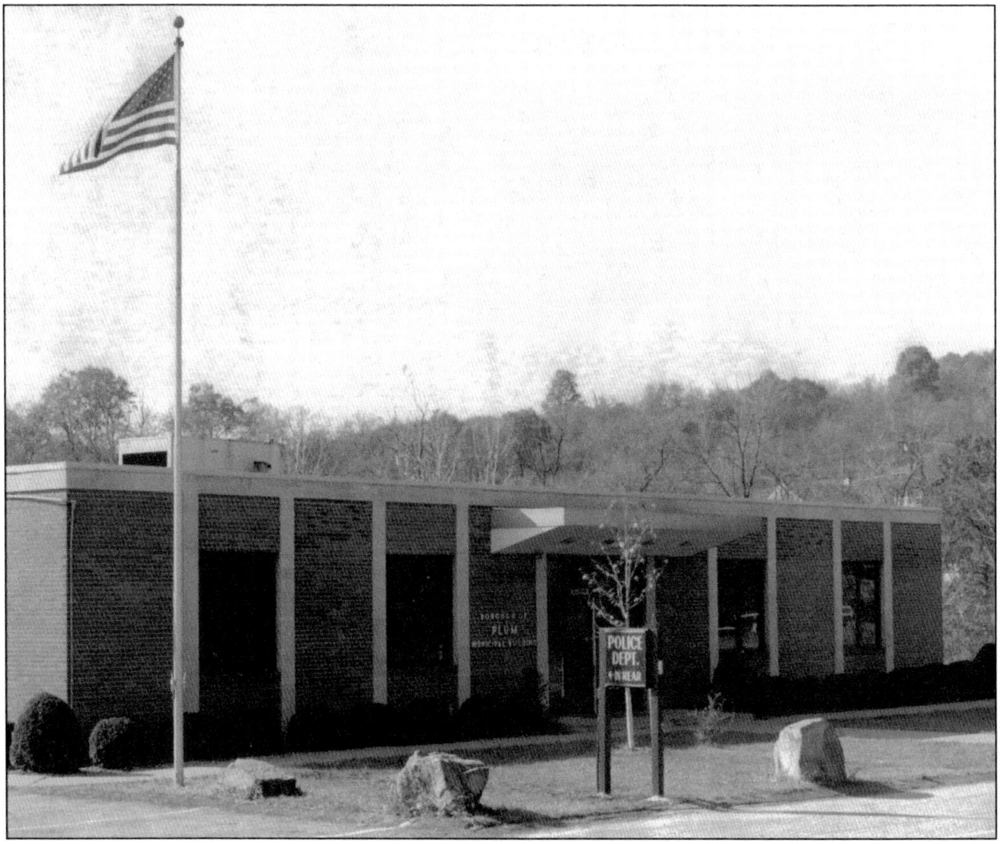

Orin D. Sampson and Mayor Anthony E. Oblock held a press conference in 1959 to announce the beginning of Holiday Park's development. Sampson was fond of the preservation of nature and was instrumental in establishing several tracts of land, totaling several acres, for recreational use. Oblock had an illustrious political career in Plum, serving for several terms on the school board and as mayor for over 25 years.

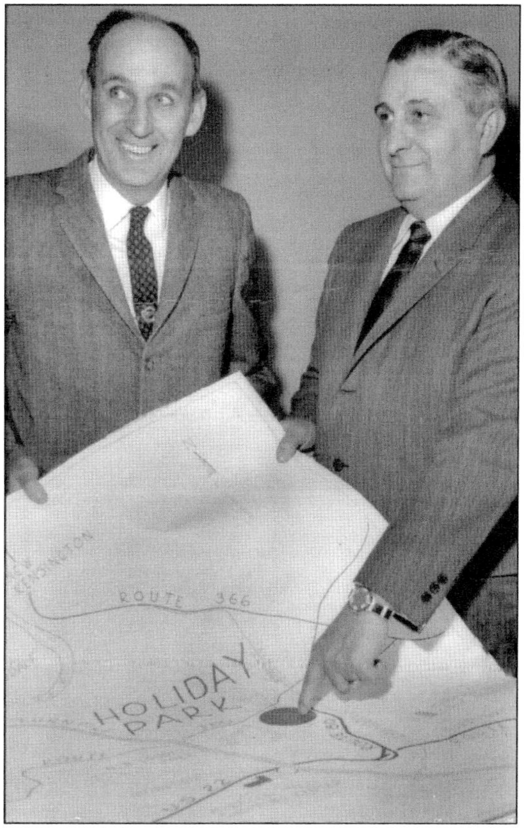

Pictured below is the Plum Borough Council in 1988. The members are, from left to right, (sitting) borough manager and secretary Alberta Horner, Steven Zelashy, and Donald Konopfel; (standing) Bruce Dice, Council President Richard Hereda, Council Vice President Thomas White, Stanley Caraher, Albert Flickinger, and Alfred Francl.

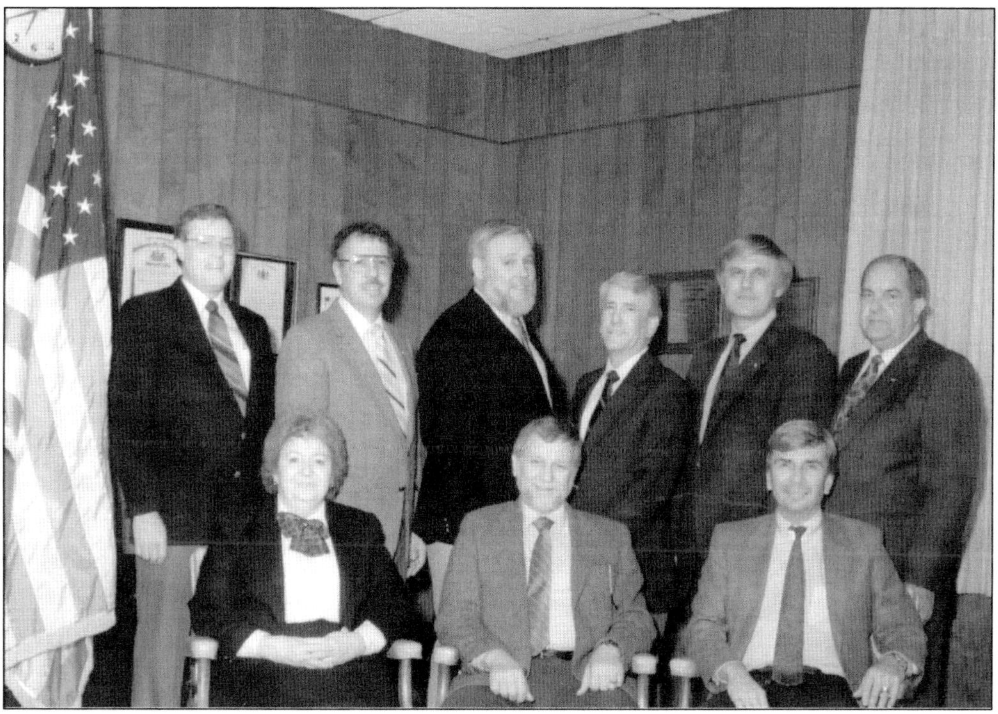

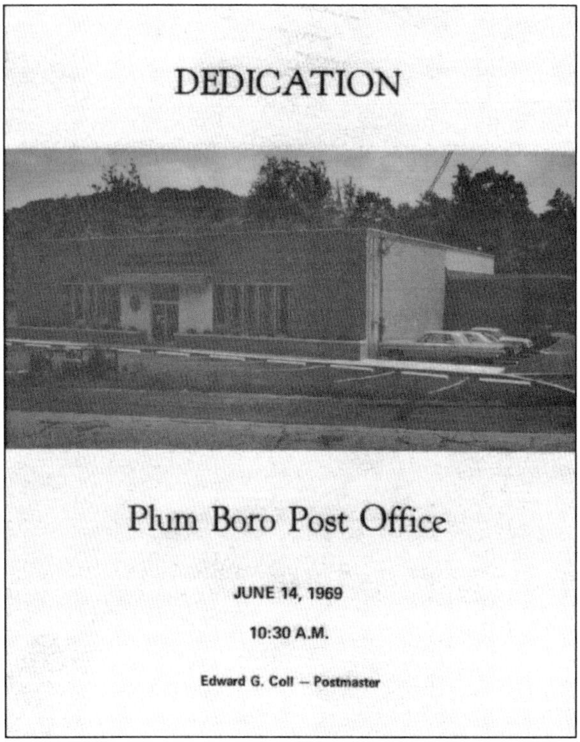
DEDICATION

Plum Boro Post Office

JUNE 14, 1969

10:30 A.M.

Edward G. Coll – Postmaster

Plum's current post office opened with a dedication service on June 14, 1969. Edward G. Coll, Pittsburgh's postmaster at the time, and Mayor Oblock were in attendance. Fr. William Hausen of St. John's Roman Catholic Church and Rev. William Ailes of the Presbyterian Church of Plum Creek offered the invocation and benediction, respectively, for the dedication program.

Holiday Park Volunteer Fire Department was founded in 1963. After much fundraising, the money was available to buy a used 1942 American LaFrance 705 GPM pumper from the Verona Fire Department. Sardis Fire Department in Murrysville served as Holiday Park's base until the Holiday Park building was completed on Abers Creek Road in 1964.

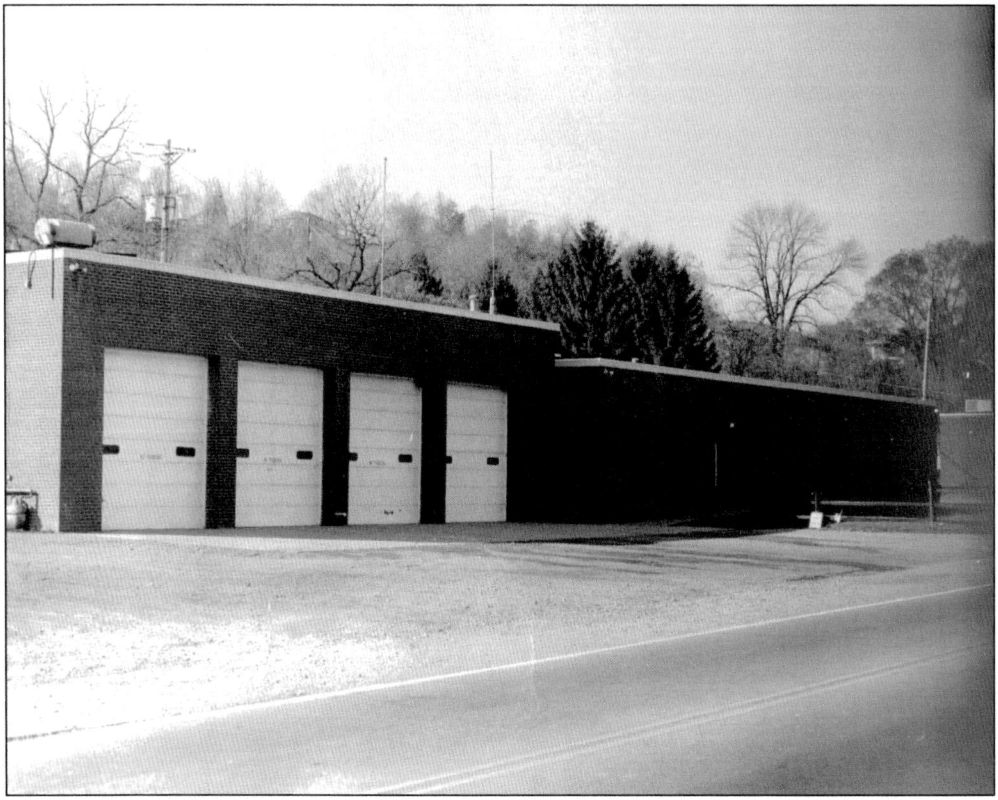

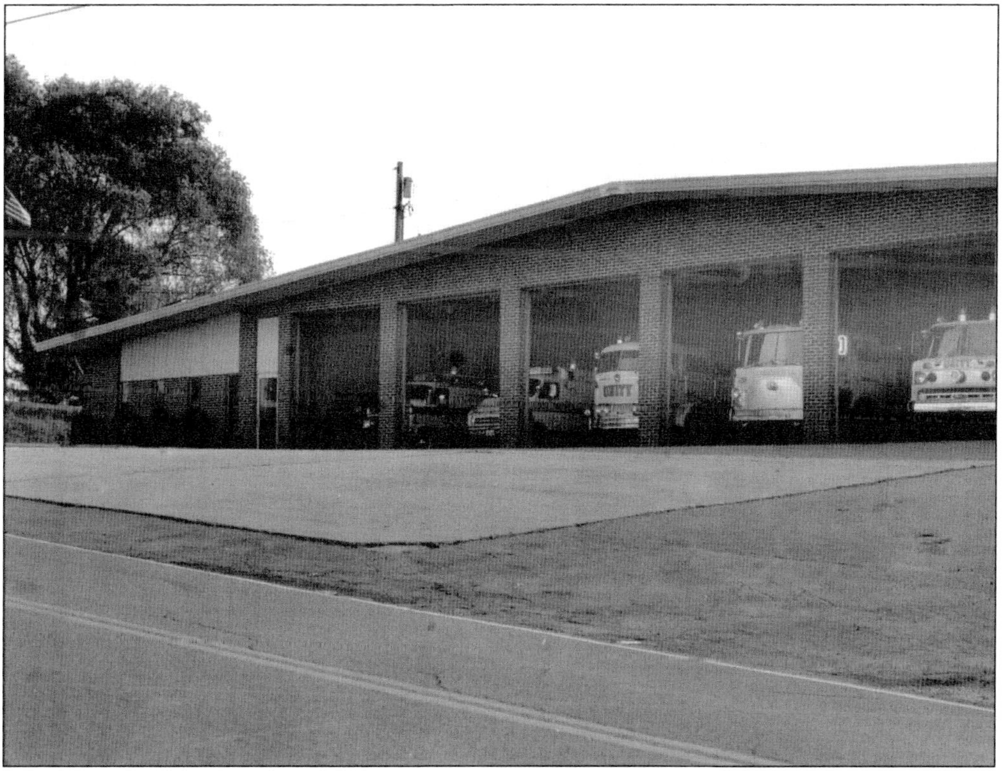

Unity Volunteer Fire Department was founded on July 9, 1925. The first president and chief was Howard M. Tarr. In 1941, Mr. and Mrs. F. McLaughlin donated land for a new firehouse. In 1973, the fire department moved to its present location on Old Leechburg Road. This year also saw the beginning of ambulance service in Unity.

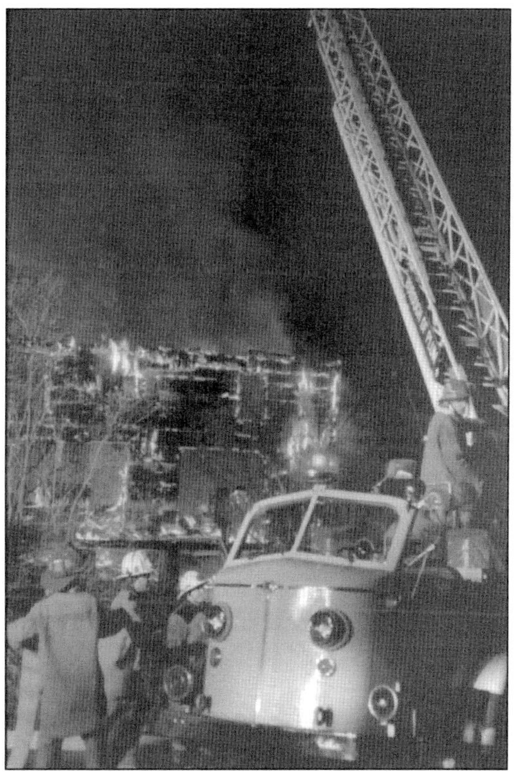

Unity Volunteer Fire Department can be seen in action during this Sardis Road log-house fire in May 1988. Plum is fortunate to be served by the brave men and women of four all-volunteer fire departments. In addition to Unity and Holiday Park, Plum's other fire departments are Renton (founded 1949) and Logans Ferry (founded 1941).

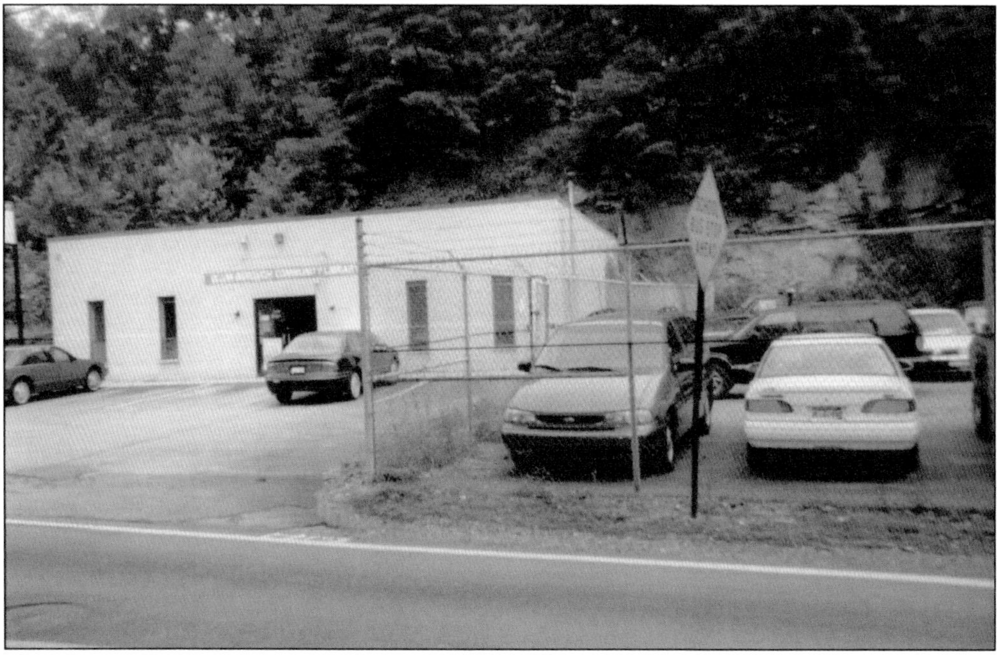

Plum Borough Community Library was considerably smaller in the not-so-distant past. It has long been a goal of Plum to have a large community library. The new library building on Center New Texas Road was the first stage of a multistage plan to expand the library. This photograph of its former location on Unity-Center Road was taken in May 2000.

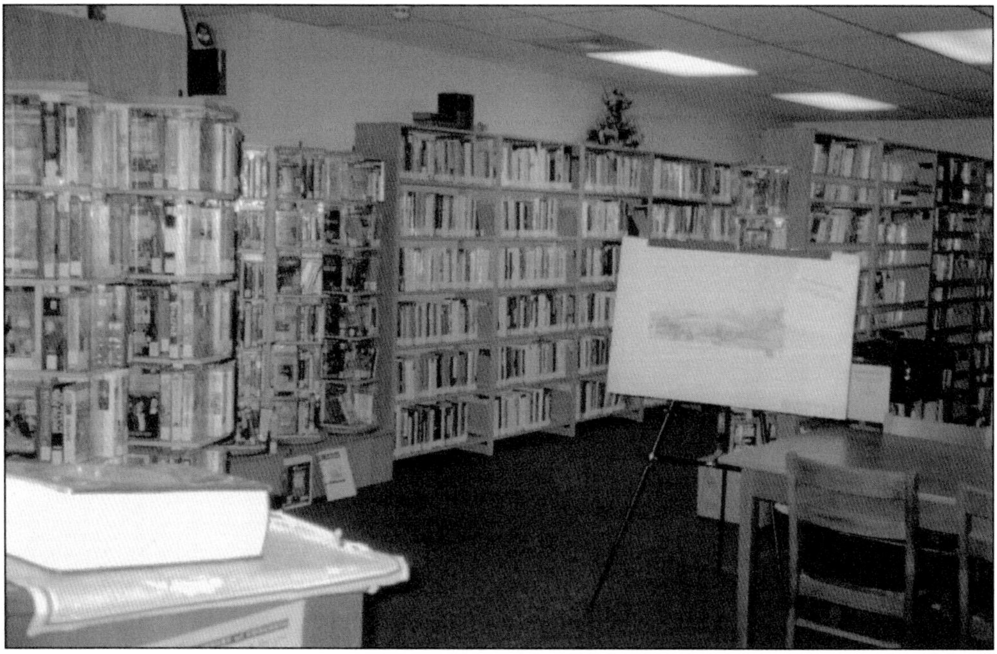

This photograph from May 2002 shows the interior of the former Plum Library. The poster board at right center displays the drawings for the new library building. Thanks to support from state grants, the new Plum Borough Community Library was built on Center New Texas Road next to the senior citizen's center. In 2010, an addition to the building was completed.

Seven

ORGANIZATIONS AND CELEBRATIONS

Civic, social, and recreational organizations play a vital role in the life of every community. They provide the framework that allows a community as a whole to enrich itself and proudly march into the future.

Plum has served as home to two women's clubs, troops of Boy Scouts and Girl Scouts, sportsmen's clubs, ethnic clubs, a historical society, a senior center, a library, a massive county park, and much more. Each has offered much in the way of education and recreation in the borough of Plum, leaving an indelible mark on the community's history. The groups listed are but a sampling of the diverse nature of such things in Plum's history.

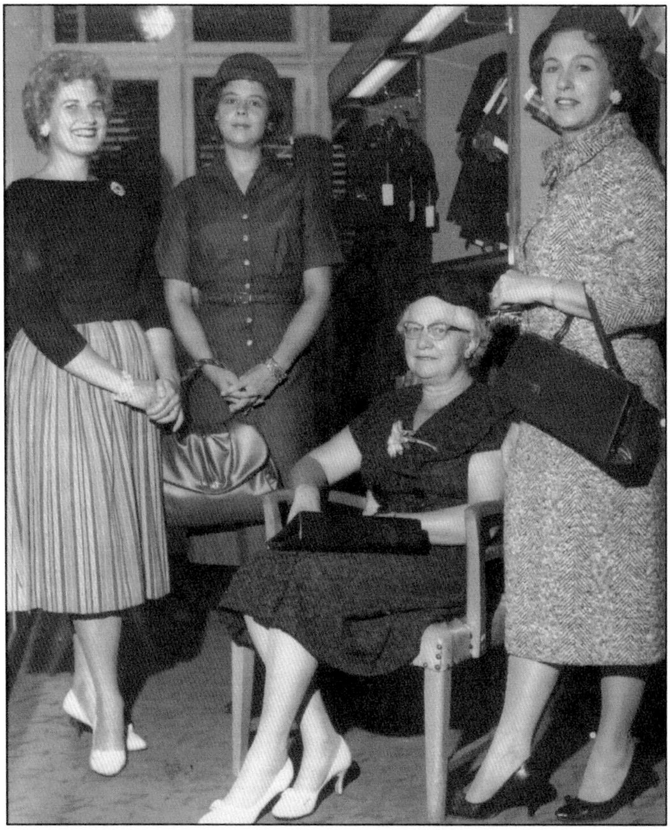

The Plum Creek Valley Women's Club was founded in 1931 with 23 charter members. During the 1940s, the club taught people about preserving and canning foods. They also hosted several victory-garden shows. Later, they made donations to the Plum Veterans Service Club, Meals-on-Wheels, Meals for Millions, St. Anthony's Home, and countless other philanthropic organizations. There were two departments within the club—a Garden Department and a Home and Hobby Department. The Garden Department was always very active. In the c. 1950 photograph at left, three unidentified women pose with Mrs. J.R. Jackson (seated). Posing outside below are, from left to right, Mrs. Paul Elkin, Mrs. George Sheffler, Mrs. W.C. Frack, and an unidentified woman.

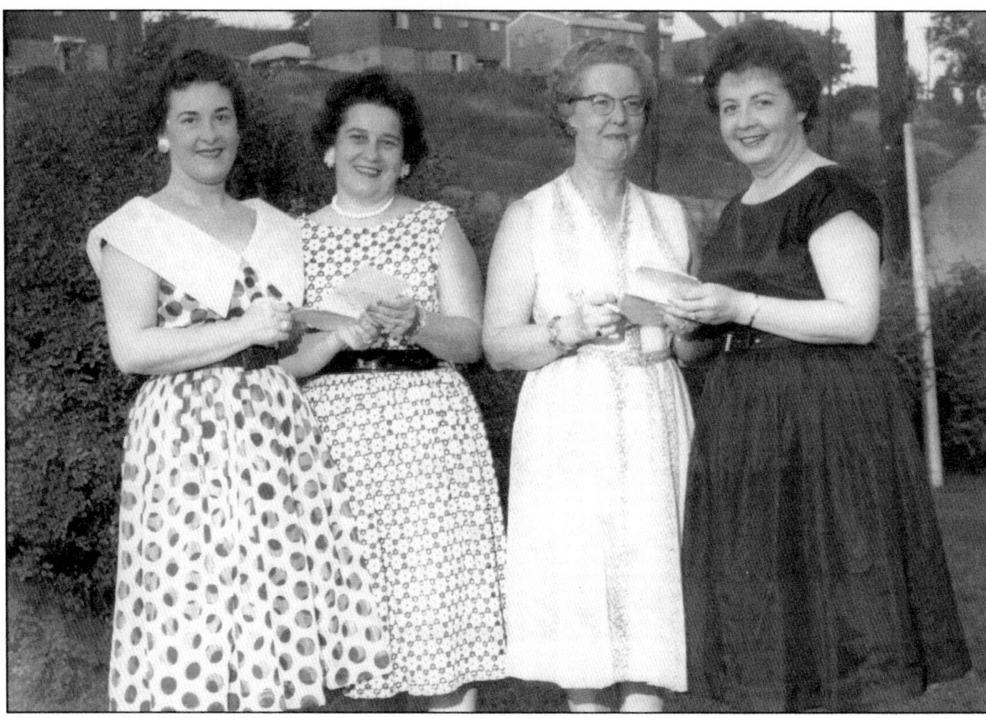

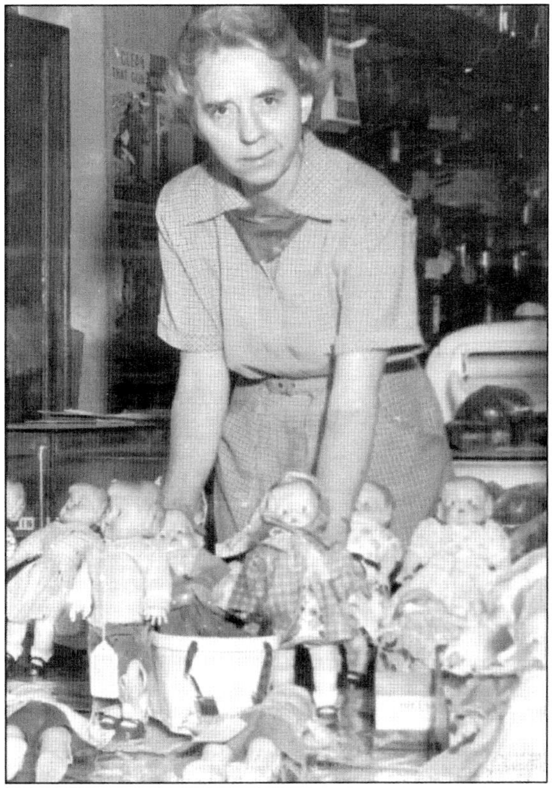

During World War II, the Red Cross conducted first aid classes in the Plum Creek Valley Women's Club clubhouse. Built in 1941, the clubhouse was erected on land donated by the Bessemer and Lake Erie Railroad. The many programs put on by the club continued into the post-war era. It hosted informative or humorous talks that were given by a wide array of speakers. Mrs. R.F. Jackson poses with dolls dressed by the women of the club in December of 1955. Below are three lovely ladies wearing their finest—most likely in preparation for a major club event—around June 21, 1956.

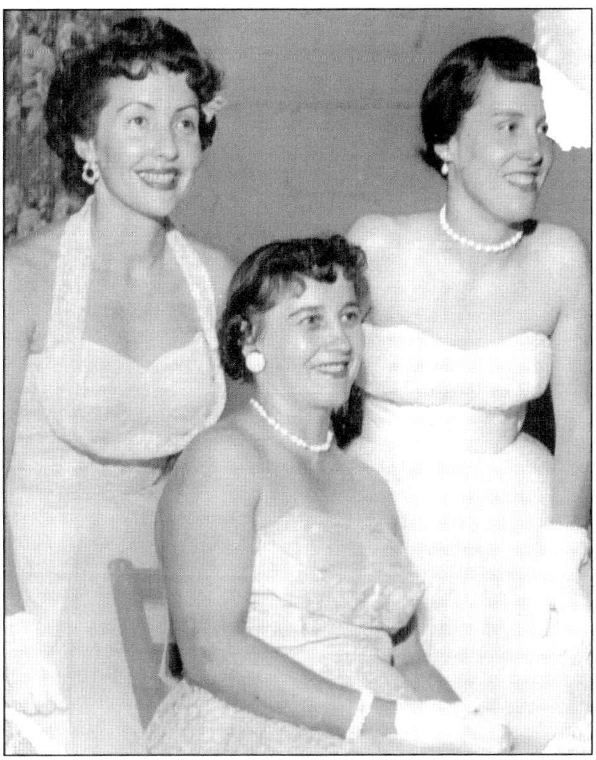

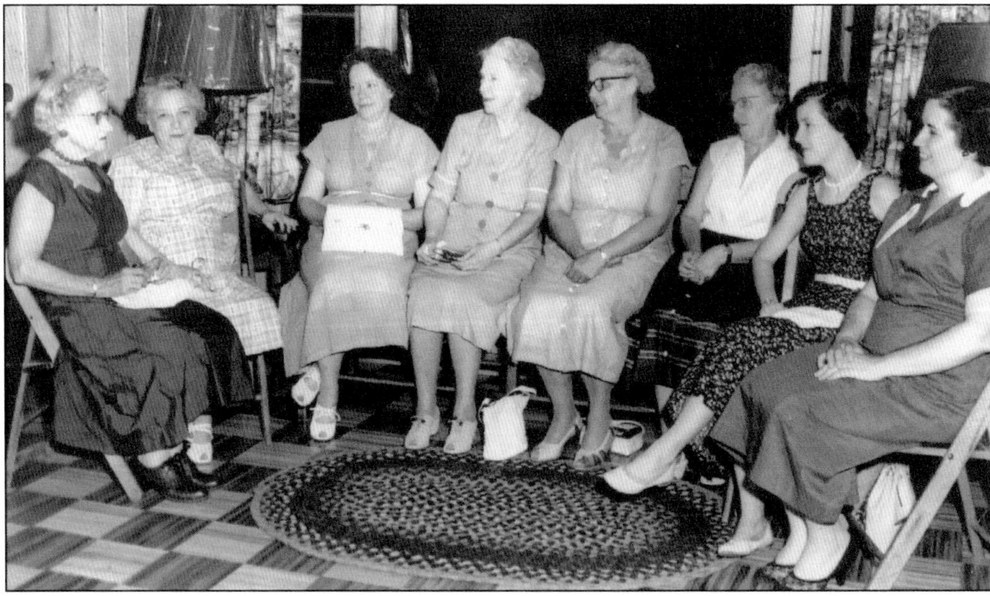

Above, a group of unidentified Plum Creek Valley Women's Club members posed for the October 27, 1955, edition of the *Valley Daily News*. Below, Mrs. Cox, Mrs. J.C.B. Poole, and Mrs. F.D. Anderson pose after having carved a jack-o'-lantern for a Halloween festivity. The Plum Creek Valley Woman's Club was not the only women's club in Plum. Holiday Park was also the base of a club, the East Plum Women's Club. It was founded on March 16, 1966, and federated on July 7, 1966. The club's objective was to develop the artistic, educational, civic, and social interests of its members as well as to advance the welfare of the greater community and to promote the programs of the General Federation of Women's Clubs.

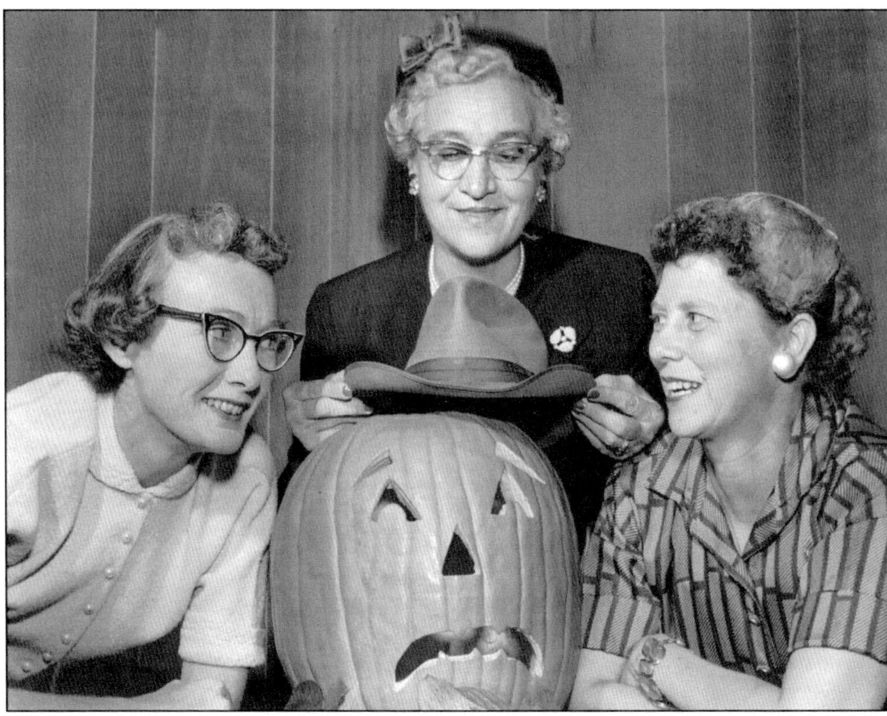

In addition to The Plum Creek Valley Woman's Club (the club's membership book is shown here) and the East Plum Women's Club, Plum was home to a variety of other social and civic organizations. Some of these organizations include the YMCA, the Slovenian Club of Center, and the Unity Sportsmen Club.

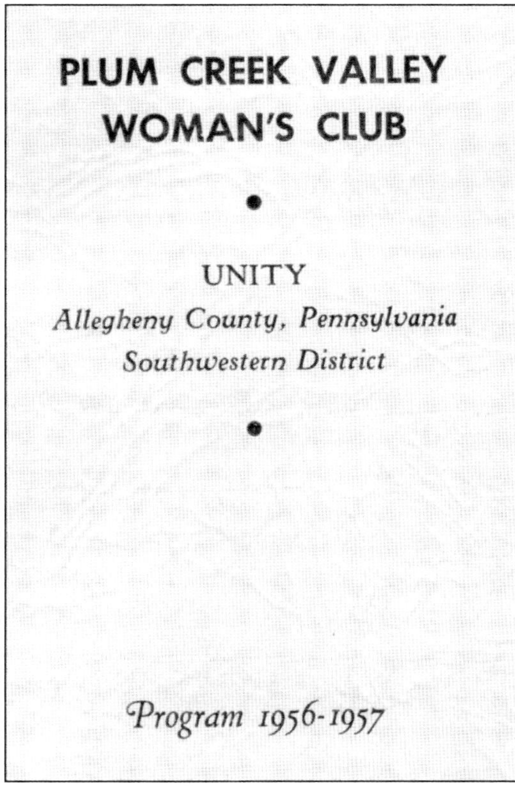

PLUM CREEK VALLEY
WOMAN'S CLUB

UNITY
Allegheny County, Pennsylvania
Southwestern District

Program 1956-1957

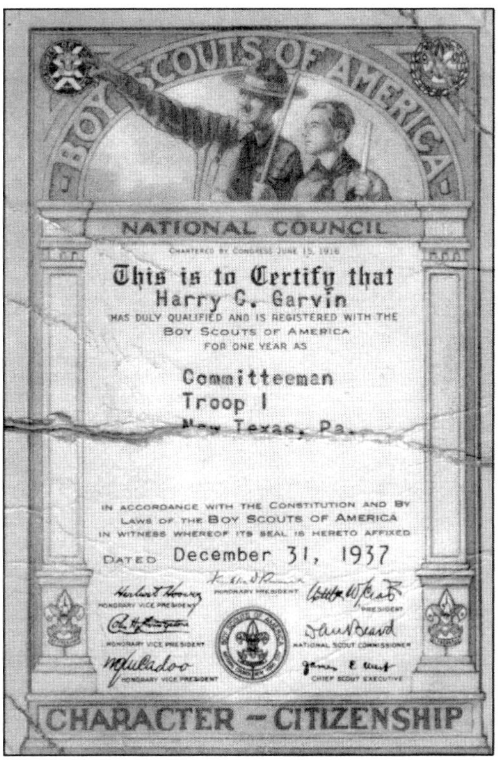

BOY SCOUTS OF AMERICA

NATIONAL COUNCIL

CHARTERED BY CONGRESS JUNE 15, 1916

This is to Certify that
Harry C. Garvin
HAS DULY QUALIFIED AND IS REGISTERED WITH THE
BOY SCOUTS OF AMERICA
FOR ONE YEAR AS

Committeeman
Troop 1
New Texas, Pa.

IN ACCORDANCE WITH THE CONSTITUTION AND BY
LAWS OF THE BOY SCOUTS OF AMERICA
IN WITNESS WHEREOF ITS SEAL IS HERETO AFFIXED

DATED December 31, 1937

HONORARY VICE PRESIDENT — HONORARY PRESIDENT — PRESIDENT
HONORARY VICE PRESIDENT — NATIONAL SCOUT COMMISSIONER
HONORARY VICE PRESIDENT — CHIEF SCOUT EXECUTIVE

CHARACTER — CITIZENSHIP

As Plum was the birthplace of William D. Boyce, the founder of the Boy Scouts of America, it is only natural that the Boy Scouts would have a presence within the municipality. This Boy Scout card belonged to Harry Garvin of Plum's New Texas community. Plum's first Girl Scout troop, which had over 20 members, began in 1958.

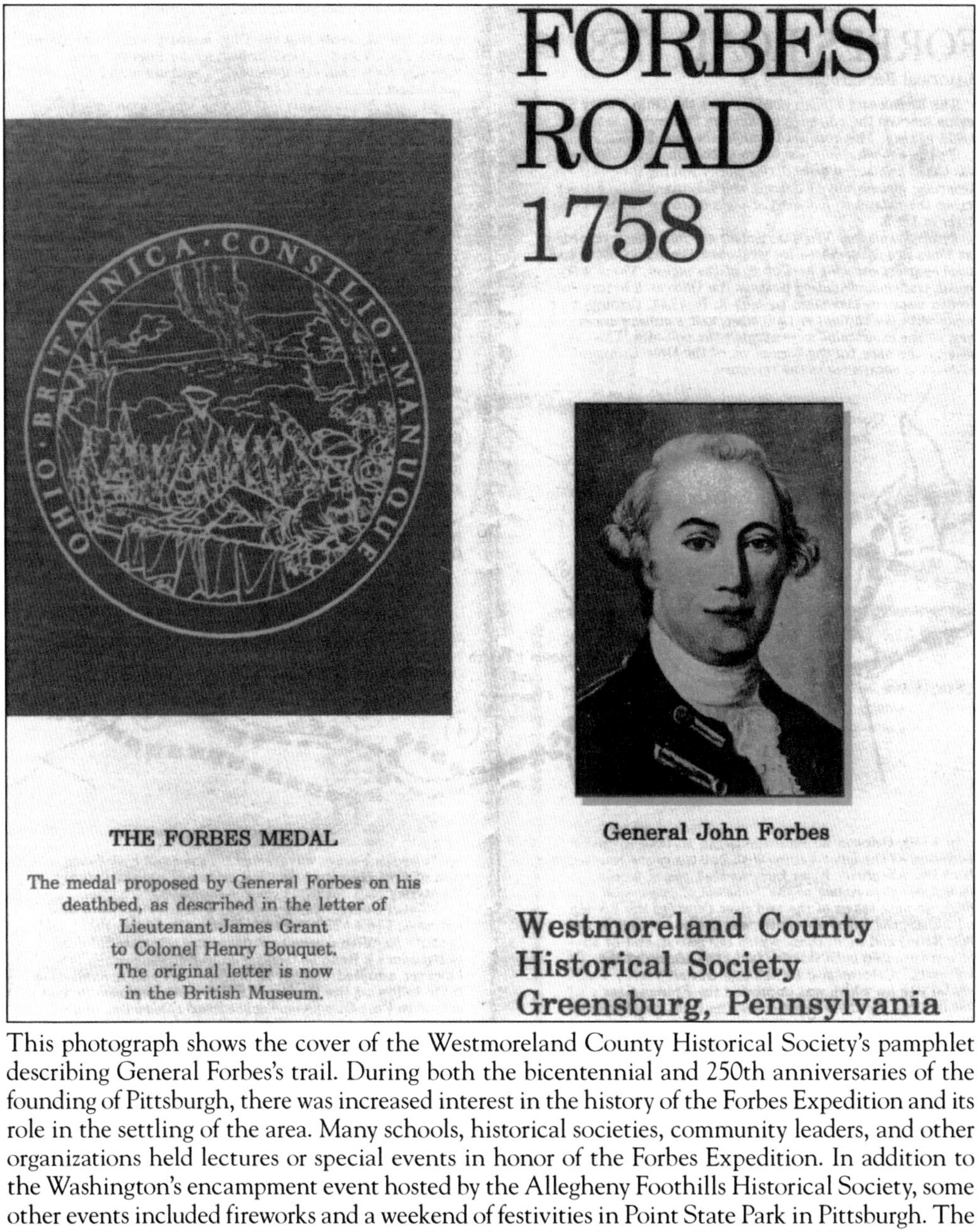

This photograph shows the cover of the Westmoreland County Historical Society's pamphlet describing General Forbes's trail. During both the bicentennial and 250th anniversaries of the founding of Pittsburgh, there was increased interest in the history of the Forbes Expedition and its role in the settling of the area. Many schools, historical societies, community leaders, and other organizations held lectures or special events in honor of the Forbes Expedition. In addition to the Washington's encampment event hosted by the Allegheny Foothills Historical Society, some other events included fireworks and a weekend of festivities in Point State Park in Pittsburgh. The Westmoreland County Historical Society hosted a series of lectures. Starting in 2006 (the 250th anniversary of the start of the French and Indian War), the Westmoreland County Historical Society began using the French and Indian War as the topic for their annual Ohio Country Conference. Each speaker in attendance focused on a topic relevant to a year of the war (1756 in 2006, 1757 in 2007, and so on).

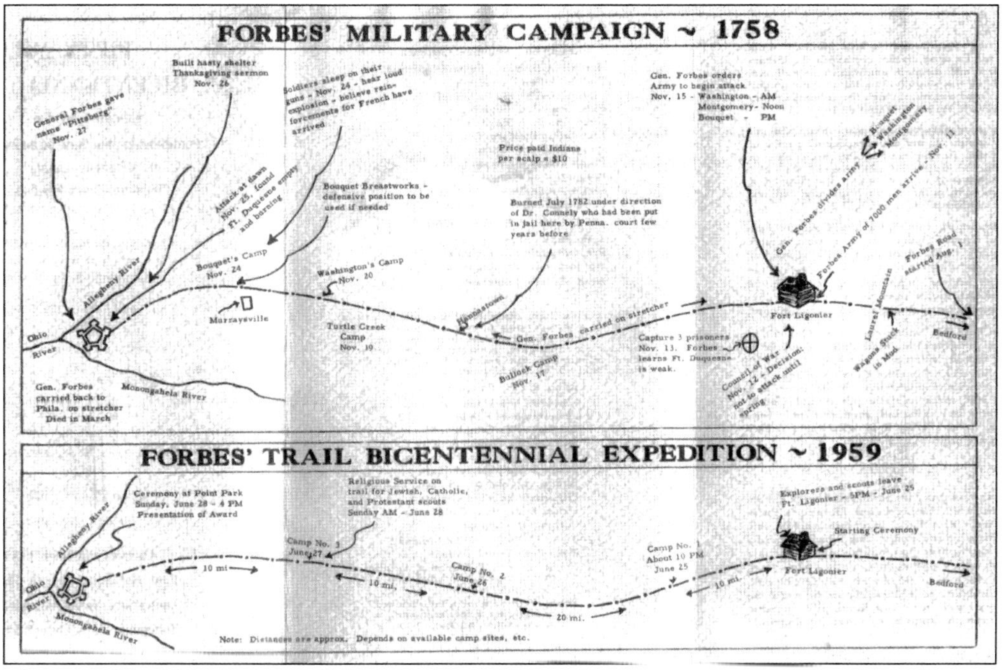

This map (above) was a part of a pamphlet commemorating the "Fifty Mile Bicentennial Hike" (right), sponsored by the various Boy Scout councils in Allegheny County. Starting on Thursday, June 25, 1959, Boy Scouts began a march from Fort Ligonier that replicated the march of Gen. John Forbes's 1758 campaign. A ceremony was held at 3:30 p.m. on June 28, 1959, at Point State Park in downtown Pittsburgh. This was one of the events that served as inspiration for the 2006 commemoration of the 250th anniversary of Washington's 1758 encampment in the area as part of Gen. John Forbes's campaign against Fort Duquesne. On arriving at Point State Park, visitors could see a small log cabin on the park's premises. The cabin was built of logs from the original Carpenter family log house.

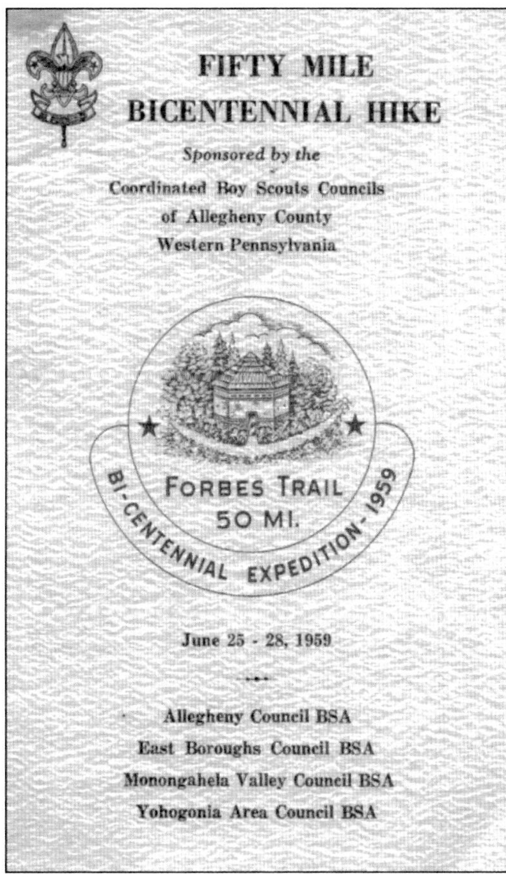

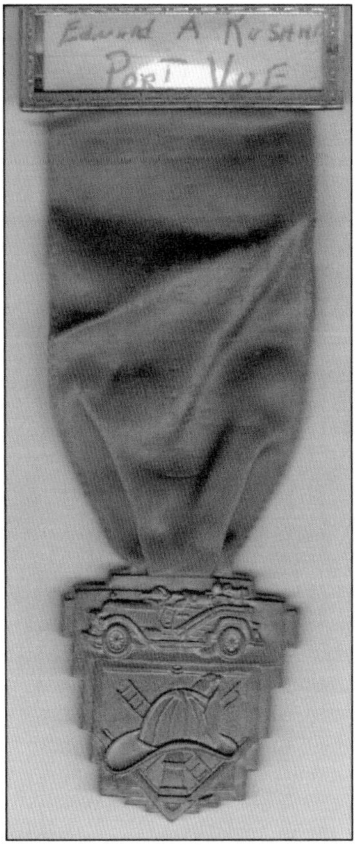

The 45th Annual Allegheny County Firemen's Convention was hosted by the Oakmont Fire Company in neighboring Oakmont. It ran from June 21 to June 27, 1959. This medal belonged to Edward A. Rushner of Port Vue, Pennsylvania. (Courtesy of the McKeesport Heritage Center.)

In 1983, a Bridal Treasures fashion show was hosted by the Allegheny Foothills Historical Society. Marilyn Hober, Dawn Yeager, Diane Atchinson, and Eleanor Broome served as models. Each woman wore a wedding dress belonging to one of their ancestors. This was one of the many festivities that the historical society put on as a fundraiser in its early years.

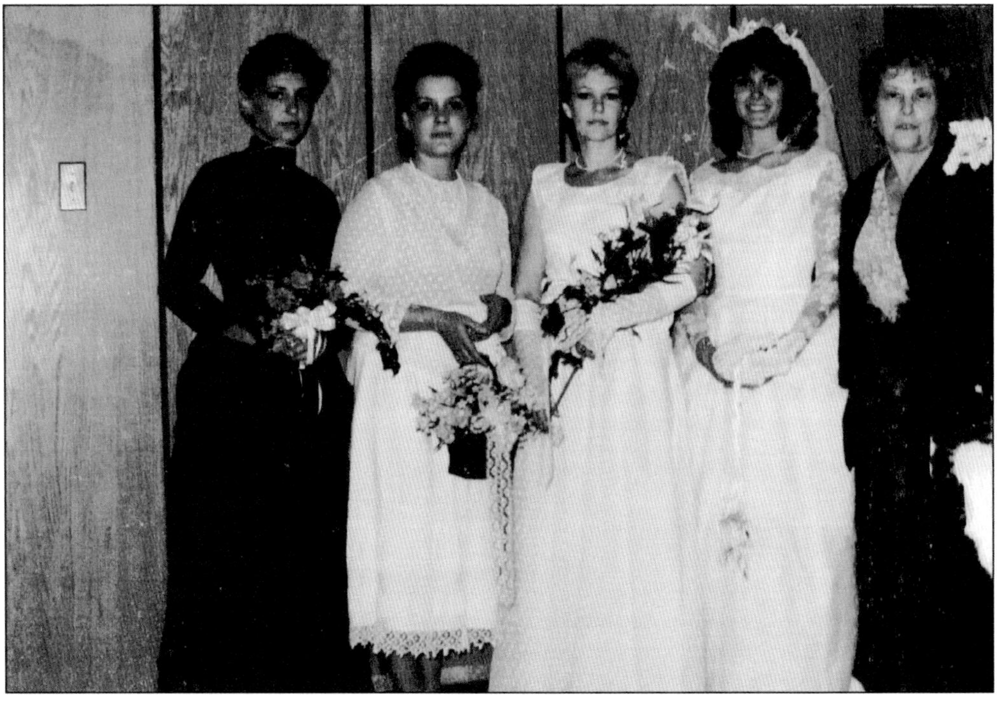

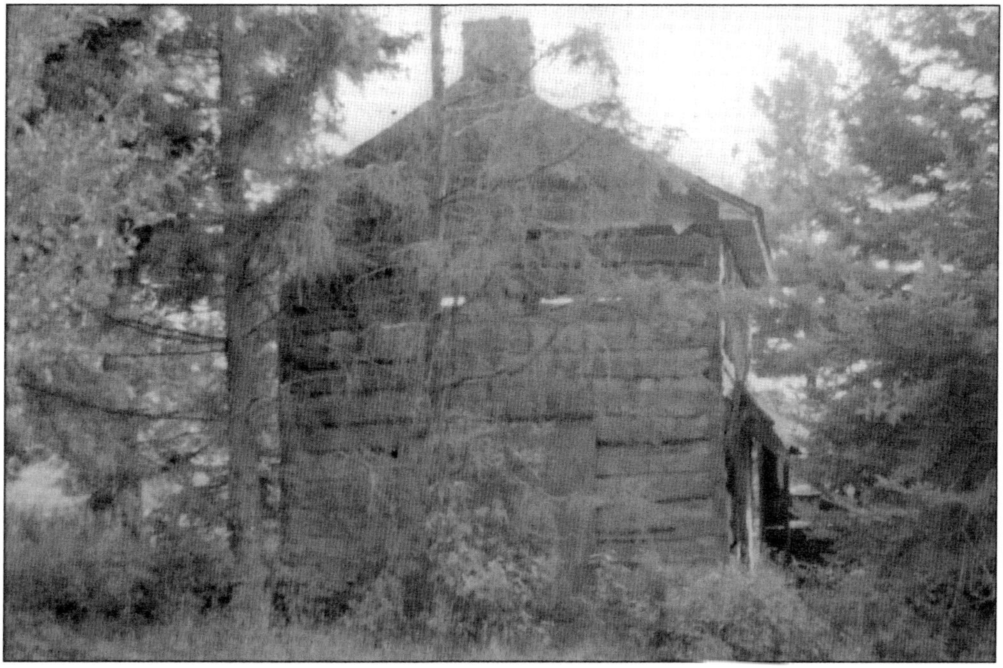

The Sloan log schoolhouse in Murrysville was purchased by the Allegheny Foothills Historical Society in 1981 and served as the source of many of the logs used for the reconstructed Carpenter log house. After the schoolhouse's dismantling, the logs were housed in the Carpenter barn, along with some of the log house's original logs, until construction of the new structure began.

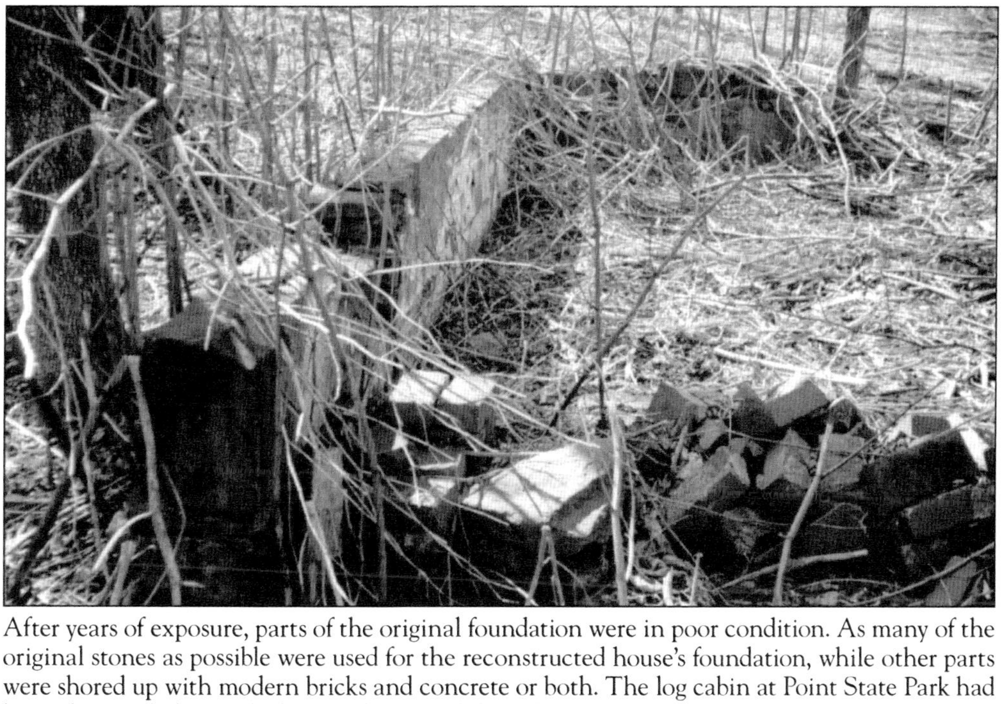

After years of exposure, parts of the original foundation were in poor condition. As many of the original stones as possible were used for the reconstructed house's foundation, while other parts were shored up with modern bricks and concrete or both. The log cabin at Point State Park had been dismantled years before, and some of those logs were used in the reconstruction of the Carpenter homestead.

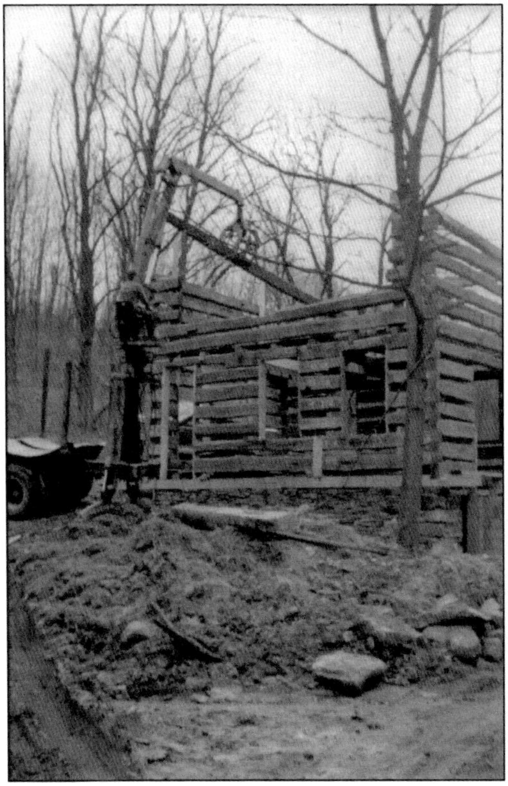

After many fundraisers (which included selling logs to sponsors), construction was ready to begin on the Carpenter log house in 1987. The original foundation was cleaned up; the logs, which had been numbered, were set in place. A wire-mesh and mortar chinking was used between the logs. In 1996, a kitchen was added to the east side of the house to allow for a larger display area.

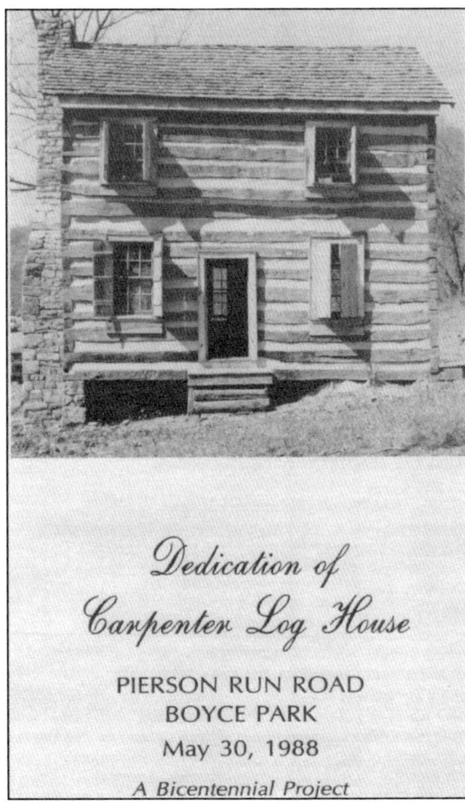

On May 30, 1988, the dedication of the Carpenter log house in Boyce Park took place. Eleanor Carpenter Broome, one of the last family members to have lived in the original homestead, was instrumental in garnering support to have the log house rebuilt. The original house was one and a half stories tall, with the sleeping quarters upstairs. The springhouse, summer kitchen, and outhouse were all detached structures.

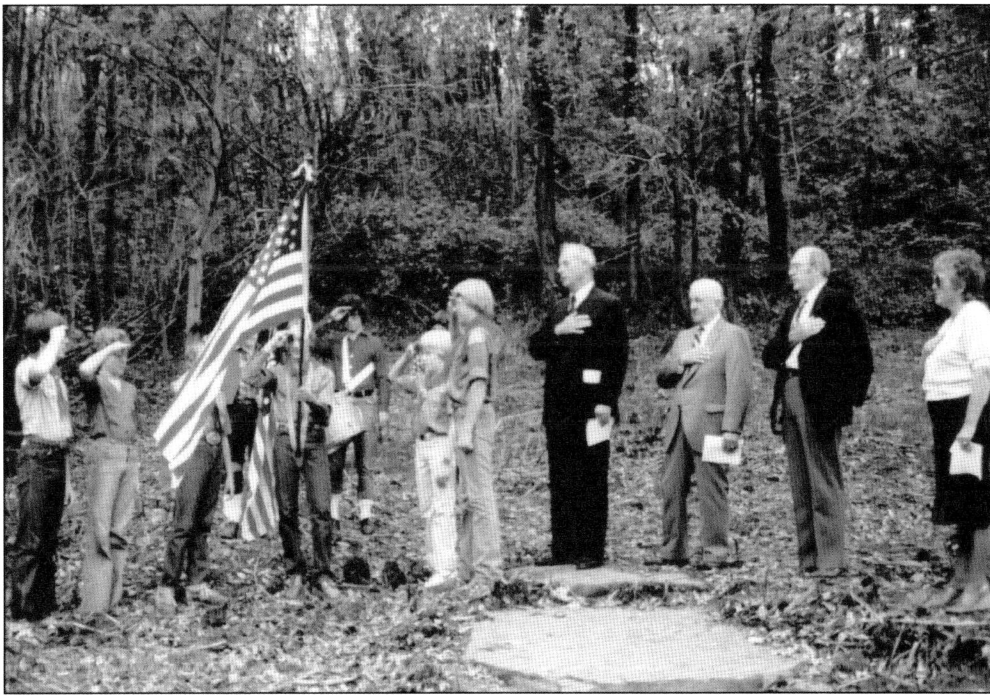

In the summer of 1982, a groundbreaking ceremony was conducted at the Carpenter reconstruction site. Several members of the Carpenter family took part, including Eleanor Broome, Susan Broome, James Stewart, Bob Yeager, and Louise Straley. Officials participating included Mayor Anthony O'Block and Jack Milberger, the county parks director. A local Boy Scout troop was responsible for the presentation of the flag.

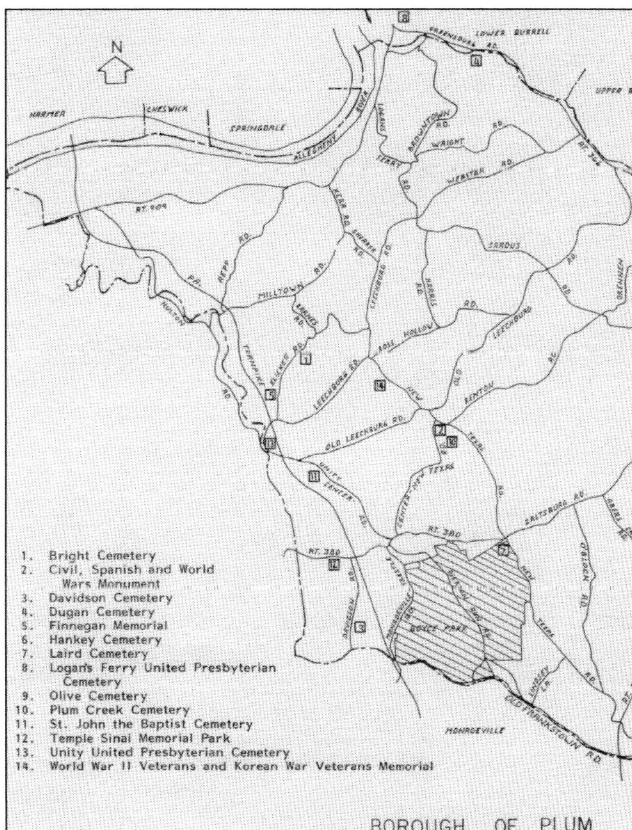

This map marking the cemeteries of Plum Borough was included as part of the program for the dedication of the Carpenter log house on May 30, 1988. The dedication of the reconstructed log house was the culmination of many years of work by various members of the Allegheny Foothills Historical Society and members of the community at large.

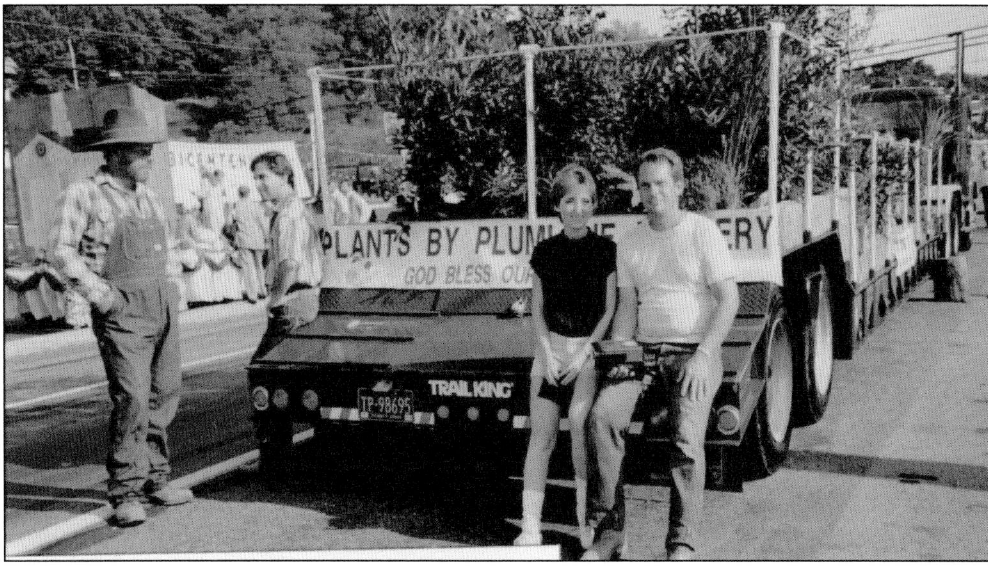

The Allegheny Foothills Historical Society entered a float at the Plum Bicentennial Parade on August 27, 1988. The bicentennial celebrations proved a fitting culmination to a decade of work by the members of the historical society. The members worked very hard to raise the funds necessary to reconstruct the Carpenter log house. The festivities also provided a source of pride to all Plum residents who appreciate their community's history.

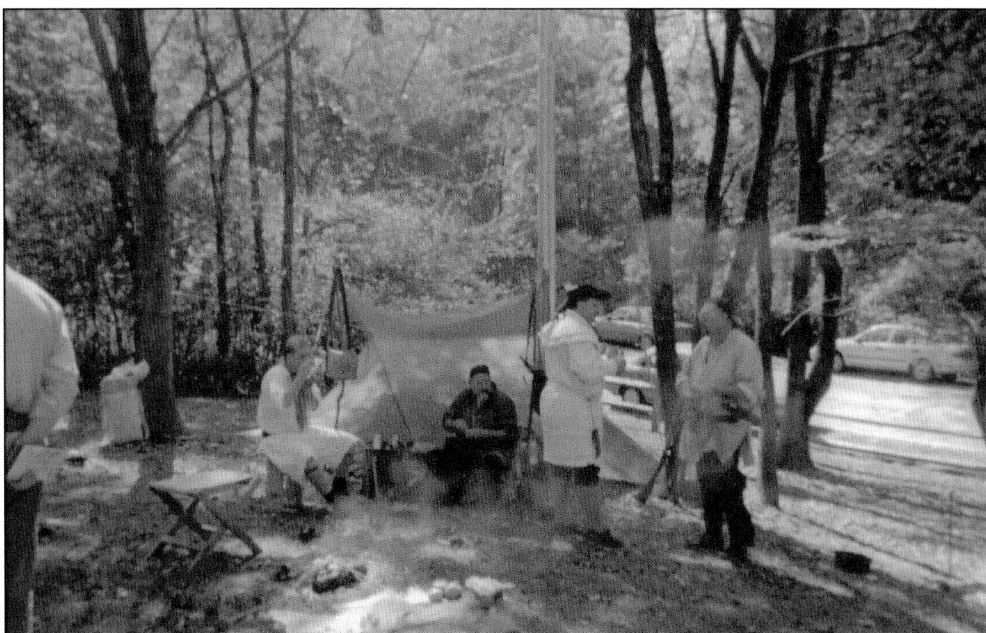

This picture was taken during the Harvest Festival in September 2001. The Harvest Festival is an annual event hosted by the Allegheny Foothills Historical Society around the end of September or the beginning of October. Reenactors and historical speakers are invited to the grounds surrounding the Carpenter log house. Various vendors are often present as well.

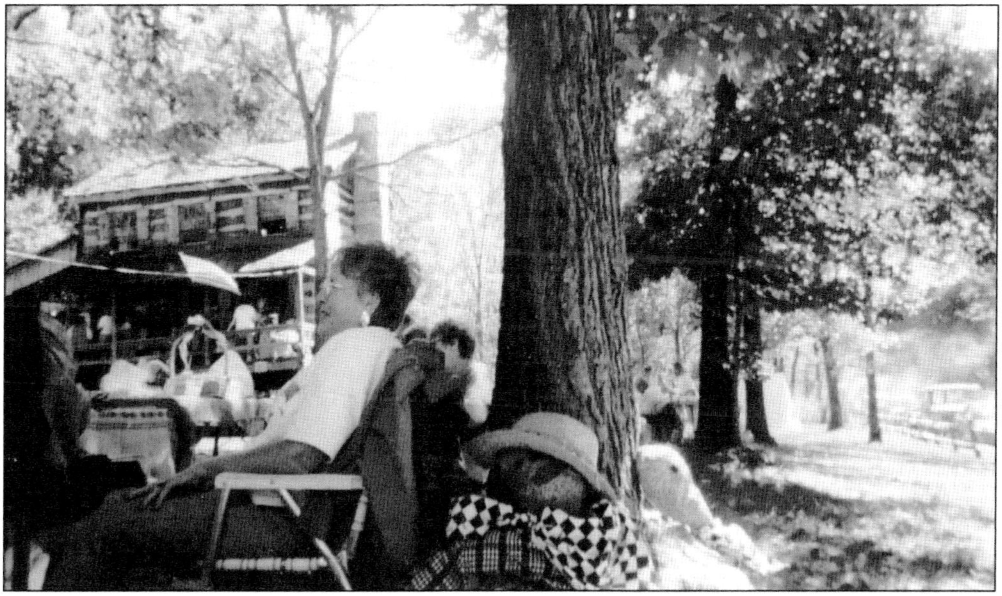

Eleanor Carpenter Broome, founder of the Allegheny Foothills Historical Society, enjoys the festivities at the annual Harvest Festival at the Carpenter log house. Although the Harvest Festival goes on rain or shine, it was replaced in 2008 (for one year only) by the 250th anniversary of Gen. John Forbes and George Washington having marched through the area. The event, which was held on October 3 and 4 in 2008, was entitled Washington's Encampment.

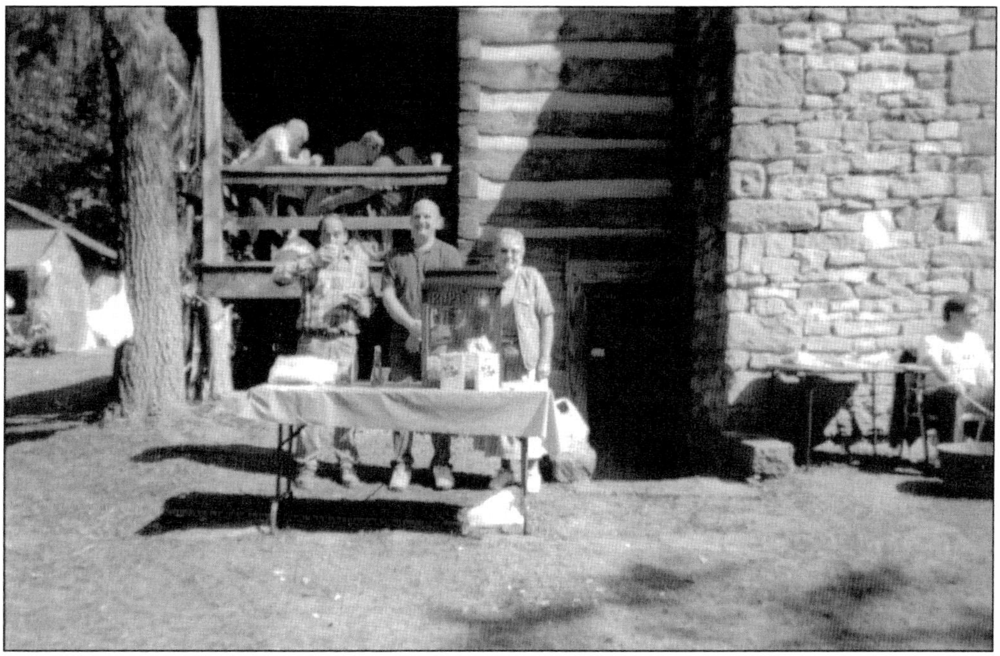

Harvest festival attendees enjoy popcorn outside of the Carpenter log house while others wait on the porch for a chance to tour the structure. The log house—which is different from a log cabin in that a log cabin is a temporary structure and a log house is a permanent structure)—is generally open for tours every Sunday from Memorial Day weekend through Labor Day weekend from 1 p.m. to 4 p.m.

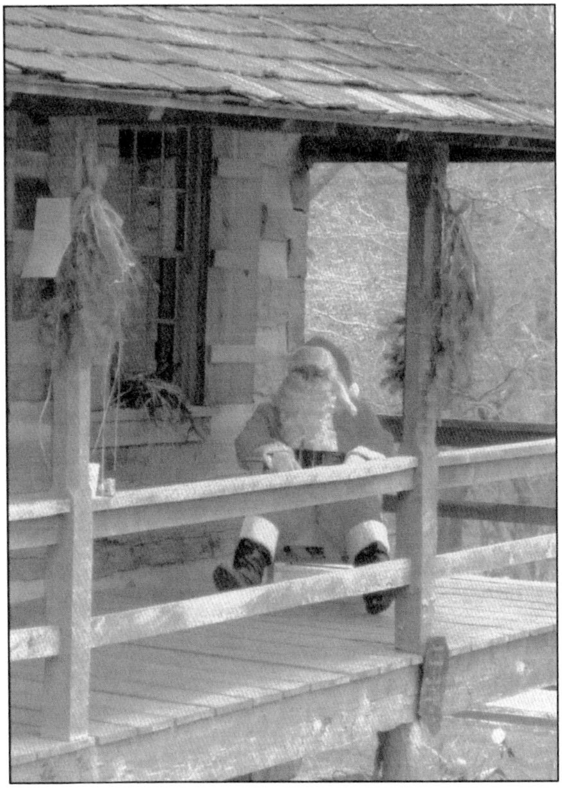

George Oblock, playing the part of Santa Claus, waits on the porch of the Carpenter log house for visitors to arrive during Sugar Plum Days in December 2003. Sugar Plum Days is a yearly favorite amongst locals. Several institutions and locales throughout the community participate by putting on programs, giving tours, and offering refreshments. Such locales include the Carpenter log house, the Plum Borough Municipal Building, the Plum Community Library, and the Allegheny Foothills Historical Society's history room inside the library. Mrs. Claus is not with Santa in this photograph, as she is usually reading stories to children at the library.

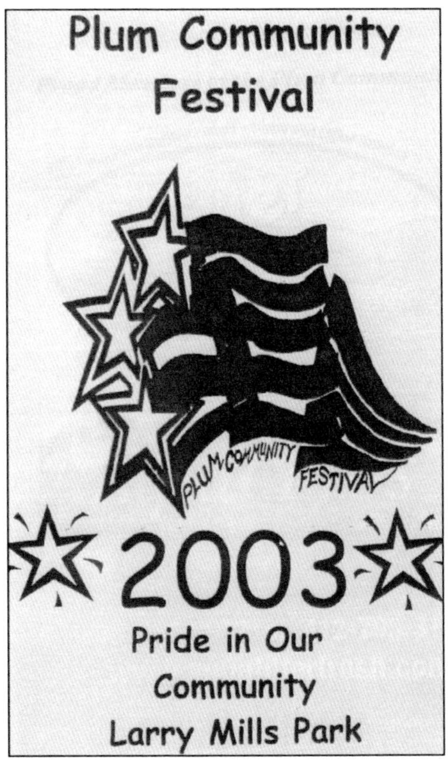

Always a favorite summertime event, Plum's annual Community Festival is sponsored and planned by Plum Borough. Shown here is the front cover of the program for the 2003 event.

Sugar Plum Days are held in mid-December. Events are held in several different locations. At each locale, children can get their "Sugar Plum Passports" stamped and become eligible to win a prize. The Allegheny Foothills Historical Society volunteers staff two different locations—the history room at the Plum Community Library and the Carpenter log house in Boyce Park.

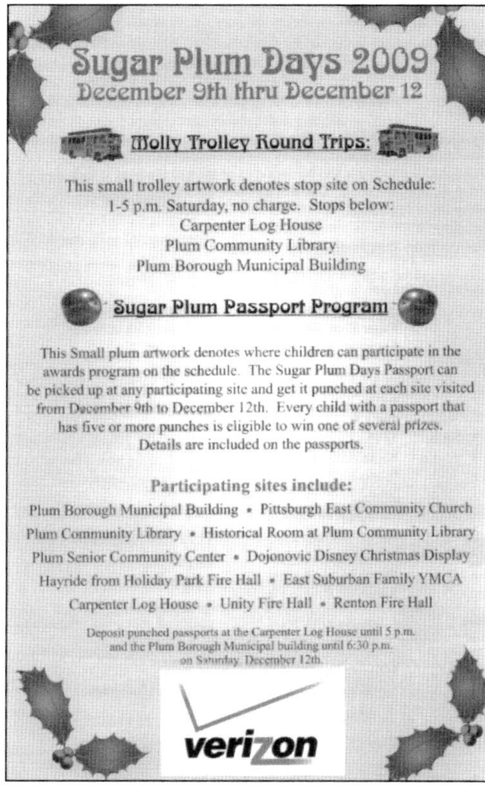

Washington's Encampment—the celebration of the 250th anniversary of the Forbes campaign's camp in the area—was held on the first weekend of October 2008. Sponsored by the Allegheny Foothills Historical Society, it included a variety of reenactors and historical speakers. The Carpenter log house and barn were utilized by reenactors, as was almost a mile of trail in Boyce Park.

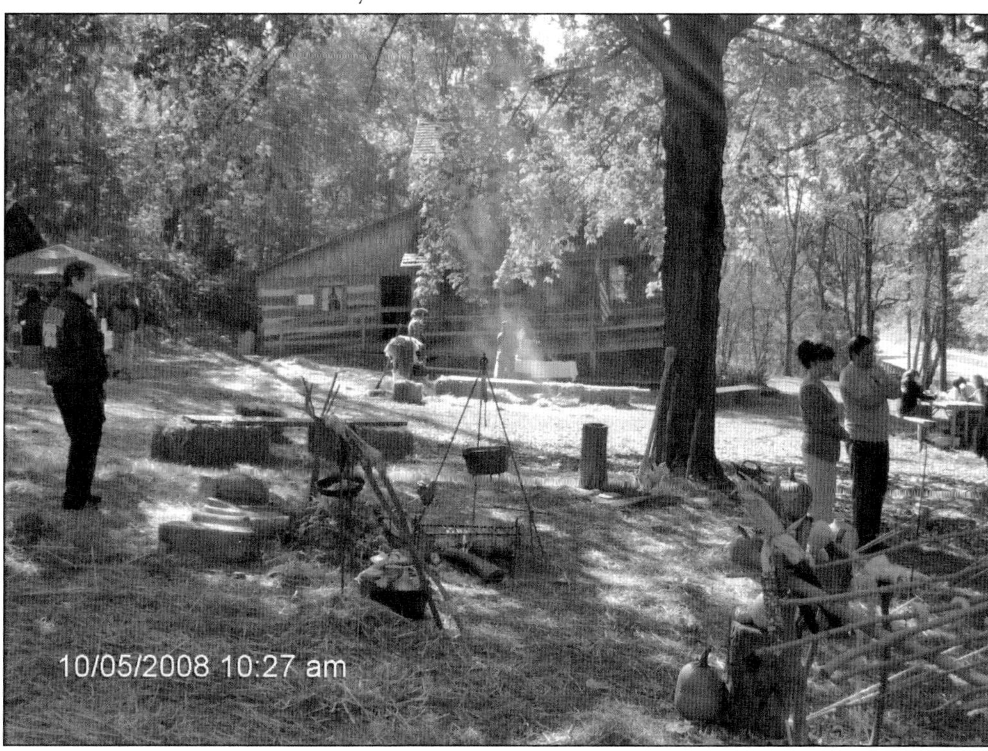

INDEX

Bibliography

Allegheny Foothills Historical Society, ed. *Where the Wild Plum Trees Grew*. New Kensington, PA: Buhl Brothers Printing, 1988.

Atlas of the County of Allegheny, Pennsylvania. Philadelphia: G.M. Hopkins, 1876.

Garlow, Jean. *Plum Borough: Our Community, Then and Now*. Plum Borough, PA.

History of Allegheny County, Pennsylvania, Vol. I. Chicago: A. Warner and Company Publishing, 1889.

Lake, Robert S. *History of Valley Heights Golf Course: 1923–1984*. Acworth, GA: 2006.

Logans Ferry United Presbyterian Church: Quasquicentennial Anniversary 1856–1981. New Kensington, PA: 1981.

Rogers, Gary. *Tales from our Towns*, Vol. I. Verona, PA: Rogers and Deturck Printing, 2005.

————. *Tales from our Towns*, Vol. II. Verona, PA: Rogers and Deturck Printing, 2010.

Wallace, Paul A.W. *Indian Paths of Pennsylvania*. Harrisburg, Pennsylvania: The Pennsylvania Historical and Museum Commission, 1965.

About the Organization

The Allegheny Foothills Historical Society was organized in January 1979 for the purpose of preserving physical properties, artifacts, documents, and other personal items for the purpose of fostering a greater understanding and appreciation of the history of the area. The society provides tours of the Carpenter log house, located on Pierson Run Road in Boyce Park. The society also operates a history room and archives within the Plum Borough Community Library.